MATT AND TOM OLDFIELD

ULTIMATE
FOOTBALL HEROES

STERLING

FROM THE PLAYGROUND
TO THE PITCH

CH00683859

DINO

Published by Dino Books,
an imprint of John Blake Publishing,
2.25, The Plaza,
535 Kings Road,
Chelsea Harbour,
London SW10 0SZ

www.johnblakebooks.com

www.facebook.com/johnblakebooks
twitter.com/jblakebooks

This edition published in 2018

ISBN: 978 1 78946 053 7

British Library Cataloguing-in-Publication Data:

A catalogue record for this book is available from the British Library.

Design by www.envydesign.co.uk

Printed and bound in Great Britain by Clays Ltd, Elcograf S.p.A.

5 7 9 10 8 6

John Blake Publishing is an imprint of Bonnier Books UK
www.bonnierbooks.co.uk

For all readers,
young and old(er)

ULTIMATE
FOOTBALL HEROES

Matt Oldfield is an accomplished writer and the editor-in-chief of football review site Of Pitch & Page. Tom Oldfield is a freelance sports writer and the author of biographies on Cristiano Ronaldo, Arsène Wenger and Rafael Nadal.

Cover illustration by Dan Leydon.
To learn more about Dan visit danleydon.com
To purchase his artwork visit etsy.com/shop/footynews
Or just follow him on Twitter @danleydon

TABLE OF CONTENTS

ACKNOWLEDGEMENTS

First of all, I'd like to thank John Blake Publishing – and particularly my editor James Hodgkinson – for giving me the opportunity to work on these books and for supporting me throughout. Writing stories for the next generation of football fans is both an honour and a pleasure.

I wouldn't be doing this if it wasn't for my brother Tom. I owe him so much and I'm very grateful for his belief in me as an author. I feel like Robin setting out on a solo career after a great partnership with Batman. I hope I do him (Tom, not Batman) justice with these new books.

Next up, I want to thank my friends for keeping me sane during long hours in front of the laptop. Pang, Will, Mills, Doug, John, Charlie – the laughs and the cups of coffee are always appreciated.

I've already thanked my brother but I'm also very grateful to the rest of my family, especially Melissa, Noah and of course Mum and Dad. To my parents, I owe my biggest passions: football and books. They're a real inspiration for everything I do.

Finally, I couldn't have done this without Iona's encouragement and understanding during long, work-filled weekends. Much love to you.

CHAPTER 1

A DREAM COME TRUE

It was 14 November 2012. This was the biggest day of Raheem's life so far – after all, you only made your England debut once. Two months earlier, he had been called up for the World Cup 2014 qualifier against Ukraine and named as a substitute. He didn't get to come on but he still learned a lot from training with the country's best players. It was hard watching from the bench, especially when the team was losing with ten minutes to go. With his pace and skill, Raheem knew he could have made a difference on the wing against a tired defence but in the end, England managed to get a draw without him.

This time, though, in Sweden, not only was

Raheem playing but he was starting. 'I'll be testing some of the younger players in tomorrow's friendly,' Roy Hodgson, the England manager, had told him as they walked off the training pitch the day before. 'You'll be starting, Raheem – we believe you're ready for this.' Roy had always had great faith in him; at Liverpool, he had given him his debut at the age of just fifteen. Raheem could only nod and flash his trademark big smile. It was the news he'd been waiting for.

In the tunnel before the match in Stockholm, he took a deep breath and let the noise of the 50,000 fans in the stadium fire him up. This was what he was born to do. Moments later, he walked out onto the pitch, holding the hand of a Swedish mascot. Just like for Liverpool, Steven Gerrard was there with him as captain and mentor. In the dressing room before the game, Stevie could see that Raheem was nervous.

'There's nothing to worry about, kid. It's no different to playing in front of the Kop at Liverpool. Don't rush things today – just do your thing and enjoy it. Something tells me this won't be your only England cap!'

Stevie patted him on the back and left him to his pre-match stretches. It was a real comfort to have such experienced teammates alongside him – these big games could be pretty scary for a seventeen-year-old.

As the national anthem played, Raheem looked down proudly at the famous three lions on his white tracksuit top. He still couldn't quite believe that he was wearing the England shirt so soon into his career. What a year 2012 had been and there was still a month of it to go. Despite being born in Jamaica, England was certainly Raheem's footballing home. His homeland would always have a special place in his heart but it was in London and Liverpool that he had developed as both a player and a person.

Just before kick-off, another Liverpool teammate, Glen Johnson, came over to give him some words of advice: 'Raheem, stay focused today. You're on the right wing and I'm at right back so we'll be working together a lot. Make those amazing attacking runs when you can but don't forget to defend too. I don't want to spend the whole game clearing up your mess!' Glen gave him a friendly slap on the back and they took up their positions ready for the start.

Raheem knew it wouldn't be an easy game; the Sweden team included experienced Premier-League players like Jonas Olsson and Seb Larsson, plus one of his favourite players in the world, the amazing striker Zlatan Ibrahimović. Raheem was really looking forward to playing against Zlatan and seeing his tricks and flicks up close. Zlatan did not disappoint, scoring the first goal after 20 minutes.

Five minutes later, Raheem found space for the first time in the match and he ran at the Swedish defence before passing to Danny Welbeck, who nearly set up a goal. Raheem could sense the Sweden fans holding their breath when he had the ball at his feet. They knew he was a threat and that gave him confidence.

Raheem was involved again as England made it 1-1. Stevie passed to him deep inside his own half and this time, rather than dribbling, he did what coaches had always told him to do – 'get your head up and look up for the pass'. He could see Ashley Young making a great run over on the left and he played a great ball out to him. Ashley did brilliantly and crossed for Danny to score.

England took the lead before half-time but the second half was all about Zlatan. His second goal was a volley, his third was a powerful free-kick and his fourth was one of the best goals Raheem had ever seen, an impossible overhead kick from thirty yards out. Watching such an amazing performance, Raheem was sure that he had the desire and the talent to be that good. He just needed to keep working hard.

With five minutes to go, Raheem was substituted. 'Well done, lad,' Roy said as he made his way off the pitch. As he took his seat on the bench, Raheem felt really tired but pleased with the way he had played. It hadn't been the dream debut he had hoped for but it had been an amazing experience to represent his country. He couldn't wait to do it again, especially back at Wembley. As a kid, he had lived around the corner from the new stadium, playing football in the streets as it was being built. To play on that pitch in front of all those fans would be unbelievable.

On the flight back to England, Raheem thought back on how far he'd come. There were times when his future had looked bleak. But thanks to football, he stayed out of trouble and learnt respect, hard work and self-esteem. He owed a lot of people for the support they had given him over the years – his mum Nadine, his teachers, his coaches. They had all believed in his talent.

Most of all, he thought about what Chris, his teacher at Vernon House, had once said to him. 'If you carry on the way you're going, by the time you're seventeen you'll either be in prison or playing for England.' Raheem smiled to himself; thankfully, he had achieved the second option. But he promised himself that this was just the beginning.

CHAPTER 2

JAMAICAN SUNSHINE

It was a special vase. One that had been handed down from generation to generation, dusted regularly and placed proudly on a shelf in the main room. The ball bounced up, almost in slow motion, and just missed the vase. But it still made the shelf shake.

'How many times have I told you, Raheem?' his grandmother yelled as she stormed into the room. 'No football in the house! The sun is shining. Find your friends and take the game outside.' She shook her head as she pointed towards the back door.

Raheem knew all about that rule. But he couldn't help it. He was only five years old and he had a lot of energy.

He looked at the floor to show that he felt bad

about nearly breaking the vase. 'I'm sorry,' he mumbled. 'I won't do it again.'

Then he raced outside into the bright sunshine, carrying the ripped ball that had almost got him in big trouble.

At the corner of the street, he saw one of his friends, Christopher. He waved. 'Want to play?'

Christopher smiled. This wasn't the first time that he had seen Raheem rush outside looking a little guilty. It usually meant that his friend had caused damage in the house by kicking the ball too hard.

'Sure. Let's ask Leon and Ridley as well. I'll get some of my dad's paint cans to use as goalposts.'

Just like that, the game was underway. That was the beauty of living in Jamaica. Raheem never had to worry about the weather. It was almost always sunny.

Even at such a young age, Raheem and his friends knew all about 'scrimmage', which was a popular style of football on the island. The goals were small and the rules were non-existent. It was a game for 'showmen', where skills were encouraged above all else. Scoring goals was still important but performing magic with the ball was encouraged even more.

Raheem had already earned a reputation among his friends in Maverley, part of the Jamaican capital of Kingston. He was skilful and competitive, but most of all he was very fast. It was almost unfair on the other boys. Raheem would just kick the ball ahead and sprint after it. No one could catch him.

'Come on, give us a chance,' Christopher complained after Raheem did his usual trick the first time he got the ball.

Raheem grinned. 'Catch me if you can!'

When he got bored of scoring goals that way, he showed off his skills. Flicks and tricks, he called it. It never took long for his friends to shout at him when he didn't let them touch the ball. 'Stop showing off, Raheem. Pass it!'

It rarely made a difference. The next minute, Raheem would be flicking the ball over a defender's head – a move known in Jamaica as a 'pile' – or knocking the ball through a defender's legs – known as a 'salad'. He was just a natural for the scrimmage style of play.

He knew all the neighbours. Some of them came out to watch the boys playing in the street, relaxing with a beer and cheering every goal. Raheem was everyone's favourite – 'dynamite', they called him.

That night, Raheem limped back into the house, exhausted from nearly two hours of football without even a five-minute break. His grandmother smiled as he wiped the sweat from his forehead. She poured him a glass of water. 'Where do you get all that energy from? It makes me tired just watching you rushing around. Wash your hands and sit down. Dinner will be on the table in two minutes.'

When his plate was placed in front of him, Raheem's eyes lit up. It was fish and potatoes, his favourite. 'Wow, you didn't tell me we were having *this*. I scored ten goals in our game this afternoon, so I think I earned it!'

His grandmother winked at him. Then her face turned more serious. 'Well, you might not have been getting any dinner at all if you'd broken that vase.'

Raheem went red, imagining how that conversation might have gone. He loved his grandmother. She was funny and always took good care of her grandchildren, but she was scary when she got angry.

After dinner, he helped bring the plates and glasses into the kitchen. While his grandmother stood at the sink, Raheem asked, 'Did we get any post today?'

His grandmother turned off the tap and turned to face Raheem, with a sympathetic look. 'Not today. But your mum is going to send another letter soon. Don't worry. I know she's thinking about you.'

Raheem nodded and tried to put on a smile. His mum had moved to England a few months ago and he really missed her. She had promised that they would not be separated for long.

His grandmother finished the bedtime story, closed the book and tucked Raheem in. 'Night night, little man. Sweet dreams.'

'Night night,' Raheem replied. Before he turned off his lamp, he opened the drawer by the side of the bed and took out a crumpled envelope. This had become part of his routine lately. It was the most recent letter from his mum. He read it twice, kissed the paper and put it back in the envelope. He knew that they would be reunited soon.

Thousands of miles away in England, his mum lay awake after a late night at work. Nadine was tired but she couldn't sleep. Her mind turned to her children – and, in particular, little Raheem. What would he be doing at that moment? Was he missing her? Did he understand why she was doing it? It was the last question that troubled her the most. Raheem was still so young and she had struggled to explain why she was moving away.

But she just had to leave Maverley – for her sake and for her children's future. Every year, it became a more dangerous place with all kinds of crime and lots of local gangs. None of that was affecting Raheem yet, but what would happen when he was a teenager? It would be so easy to get caught up with the wrong group of friends. With the clock ticking, Nadine had made her decision. She would find a way out and make sure that her children had every chance of staying on a safer path.

Not that it was easy, of course. Tears had streamed down her face as she waved goodbye to Raheem and it felt as if she had cried throughout the whole flight to England. But once she landed in London, she had forced herself to be strong. Everyone was depending on her. If she was going to create this new life, she needed to find a job and a place to live.

Things had fallen into place quickly. She had found a vacancy on St Raphael's housing estate in north-west London straightaway and a hospital job nearby. She then began to put money aside into a white envelope, ready for bringing her family to London as soon as possible. Months later, the envelope was starting to bulge.

Thinking about Raheem always made her smile. He was such a cheeky little boy, full of energy and love. She reached for the notepad on the floor next to her bed. 'Time for another letter,' she said quietly. 'It won't be long until I have good news to share.'

CHAPTER 3

LEAVING THE SUN BEHIND

One morning, as he sat down in his usual chair for breakfast, Raheem's world was turned upside down. His grandmother gave him a sad smile and ran her fingers through his hair.

'Raheem, your mum called last night. She's been making plans. You're going to join her in England.'

Raheem looked confused. He didn't know where England was, or if he would still be able to meet up with his friends. He had so many questions but before he could launch into the list, his grandmother was giving him a plate of plantain and telling him more about the move.

'You leave in two weeks. That means you need to

start thinking about everything you want to pack. I'll give you one of my suitcases and we can pack it together. Then you're going on an airplane.'

Raheem's eyes widened. He had seen airplanes on television and he even had a toy plane that his grandmother had bought him last year for his birthday.

'Your mum has a place for you to live in London, the capital of England. She says there are lots of other boys in the neighbourhood. I'm sure you'll make lots of new friends.'

'I like the friends I have now.'

His grandmother paused. She had expected this. Raheem spent so much time with Christopher, Leon and the other boys who lived on their street. She wanted to make this move as easy as possible, but Raheem would be crushed to find out that he might never see his Maverley friends again.

'I know,' she replied. 'But football is even bigger in England. Your mum said it's all anyone ever talks about. There will leagues for you to join and coaches to help you get even better.'

Raheem shrugged. This was all happening so fast.

He was excited that he would see his mum. He missed her. But England? He didn't know what to think.

'What school will I go to? Can I bring my football? How will we know where to meet Mum?' He was talking faster than ever as new thoughts popped into his head.

His grandmother walked over to him and put a hand on his shoulder. 'Raheem, I don't have all the answers. But I promise you one thing: everything will be OK.'

Raheem heard footsteps in the hallway. 'And I'll be with you to make sure everything is OK, little man,' a cheerful voice called. His sister, Lakima, appeared in the entrance to the little kitchen. 'You can hold my hand if you get too scared,' she added with a smile.

'I'm not scared,' Raheem shot back, not realising that it was a joke and his sister was hoping for that exact reaction. 'Nothing scares me.'

Lakima came over and hugged her little brother. Raheem tried to wriggle away but his sister's arms were too strong. Kimberley, Raheem's other sister, rushed in to join the hug. 'As long as we're together, we'll be fine,' Lakima said, patting his cheek.

The next day, Raheem raced into his bedroom after another afternoon of football in the street. A brown suitcase was propped up next to his bed, with a short note on it. 'Ready for you to start packing,' it said, in his grandmother's handwriting.

Raheem sighed. He quickly decided that packing was boring. He wasn't sure which clothes and toys to pack so he just piled everything into the suitcase, pulled down the top and sat on it to make it close. 'Grandma, I've done it!' he called.

Moments later, Lakima walked past. 'Raheem, you don't need to pack everything! Leave some of these things here for when we come back to visit. My teacher said England is cold and rainy, so you don't need all those pairs of shorts.'

Cold and rainy? Raheem didn't like the sound of that. Why had his mum picked England when she could have stayed in sunny Jamaica? That didn't make any sense to him.

When the big day finally arrived, Raheem felt

nervous. He hugged his friends Christopher and
Leon. 'I promise I'll write you both a letter as soon as
we get there. Then we can plan our next match.'

As they carried the suitcases out into the street
ready for the drive to the airport, Raheem suddenly
remembered that he had forgotten one important
item. He darted back through the house and opened
the back door. Hidden away out of sight was
Raheem's football, which had started off white and
shiny but now had pieces of leather falling off it. He
tucked it under his arm and rushed back to join the
rest of the family.

When he appeared clutching the football and
scampered over to put it in his suitcase, everyone
laughed. 'Well, you couldn't travel without that,
could you?' his grandmother said, laughing so much
that she almost fell over.

Five minutes later, Devon, a friend of the family,
arrived and the cases were loaded into his car. As they
began their journey to the airport, Raheem watched all
the familiar places whizz by and wondered how long
it would be until he was back in Jamaica.

CHAPTER 4

LONDON LIFE

As the doors of the airplane swung open, Raheem was jumping up and down. 'Is she there? Is she there?' he called to Lakima who was just ahead of him.

'I can't see yet. There are so many people out there. Oh wait, there she is! On the right.'

Raheem saw her too – his mum. It had been months since he had seen her but it felt like years. 'Mum!!!' he screamed, running towards her and jumping into her arms.

Nadine couldn't remember the last time she had felt so happy. She hugged Raheem and held on tightly, kissing the top of his head. 'I've been looking forward to this day for so long. I've missed you so much.'

All around them, other travellers were finding their families or the taxi drivers who were ready to take them to their next stop.

'Let's go, kids!' she said, with a wide grin. 'We're taking the bus and we need to get our tickets over there.' She pointed to a small counter against the wall. Moments later, they had their tickets and were walking outside to the bus stop.

The first thing that Raheem noticed was the cold. As he stepped out of the airport, clutching his mum's hand, a big gust of wind made him stumble. He shivered. It had been hot and sunny when they left Jamaica. This felt like a totally different world. Not for the first time, Raheem was unsure whether he was going to like England.

'Raheem, you're very quiet,' Nadine said as the bus was speeding towards north London. 'I know this is a big change but you'll get used to it. You'll have so many places to explore.'

Raheem didn't reply. He was too busy looking out

of the window and playing with his toy car.

He finally spoke ten minutes later. 'Will I have my own room?'

Nadine smiled. 'You'll have to wait and see,' she said, winking at him. 'There's a park just across the road and I'm sure you'll enjoy taking your ball over there and meeting the other boys.'

Raheem had cheered up by the time they arrived at St Raphael's. He walked closely behind his mum, both of them looking around at their new surroundings. Some of the neighbours were watching as they carried their cases up the stairs. One of them smiled and waved.

'Hi, Trudi!' Nadine called. 'Come over and meet my family later on. We're finally all together again!'

That night, Raheem lay in his new bed and thought about everything that had happened in the past twenty-four hours. This was a new adventure but a scary one. He hoped he would make friends quickly and that his football skills might make that easier.

Nadine stood in the doorway to Raheem's room,

peeking round the door. 'I hope I've done the right thing,' she whispered to herself. The dangers and 'no go' areas in Maverley were no secret, but north London had its own dangers. She had seen some worrying things during her time at St Raphael's but she was confident that her family would be safer here.

Raheem didn't waste any time in introducing himself to the other boys. At first, it was just kicking a ball around on the estate. He found a few other boys his age and they were always happy for Raheem to join in. Any time that he had a ball at his feet, he felt right.

But when Raheem started school in north London, everything felt wrong. It was very different to his experiences in Jamaica and having to adapt was very frustrating. He tried to pay attention to his teachers but he found it very hard to concentrate. His mind would wander: usually he was either thinking about football or talking to his friends. But it landed him in trouble. Time and time again, Nadine was called to see the headmaster and was told about Raheem's latest incident.

'Raheem, you've got to listen to your teachers,' she told him on the walk home one afternoon. 'The school is running out of patience. Keep quiet and work hard. That's all I'm asking.'

He nodded, then looked at the ground. He hated letting his mum down, but he hated school too. Sometimes he was naughty – he knew that – but sometimes it just felt like he couldn't focus on what his teachers were telling him. Was that really his fault?

Things at school went from bad to worse. Eventually, the headmaster lost patience and Nadine received the call she had been dreading: Raheem was being asked to leave the school.

Nadine knew she had to act quickly, or else Raheem might spiral away from an education and into the kinds of activities that she had worked so hard to protect him from. 'I have to get this next decision right,' she told one of her friends on the estate. 'Raheem needs to be at a school where the teachers understand his personality.'

As she researched her options, the decision

became much easier. There was a school that seemed perfect for getting Raheem back on track: Vernon House Special School.

CHAPTER 5

NEW SCHOOL, NEW START

'Are you nervous for your first day?' asked Lance, one of the many boys who played football with Raheem on the estate.

'Not really, I needed the change. My last school just wasn't for me. I'm looking forward to starting fresh.'

Raheem meant it, even if he was a bit embarrassed about changing schools. It was only temporary, until he could improve his behaviour in class. He knew he could beat his learning difficulties, just as he had learnt to beat defenders on the football pitch. He just needed a bit more care and attention than a big school could offer him. At Vernon House, there were only six pupils in each class, so he wouldn't get the chance to be naughty.

When Nadine dropped Raheem off at school on his first day, the headmaster met him at the gates and took him to his class. 'Raheem, this is your new teacher, Mr Beschi.'

They shook hands. Chris Beschi was used to moody kids who wouldn't take their eyes off the floor, so it was nice to see Raheem's big, shy smile. He knew immediately that this was a good-natured boy that he could really help. 'Nice to meet you. I hear you're a keen footballer?'

Raheem grinned. 'Yes! Do you play football here?'

It was Chris's turn to smile. 'Do we play football here? Yes, of course we do!'

Raheem liked Vernon House for many reasons, but it was the football that was closest to his heart. This was school and yet they let him do what he loved most for two hours every day. Sometimes it was just the pupils playing amongst themselves but Raheem preferred it when they played ten-a-side, with five kids and five teachers on each side. It didn't take long for everyone to become aware of his talent.

'Raheem, we'll have you on our team,' Chris shouted as they all lined up in the playground.

'Sir, it's not fair!' the other kids complained. 'Whoever has Raheem always wins – it's like having a sixth adult on your team.'

Chris loved watching Raheem play football. In the classroom, he could sometimes get frustrated when he didn't understand something. But on the pitch, that energy and frustration was converted into something positive and amazing. He never stopped working for his teammates, even when they gave up. With the ball at his feet, Raheem's eyes lit up and the smile never left his face. He could run rings round the other players and he had perfected every trick imaginable.

Not only this, but football also allowed Chris to see Raheem's true intelligence. He was always thinking, trying to find new ways of creating goals. He knew exactly when to go forward and when to pass backwards and start the attack again. For an eight-year-old, he had some great ideas. 'Sir, in the

next game, I'm going to play through the middle,'
Raheem told him after class one day. 'I'll get more of
the ball there and it's harder for the defenders when
they don't know if I'll go left or right.'

Every week, Chris took Raheem and his fellow
pupils on a mile-long walk to take photographs
of a building development for a school project. It
wasn't just any old site, however, especially not to
Raheem. It was the new Wembley stadium, still
under construction. Every time he looked up at the
massive arch and the huge steel structure, he felt a
shiver of excitement.

'One day, I'm going to play in that stadium in
front of thousands of fans,' Raheem announced to
everyone. None of the other boys laughed – they
knew he wasn't joking. It became the dream that
kept him focused.

Playing so much football was really helping
Raheem to concentrate back in the classroom. And
in such a small group, Chris was able to build up his
confidence about learning. 'A lot of that frustration
comes from you thinking you're not clever,' he told

Raheem. 'But you are – you just need to believe in yourself like you do on the football pitch.'

Although his behaviour was certainly improving, there were still moments when Chris saw the youngster's wild side. Raheem was mischievous more than anything, but it was easy to see how he could slip into bad habits. Chris was determined to keep him on the right path to success. After one training session where Raheem showed both his dazzling ball skills and his temper, he told him: 'If you carry on the way you're going, by the time you're seventeen you'll either be in prison or playing for England.'

The words stung Raheem and he never forgot them. If those were his two options, he knew which one he wanted – and he would work as hard as possible to make that a reality.

CHAPTER 6

DREAMING BIG

The more Raheem played, the more he loved it.
Football had become the number one priority in his
life. Each day revolved around it. And with every
impressive performance, he allowed himself to dream
of making it as a professional.

His friends could not believe how easy everything
was for him, whether it was a game in the street or
a proper match (for the school). Before long, all the
local boys knew about his tricks and flicks.

'There's nothing I can't do with the ball,' Raheem
told Darren proudly one afternoon.

'Are you sure you aren't Brazilian?' Darren joked.

'You can call me Heemio if you want. I think I'd fit
in well with Ronaldo and Ronaldinho.' Raheem had

first seen Ronaldinho's skills when England played
Brazil at the 2002 World Cup. Usual school lessons
had been cancelled for the morning so that all the
boys could crowd into a classroom to watch the
game on a big television. Even though Raheem was
cheering for England, he loved the way Ronaldinho
played and spent the next few days trying to copy the
free-kick that Ronaldinho lobbed past David Seaman
for the winning goal.

Darren laughed at the idea of Raheem playing on
the wing in a Brazil shirt and teaming up with the
stars to leave defenders looking silly.

'Those kinds of players aren't afraid to try things,'
Raheem said. 'That's how the game is meant to
be played. The tricks don't always work but it's
entertainment. Even if it only works once or twice
per game, it could be the difference between
winning and losing.'

Raheem soon had another idol to learn from –
this time at his favourite team, Manchester United.
Cristiano Ronaldo was one of the club's summer
signings. Ronaldo could make the ball do amazing

things, even as he was sprinting forward, and he was only seventeen.

'He has so much confidence and he never gets scared if he loses the ball a few times,' Raheem explained to anyone who would listen. 'He's going to be the best player in the league. Just give him a couple of years.'

His friends laughed. Raheem was known for his bold claims – and he was often right.

At school, most of his class supported one of the London teams – some Chelsea, some Arsenal, some Tottenham and even a few QPR or West Ham fans. Raheem was happy to claim Ronaldo as his own hero and let the others pick their own.

Every Saturday night, Raheem would wait for his mum to fall asleep and then sneak downstairs to watch *Match of the Day*. He turned the television on and quickly lowered the volume. He watched the Manchester United games closely, paying special attention to Ronaldo so that he could copy the tricks in the street the next day.

That was how it usually worked. Raheem would

see a clever skill on *Match of the Day* and then he'd practise it over and over again until he had mastered it. Next, he would test it in games on the estate. The end result was usually some bruised ankles but some spectacular goals.

One evening, Raheem was in an especially good mood. And that meant he was in unstoppable form once the game started. 'Heemio, play the through ball!' Ollie screamed. But, as usual, Raheem had other ideas. He darted forward, fooling one defender with a stepover and another by swerving to the right. As the last defender raced towards him, Raheem flicked the ball up and over the defender's head, then volleyed it past the goalkeeper.

He raised his arms in the air. To his left, a group of boys and girls from his school chanted 'Heemio! Heemio! Heemio!' Raheem smiled at that. He was becoming a local celebrity. Sometimes that meant the older boys tried to push him around – otherwise his speed could embarrass them.

Raheem was eager to play on a bigger stage, and he wasn't shy about aiming high. 'Mum, I want to play in the Premier League one day,' he announced one morning at breakfast.

'Well then, we better make sure the scouts know where they can find you,' Nadine replied.

'I know I can do it. I just need a team to take a chance on me and be willing to give me a proper trial. Then I'll let them see all my tricks.'

Nadine smiled. It was nice to see her son being so passionate about football, even if he wasn't treating his schoolwork with the same excitement. But she was used to it by now: it was football, football, football in her son's life.

CHAPTER 7

COPLAND HERO

'Mr Lawrence!' Lakima called through the fence. It was getting dark and the Copland Community School football coach was collecting up the balls after a training session. 'You need to let my brother, Raheem, play – they say he's the best player on the estate!'

Paul Lawrence liked Lakima's passion but he hadn't even heard of Raheem. 'OK, what year is he in?'

'No sir, he's not at Copland yet – he's still at primary school. But he'll be coming here in a couple of years.'

After Lakima told him about her younger brother, Paul told her that he would take a look at him when he joined the school. There were a lot of kids that came to him, each of them claiming to be the best footballer on St Raphael's estate. Most of them were good but not as good as they thought they were.

However, Lakima kept asking him and after the sixth time, Paul finally agreed. If she was that determined, then he had to see this kid play. 'OK look, if you'll stop nagging me every day, I'll let him join in. Tell him to come down to practice tomorrow night at five.'

When Raheem turned up with his sister, Paul couldn't believe how small he was. The boy was only two years younger than most of the Copland players but, compared to them, Raheem looked like a baby. He was very shy and didn't talk to the other boys as they got ready for training. He stood on his own and practiced keepy-uppies. He was certainly good at that.

But as soon as the practice began, Raheem came alive. Every time he got the ball, he dribbled round three or four players with speed and skill. He could be a little greedy at times but he had some amazing tricks and when he couldn't go any further, he would pass to a teammate or score a goal. Paul knew he was watching something special. Raheem was fearless, even when defenders used their strength to try to push him off the ball. The kid seemed to love the challenge of playing against older boys.

'Nice work, Raheem!' Paul shouted from the touchline, clapping loudly as the kid fired a shot into the net for a second time. If only he was a few years older, the coach thought to himself; this kid would be great for the Copland team. The smile never left Raheem's face while he played; Paul loved to see kids enjoying football that much. For the full hour, Raheem never stopped running up and down the wings. The opposition players were exhausted by the end.

'I told you he was good!' Lakima joked as the training session ended.

'He's not just good – he's incredible!' one of the team replied. 'Sir, how can we get him in our team? We could win the cup with him on the wing.'

'We can't, I'm afraid – he's too young,' Paul said, patting the boy on the back. 'Raheem, well played today. Your sister was right about you – you're the real deal! As soon as you're a student here, I promise, you'll be one of our stars. Lakima, make sure he joins the school in two years, OK?'

Raheem couldn't wait to join Copland. They had one of the best football teams in London. And from the school playing fields, he could see the new Wembley stadium being built in the distance. He thought of it as his home ground. 'I'm going to play there one day,' he told Lakima.

Raheem's football skills were the talk of the estate but he wanted to test himself against other kids at other schools. He knew he was ready and he wanted to win trophies. His mum Nadine was really happy – finally her son had a focus in his life. After some difficult years, Raheem was really improving in class and he was doing well at school. And it was all because of football – she used to hate the sport but now she loved it.

'Mum, can I go out and play for an hour please?' Raheem would ask after school. 'Lakima can keep an eye on me and I'll be back for dinner!' Nadine couldn't argue with that. If it kept her son out of trouble, he could play football all day long.

When he finally arrived at Copland, Raheem went straight into the school team. After the first practice, Paul went over to him and shook his hand. 'Wow, you certainly haven't lost your talent!' The coach laughed. 'You're even better than I remember. It's great to have you here.'

When Raheem was still in Year Seven, he was the captain and star of the Year Eight team. 'We've changed the rules for you,' Paul explained, with a big grin. With Raheem cutting inside from the left wing and scoring and setting up lots of goals, Copland beat team after team and made it all the way to the Brent Cup Final. 'Raheem could play for the Year Elevens and he'd still be the best player there,' Paul told the school's headmaster with pride.

'Right boys, let's go out and show them how good we are,' Raheem said before the game, proudly wearing his white captain's armband over the school's blue shirt. Away from football, he was still very shy but on the pitch he was a confident leader. He could see that some of the players were a bit nervous about the big match; he, on the other hand, couldn't wait. He wanted his fearlessness to rub off on his teammates. 'We've got nothing to be scared about – we can win this!' he shouted, rushing around to give everyone a high five.

In the final, Raheem was man of the match. The opposition had heard about him and they tried to kick him at every opportunity but Raheem was just too quick and too good for them. He was the best player by a mile. At the final whistle, the Copland players lifted their star player high into the sky as they celebrated their victory. 'I love winning,' he told his mum that night as she came into his room to say goodnight. 'It's the best feeling.'

'Something tells me you'll be winning plenty more trophies in the next few years,' Paul told Raheem as they stood in the school corridor. They were looking at a new photo framed on the wall – it was a picture of Raheem lifting the Brent Cup, with a massive grin all over his face. The caption underneath read: 'Man of the match Raheem Sterling, who scored a hat-trick and set up the other two goals.'

CHAPTER 8

CATCHING THE EYE

Nadine had been told many times how much talent Raheem had and she could see how important his skill was in helping him to stay away from the gang crime on the estate. She could teach him manners and respect but she couldn't do everything.

'The more football you play, the better, that's what I think!' she told Raheem at dinner one night. Lakima rolled her eyes; since he'd started playing football, Raheem had become the golden child, and he always got his way. 'When you let off steam on the pitch, you're an angel at home and at school.' He couldn't have been happier to hear his mum say that. Playing football was what he loved most of all.

Raheem enjoyed playing on the estate with his

mates but by the age of nine, he was ready for bigger and better things. He wanted to play proper matches on proper pitches against proper teams. He wanted to wear a team kit and win trophies. Clive, a local youth worker, started taking him to Roe Green Park to practise.

'You've got so much talent!' Clive told Raheem one evening as they played one-on-one until it got dark. He was exhausted; Raheem always kept him on his toes with his stepovers and nutmegs. 'If you keep working hard, you really could be the next Ronaldinho!'

Thanks to Clive, Raheem started playing for a local church team, Alpha and Omega, in the evenings and at weekends. They had a good youth side and it was the challenge he needed. Clive always picked him up from the estate and took him to the games. He always found Raheem waiting for him outside, practicing his keepy-uppies.

'Do you ever rest or sleep?' Clive joked. 'I don't think I've ever seen you without a football at your feet!'

Raheem quickly became the star of the team. He

was still small for his age but that just helped him to take defenders by surprise with his tricks. They just couldn't take the ball off him. Clive watched with pride as Raheem scored goal after goal. Despite being the best player on the pitch in most games, he was always modest and his teammates liked that about him.

The only problem for Raheem was losing – he couldn't stand it. He had got better at controlling his frustration but sometimes he just couldn't help it. Word had quickly spread across the league about Raheem and opposition teams would be rough with him in order to try to stop him. They would push him and kick him in the back of the leg when the referee wasn't looking. Raheem tried to stay calm but if he wasn't getting free-kicks and his team weren't playing well, he would lose his cool.

It was Clive's job to deal with Raheem's disappointments. 'Look, you can't win every time,' he said one day as they sat in the car outside his home after a particularly bad defeat. Raheem hadn't said a word on the journey. 'Life just isn't like that.

Sometimes you'll lose and you have to learn to deal with that in the right way. That's what sportsmanship is all about.'

'But they were cheating!' Raheem complained.

'That might well be true but things aren't always fair. Part of growing up is accepting that things don't always go your way.'

Raheem promised to think hard about this advice. He agreed that getting aggravated was a waste of his energy and talent, especially when he was playing so well.

Clive wasn't the only one paying attention to Raheem. Peter Moring, a youth coach in the area, had first seen him playing for Oakington Manor Primary School. He'd been amazed by the kid's ability – it was so rare to see someone stand out so much at that age. When he then saw Raheem running rings around teams for Alpha and Omega, he knew that he was watching something special.

Peter knew he had to act. He decided to speak to one of his contacts connected to the team. 'Tell me more about the little left winger. No one got near him in today's game. Have you had many scouts watching him?'

It wasn't a surprise that people were interested in Raheem but Alpha and Omega didn't want to lose their star player. Plus, the coaches weren't sure that Raheem was ready for the pressures of professional academies just yet. He was still a very raw talent and he needed to be more consistent. He was definitely still learning.

The reply was clear: No scouts so far, but Raheem isn't going anywhere right now anyway.

Peter grinned when he heard that news. When he wasn't coaching, he was doing occasional scouting for QPR. If he saw a particularly good kid, he let QPR know. This was one of those times.

He made the call. 'I've just watched a terrific talent. His name is Raheem Sterling. I'll send over all the details but you should think about getting one of the Under-16 coaches out to watch him before another club snaps him up.'

CHAPTER 9

RAHEEM PARK RANGERS

'Welcome to the Queens Park Rangers School of
Excellence,' John O'Neill, the Under-16s coach,
told Raheem and Nadine when he met them at the
entrance. 'We're really glad that you could come
down tonight.'

John had taken his friend Peter Moring's advice to
have a look at the Alpha and Omega left winger. 'You
won't regret it!' Peter had told him and he was right.
One cold evening, John watched as Raheem dribbled
past one player after another for ninety minutes. It
was like watching a man among boys, only Raheem
was one of the smallest players on the pitch. The
kid had everything that the academy looked for in a

young player: composure, desire, work-rate and, of course, lots and lots of talent.

After the match, John asked to speak to Raheem. Reluctantly, the Alpha and Omega coaches agreed.

'It's great to meet you,' John said, shaking Raheem's hand. 'You were brilliant tonight – what a game!'

'Thanks,' Raheem replied with a shy smile. He didn't feel very comfortable talking to strangers, even about football. Clive stood next to him, ready to step in and help if needed. It was good to have his support.

'My name is John O'Neill,' the coach went on, 'and I'm one of the youth coaches at QPR. We're always looking for exciting young players like you. How would you like to come and train with us?'

Raheem couldn't believe it – a Championship side wanted him to try out for their academy. It would be a big step up from the local league but he felt ready to test himself against the best young players. He couldn't stop smiling. He couldn't wait to tell his mum and his friends on the estate. 'That sounds great!'

Before the training session began, John showed
Raheem and Nadine around the facilities. Compared
to the changing rooms at Alpha and Omega's ground,
it was like walking around Wembley stadium.
Raheem couldn't wait to play on their beautiful
green pitches. 'We used to be a big club,' John told
them, 'and we're on our way back up to the top.
Youngsters like you are our future – with your help,
we can get back to the Premier League!'

The Premier League – that was where Raheem
dreamed of playing. Cristiano Ronaldo, Thierry Henry,
Ryan Giggs; he wanted to follow in the footsteps of his
heroes. He wanted to play in front of thousands of fans
who chanted his name. Queens Park Rangers seemed
a great place to start his journey.

With Nadine working evenings at the hospital,
Raheem would take the bus on his own from the
St Raphael's estate over to the QPR academy. From
day one, everyone at the club was amazed at how
good Raheem was. And how tough he was too; for
someone so small, he could really battle with the
big boys. He started with the Under-12s and was

unstoppable. He was involved in every goal they scored, whether it was a shot or a pass.

'I think we should start calling you Raheem Park Rangers!' Steve Gallen, the youth development manager, joked after Raheem scored all five of the team's goals in an important win.

Unfortunately, the other youngsters just weren't at the same level and Raheem was often on the losing team, despite his best efforts. He had grown up fast in many ways but he still found it very hard to accept defeat, especially when he had tried so hard and done so well.

'What more can I do?' he complained to Steve on the sidelines one day, with tears streaming down his face. 'I can't play in every position!'

'Don't worry, kid – you were great!' Steve replied, but he knew this couldn't go on. Raheem was just too good for the Under-12s and the club needed to do everything to keep their bright young star happy.

So when Steve took over as Under-14s coach soon afterwards, he knew straight away who he wanted to add to his team.

'Raheem, you're coming to play for the Under-14s,' Steve told him after another practice where he'd been head and shoulders above the rest. 'I think you're ready for the next level up. I warn you, though – you'll be up against some very strong kids who won't like you trying to do your tricks!'

'Don't worry, coach,' Raheem replied. He wished people would stop talking about him being too small all the time. 'I can handle myself!'

'Coaches will think your size is a problem,' Peter Moring told Raheem very early on during his time at QPR. He'd lost count of the number of excellent kids that he'd seen come and then go just because they weren't big enough. He really didn't want that to happen to someone as special as Raheem. 'So you have to be so good that they can't use that excuse,' he added. 'You might not have the strength but you've got plenty of skill!'

Even for the Under-14s, Raheem stood out. He had a calmness on the ball that most kids just didn't have. Where others ran around like headless chickens in the centre of the field, he found space and moved with grace until that electric burst of speed. Steve could tell that Raheem was really thinking on the pitch; his head was always up, looking for the best way to create a goal. It was so exciting to watch a player develop like that. Steve just hoped that Raheem would stay at QPR long enough to sample first team football.

CHAPTER 10

THE KING OF CASSIOBURY PARK

With things going so well for him at QPR, Raheem was the subject of lots of attention. Tom Walley had seen plenty of brilliant young players during his many years as a youth coach in London. He had worked with future England internationals David James and Ashley Cole. In Raheem, he saw that same superstar potential.

'He's got that bit of quality,' Tom said to himself when he first saw Raheem play. With his experience, Tom knew he could help him to achieve his dream of playing in the Premier League. He decided to take Raheem under his wing.

At Cassiobury Park in Watford, Tom watched

as Raheem played with a friend. With jumpers
for goalposts, Raheem attacked again and again,
using every trick he had to take the ball round his
opponent. Every now and then, Tom shouted some
advice but mostly, he just watched with amazement.
Very few kids had such natural ability on the ball.

'Raheem, I've organised a five-a-side game for next
week,' Tom said when the boys had finally stopped
playing. His friend lay on the grass breathing hard
but Raheem looked fresh and ready to play again. 'All
of the best youngsters in London will be in one place.
It should be fun and I want you to be there.'

Raheem nodded with pride. He didn't need to be
asked twice if there was a game of football going on,
especially one where he could test himself against the
best. He'd be there, even if he had to walk all the way.

When he arrived for the game, Raheem recognised
a few of the other kids from the school and club
football he had played. He knew how good they
were but he refused to let nerves get the better
of him. This was where he belonged and he was
ready to prove it. The pitch was in the back garden

of former Tottenham and England midfielder Tim
Sherwood. Sherwood was now on the coaching staff
at Tottenham; Raheem knew that it was the perfect
opportunity to impress a Premier League club.

Raheem came back week after week to play in
these matches. He loved the challenge and he was
learning so much from Tim and Tom. With them
looking after him, he was destined for great things,
just as long as he could stay focused on his dream.

The enthusiastic young player loved running when
he had a ball at his feet or a goal in front of him.
Just running for the sake of running, however, was
something he hated. 'What's the point? It's boring'
was his usual complaint. The worst part of training
with Tom was the 'Dustbin Run'. Every week, he
would make them do shuttle runs between two bins
placed 150 metres apart. Tom would time them and
record their results.

'Kids, stamina is crucial,' he told them when he
heard their loud groans. 'You'll thank me for this one
day. It's one thing to be able to run a fast fifty metres
but it's a very different thing to do it again and again

for a whole ninety minutes. That's what you have to do at the top level.'

The first three or four runs were fine but by the fifth, Raheem's legs felt heavy and he found it hard to breathe. It was like he was swimming through treacle. 'Keep going!' Tom would shout to encourage them when they looked like they were struggling. Usually, Raheem could keep going until he was told to stop but one day, he just didn't want to do it anymore. On his sixth shuttle, Raheem threw himself to the ground, panting.

Tom had a firm word with Raheem in the changing room afterwards. 'Look, I know it's hard and I know it's not much fun but I don't ever want to see you give up like that again. You've got a lot of talent but if the dedication isn't there, you won't reach the top. I've seen it a million times, trust me. Do you think Cristiano Ronaldo just stops running when he feels like it? No, he keeps going until he can't do anymore.'

Raheem nodded to show that he had understood. He needed to make sure his attitude was right at all times; he hated quitting as much as he hated losing.

'Character,' Tom said, his favourite word. 'That's what the best players have. Character makes a career. Tell yourself that the next time you feel like you can't be bothered.'

Raheem learnt his lesson and kept getting better and better under Tom's watchful eye. Back at QPR, he had outgrown the Under-14s and the Under-16s. They were trying to keep their star player away from the spotlight, so that other clubs didn't tempt him to move. He loved QPR, but he was starting to feel like he needed a change.

'Mum, would you be upset if I said I wanted to leave QPR?' Raheem said at dinner one night.

Nadine was silent for a minute while she chose her words. She could see that her son wasn't happy but she didn't want him to rush into anything. 'No, of course I wouldn't be upset, but I want you to think long and hard before you make a decision. They've been very good to you (and this whole family) but if you feel it's time to aim higher, then I'll support you all the way.'

CHAPTER 11

TIME TO MOVE ON

Steve Gallen wasn't going to lose Raheem without a fight. So when he was aged fourteen, Steve had him playing for the QPR Under-18s. Raheem looked tiny next to some of the giant defenders he was playing against. But that never stopped him, even though some of them were three or four years older than him.

'Why would I be scared?' Raheem replied when one of his teammates asked him. 'I know I'm good enough to beat them every time. The only way they can win is by fouling me, and that's what the referee is for!'

With such self-belief, there was just no stopping

Raheem. Suddenly, he became a local celebrity, but not everyone on the St Raphael's estate was happy for him. Due to his busy football schedule of practices and matches, Raheem was spending less and less time with the friends that he'd grown up with. They didn't like it and when he returned from training on the bus one night, they surrounded him.

'So you think you're too good for us now, is that it? Just because you're a football star, you can't hang out with us anymore?' said one of the kids who used to call him 'Heemio' when they played in the streets. In all, eight of them were blocking Raheem's path, and he felt uncomfortable.

That night, he spoke to his mum about it. 'Son, they're just jealous of your success,' she told him. 'It's tough growing up on this estate – very few get an opportunity like you have to escape and chase a better life. And it's hard for them to watch you doing so well. But when you're playing in the Premier League, I'll bet they'll be your best friends again, asking for free tickets! Try to ignore it but let me know if you have any more trouble.'

Raheem didn't want his childhood friends to hate him but he also wasn't going to let them stop him from achieving his dream, especially if they were simply jealous of him. He knew that scouts from Arsenal and Chelsea, two of the biggest clubs in the world, were watching him play.

QPR knew his potential too, but Steve was determined to keep Raheem in the youth squad for as long as possible.

'Kid, we want you to sign your youth terms here,' Steve said in a meeting with Raheem and Nadine. 'You're the best young player we've had at this club for a long time and we all know that you'll go on to bigger and better things. But for now, I think this is a great place for you to be. We'll keep looking after you as we have for the last three years.'

Raheem talked it through with his mum and decided it was the right thing to do. Signing youth terms didn't mean he couldn't then play for someone else, but it meant that a club would have to pay money to buy him. That way, QPR would get a transfer fee for all their hard work in developing his talent, and Raheem would feel he had paid the club back for all their support.

It was very rare to see a crowd of more than one hundred people at a QPR Under-18s game. And usually there were far fewer than that – a few scouts but mostly just the young players' friends and family. With Raheem performing so well on the left wing, however, suddenly the numbers quadrupled. Word had spread about QPR's latest wonderkid and everyone wanted to see him play. Raheem didn't disappoint; he loved to entertain people with his tricks.

'How does it feel to be the talk of the town? We heard there were scouts from Man City, Chelsea, Liverpool and Fulham at the game last week. You need to get yourself an agent!' his teammates teased him. They were really pleased for Raheem, although they had no idea what they would do without him if he left.

A lot of people had come to watch but no one had made an offer for him yet. Raheem was worried that Premier League clubs might be put off by not only his size but might also be frustrated about his behaviour in the past. 'Baggage' they called it – he was from a tough estate and at times his attitude was equally tough. But he was still a child trying hard to learn how to be an adult. 'One of the top teams will take a chance on me,' he told himself in an attempt to stay positive.

Steve spoke regularly with Nadine to try to keep Raheem happy. They had a lot of respect for each other as key figures in Raheem's life, and they both wanted the best for him.

'I just think it might be time for him to move on,' Nadine told Steve. 'He needs a change of scene and I don't just mean QPR; I think he needs a new start, away from London. Of course I don't want to see him leave but Raheem has too many distractions around here, too many people who could be bad influences.'

Steve understood but he had one last card to play. He called his young star into his office the next day. 'Raheem, you'll be playing for the QPR reserves this weekend. Do you think you're up to that challenge?'

'Of course!' Raheem replied with a massive grin. He was only fifteen and he was going to be playing with proper professional footballers.

Raheem did well in a very physical game. He was exhausted when he came off the pitch and the next day he had plenty of cuts and bruises. But his only thought was 'I want to go out there and play again!' He was really grateful for all of the chances that QPR had offered him but he couldn't help feeling that his time there was coming to an end.

'Steve, I'm sorry but I need to go,' Raheem said after training one day. Steve could see how upset the kid was to be saying this. He had tried so hard to keep Raheem at QPR but he knew he couldn't stand in his way any longer.

Raheem added: 'I know that there are scouts watching me and it's time for me to move on.'

CHAPTER 12

A RED IN THE MAKING

When Lee Anderson saw Raheem play for the first time, he got straight on the phone to his brother, Mark. 'You have to come down to QPR straight away,' he told him. 'Their left winger is incredible. He's not a big lad but, boy, can he play football!'

Mark was a youth scout for Liverpool Football Club. Lee would often call him to recommend players but he had never heard his brother sound so excited. 'This kid must be the real deal,' Mark thought to himself. He needed to make a trip to London.

At the QPR Under-18s' next match against Crystal Palace, Mark saw straightaway that he wasn't the only scout watching Raheem. He had never seen so many people at a game at this level. 'This is going to be good,' he said to himself as he waited for the game to kick off.

Mark wasn't disappointed; in fact he couldn't believe his eyes. Raheem's height wasn't ideal but the kid had more tricks than a magician. And he had a good 'football brain' as they said in the scouting trade; Raheem knew when to dribble, when to shoot and when to pass or cross to a teammate. You could teach some of that stuff but the best players already had it.

'When he runs at defenders, that pace is frightening,' Mark Warburton, the Brentford scout, said over a half-time cup of tea. Normally scouts kept their thoughts to themselves about players but there was no point in hiding anything when it came to Raheem. Every club wanted him. 'And he's got end product too – for a fifteen-year-old kid, that's a winning combination!'

In the second half, Raheem was just as impressive. What Mark Anderson really liked was the consistency of his play. He'd seen so many quick-footed wingers who would do one nice thing in a game but then a string of bad things. With Raheem, nothing was a fluke; he could play great passes every time and he could put in perfect crosses.

'How does a kid that small have enough power to do that?' Mark asked the man standing next to him, as Raheem scored with a brilliant shot into the bottom corner. The man had no answer for him.

Mark went back again and again to see Raheem play – and he did something special every time. He was exactly what Liverpool needed but Mark wanted to be sure about his attitude. He worked really hard on the pitch but, just occasionally, there was a flash of frustration.

'Man City, Chelsea, Tottenham, Arsenal – they've all had scouts down here,' Mark Warburton told him when he asked about Raheem's background. 'But none of them have made an offer – they say he's too small with too much "baggage". He's not from the best part of London but so far he's doing a decent job of keeping himself out of trouble. There's no way he's coming to Brentford so I can be honest – if I was you, I'd take a chance on him. If you look after him well, he could be one of England's best players in a few years.'

When Mark Anderson heard that Fulham had put in a bid for Raheem, he knew it was time to act. He called Frank McParland, the Academy Director at Liverpool FC.

'Frank, how soon can you come to QPR? There's a kid here that you really need to see. You know I don't say this often – he's the best thing I've ever seen. He's got some rough edges but we need him in our team!'

When Frank saw Raheem's talent, he agreed with Mark's assessment. They started to make their plans for persuading him to sign for Liverpool. They spoke to Nadine and other people close to Raheem. Their message was simple: 'Liverpool is a great club and the perfect place for Raheem. We'll really look after him, keep the distractions to a minimum and help him to become one of the best players in the world.'

'Raheem, come up to Liverpool and we'll show you around our training facilities,' Frank said with confidence. 'I promise you'll love it there. Once you see what we've got and meet some of the people, you'll know it's the right move for you.'

CHAPTER 13

A WELCOME FROM THE STARS

Mark Anderson drove Raheem and Nadine to Melwood, Liverpool's training ground. On the way they talked about Liverpool's future plans and how they were desperate to become the biggest club in English football again. 'You can be a huge part of that project, Raheem,' Mark told him. He liked the sound of that.

As Melwood came into view, he couldn't believe the size of the place – it was like a city of its own. It was totally different to what he'd known at QPR. Mark could see the surprise on the boy's face. 'It's quite impressive, isn't it?' he said and Raheem just nodded.

At the entrance, they were met by Frank McParland, the Liverpool Academy Director, and Rafa Benitez, the Liverpool manager. Rafa was wearing his club tracksuit with his initials, 'RB', under the liver bird on the club crest. Raheem couldn't believe that such a famous coach was taking the time to meet him. 'Wow, they must really want to sign me,' he thought to himself. They all sat down together and Rafa took charge of the meeting.

'This is one of the biggest clubs in the world but we want to make it *the* biggest club,' he said. 'In order to do that, we need a mix of great, experienced players and the best young talent. We'd love you to come and play here, Raheem. We see you as the future of this football club.'

It was a powerful speech and Raheem began to picture himself in the classic red shirt, celebrating another great goal with the fans at Anfield. He could tell that Liverpool would be a great club to play for. He looked over at his mum and she looked impressed too. Rafa then took Raheem on a tour of the facilities.

Raheem had never seen so many football pitches in one place, and the gym was the size of a shopping centre. They had all of the best equipment, plus an amazing swimming pool. There were lots of physios there helping players recovering from injury. 'As you can see, we really look after our players here,' Frank said as they moved on to the changing rooms.

As they made their way along the corridor, Steven Gerrard, the Liverpool captain, and Fernando Torres, Liverpool's superstar striker, came walking towards them. Raheem was totally star-struck. He was in the same building as two of the best players in the world. And instead of going straight past them, they stopped to chat.

'Stevie and Fernando, this is Raheem Sterling. He's one of the best young players in England and we're trying to persuade him to sign for Liverpool,' Rafa told them.

'Nice to meet you, I've heard a lot about you,' Stevie said, shaking his hand. Raheem couldn't believe that he was actually standing next to Steven Gerrard. He wanted to touch him to make sure it wasn't a fake. The whole day had been an unbelievable experience. 'Look, you've got to sign for Liverpool!' Stevie went on. 'This is the best football club in the world. Just you wait until you play in front of the fans here – there's no feeling like it.'

Fernando spoke next, asking him how he was enjoying the tour. 'The facilities are pretty incredible, aren't they? This is a great club to play for.'

Raheem didn't say a word – he couldn't, he was tongue-tied. If Steven Gerrard and Fernando Torres were telling him to sign for Liverpool, then surely he should sign for Liverpool, shouldn't he? Liverpool was a very different city from London but this was a top club with lots of money, a great history and brilliant footballers to learn from. Going to Fulham would mean he was still close to home but they were unlikely to ever challenge for the Premier League title, or to play in the Champions League.

Raheem had made up his mind, or at least Liverpool's superstars had made it up for him.

'Mum, I'm ready to sign,' he said on the train back to London. 'They clearly really want me and I can really picture myself playing there. What do you think?'

'Son, it has to be your decision,' Nadine told him. 'I'm worried about you leaving home and how the change will affect you, but I'm your mother so that's to be expected! I liked that the manager and the players came to meet you – I thought that was a very nice, personal touch. I'm sure they don't do that for every youngster that they sign for the academy!'

His mum was right; it would be a massive change for him but his mind was made up.

Liverpool paid QPR £500,000 for Raheem but if he did well, the fee could end up being as much as £2 million. It was a lot of money for a fifteen-year-old. Suddenly, he was the talk of the football world. There would be a lot of pressure on him to fulfil his potential but Raheem was determined to become a superstar.

'In a few years, that will seem like a bargain!' he joked with his family.

CHAPTER 14

LEAVING LONDON

'Hi Raheem, nice to meet you. I'm Sandra and this is Peter. Welcome to your new home!'

In Liverpool, Sandra and Peter seemed like really lovely people, but Raheem could already tell that it would be very strange living with people other than his mum and siblings. As his new 'house parents' showed him to his room, he felt like everyone he loved was a long way away. He could feel tears filling his eyes but blinked them away. As soon as Sandra and Peter left him to settle in, he called home.

'Hi, son,' Nadine answered straightaway. She was glad to hear his voice. 'Everything OK? How was the journey? How's your new room?'

'It's a lot bigger than my old one but... it's not the same,' Raheem replied. He didn't want to cry or worry his mum. It would just take some time to get used to his new situation. 'It feels really weird not having you guys around. You will come and visit, right?'

'Of course! As soon as you know when your first match is, we'll be there to cheer you on. It's only two-and-a-half hours on the train.'

Raheem had found it really hard saying goodbye to all his friends in London. He would miss all of the football matches in the parks around Wembley and at Copland Community School. He had learnt so much there and he had a lot of people to thank for helping him to stay out of trouble.

That night, Sandra cooked Raheem's new favourite meal: mac and cheese with salad. His mum must have told them on the phone. Over dinner, they talked about him growing up in London and his love of football. The food was great and the couple made him feel right at home. Peter was a big Liverpool fan, so he was excited to have a future star living in their house. 'You said you play on the wing? Well, when you become the next Stanley Matthews, don't forget about us! A free ticket every now and then would be nice!'

Raheem laughed – he didn't know who Stanley Matthews was but he promised that he'd get Peter a season ticket if he became an Anfield legend. They watched a bit of television together and then it was time for bed. It took Raheem a little while to get used to his new bed but he was soon fast asleep at the end of a very long and tiring day.

The next morning it was time to start at his new school. Raheem used to hate school but since his days at Vernon House, he was much happier in class. Football had really helped with his concentration and he was a clever kid when he tried hard.

Sandra dropped him outside Rainhill High School.

'Good luck, Raheem! Hope it goes well today,' she shouted to him as he walked towards the gates.

It was always hard to start again at a new school but luckily there were quite a few other Liverpool Academy players at Rainhill. They helped him to settle in and being a really good footballer certainly made it easier to make friends with the other boys. Just like at Vernon House and Copland, Raheem spent every spare minute out on the school playing field. Expectations were high and he had a few things to prove.

'I read about you in the newspaper!' one of his classmates told him. 'Wow, I'm playing with someone who's worth £2 million!'

Raheem didn't mind the extra attention from the others and he knew that all their jokes were light-hearted. They quickly saw how good he was on the field and welcomed him into their group. Some even found out about his nickname and started calling him 'Heemio', which really made him feel at home.

Although school was going well, Raheem couldn't help missing London. Back at his new home, he spent hours alone in his room listening to music and thinking about his friends and family. He didn't regret his decision to join Liverpool Football Club but he wished that he had his mum and sisters around for support.

'We'll be up to visit next week, Raheem,' Nadine told him on the phone. She was upset to hear her son sounding homesick. 'You'll have to show us around. Are there any good Jamaican restaurants in Liverpool?'

Raheem had no idea – he didn't really go out very much. If he wasn't at Rainhill and he wasn't training at Melwood, then he was back at Sandra and Peter's house. They were looking after him really well and he was starting to think of them like his second parents, but he couldn't wait to see his real mum. He had a whole new life that he wanted to share with her.

Nadine enjoyed her trip to Liverpool but she was in tears as she said goodbye to Raheem. On the train home, she thought long and hard about the situation. 'I have a good life and a good job in London but I want to be near my son,' she told herself. 'I'm sure I could get a job up in Liverpool and the kids would quickly get used to a new city...'

By the time she phoned Raheem that night, Nadine had made up her mind. 'Son, it might take a little while to sort out but I've decided that we're moving up to Liverpool. I can't leave you up there alone at your age – you need your mum by your side!'

Raheem was over the moon at the news. He jumped up and down on his bed, and he had a huge smile on his face. With his family around him again, there would be nothing stopping him from achieving his Anfield dream.

CHAPTER 15

FEARLESS

As he began his Liverpool career, Raheem showed no signs of the pressure while on the pitch. He was still only fifteen years old and he saw no reason to be scared of anything. He was just starting his journey to the very top and he was keen to impress his new coaches. Before he'd left London, Tom Walley had given him some advice. 'That £500,000 price-tag? Ignore it – it means nothing. Just keep playing the way you've always played with that smile on your face. You'll soon be worth fifty times that much!'

Raheem's size was the only worry, but he knew he had the skills and speed to get around that. 'Plus, I'm stronger than I look!' he joked with his new youth teammates, some of whom were nearly a foot taller than him. Wearing the Number 7 shirt, Raheem started on the left wing. Even though he was right footed, he had always felt at home on the left. It meant he could cut inside to shoot or cross with his right foot. But he wondered whether defenders would start to figure that out, now that he was playing at a higher level.

It was another test that he passed with flying colours. When it came to football, he was just a natural. In game after game, he danced his way past defenders who were much bigger than him, twisting one way and then the other. Every time he got the ball, he took it forward without any hesitation, and attacking at amazing speed. Opposition defenders had no idea what to do with this tiny wonderkid. He was everywhere, running down the wing one minute and then drifting into the middle of the pitch the next. It was like trying to mark a ghost.

'*End product! End product!*' – by now the phrase was stuck in Raheem's head like a really catchy song. He was never greedy; having beaten the right back, he then found the pass or cross to set up goals for others. Sometimes, Raheem even scored himself, although his shooting was something he really wanted to improve.

'He's absolutely fearless,' Raheem's youth team coach told Frank McParland, the Liverpool Academy director. 'They foul him and he gets straight back up and carries on. He jumps for headers with defenders double his size! You put a bit more muscle on that kid and he'll be one of Liverpool's best players in a few years.'

Frank was impressed by the glowing report and decided to take a look for himself. He had seen Raheem's skills back at QPR but he still wasn't ready for just how good he looked amongst Premier League-level academy players. On a pitch with twenty-one other bright young talents, he was head and shoulders above the rest in every way except his height.

For a fifteen-year-old, he had everything – hunger, pace, composure, vision, technique. His final delivery was strong and consistent, whether it was a shot, pass or cross. Frank had seen a lot of youngsters come through the Liverpool youth system over the years but very few had been this special.

He got straight on the phone to Liverpool manager Roy Hodgson. 'Roy, you have to come down and see Raheem play. He's the best winger I've ever seen come through at Anfield.'

For Raheem, it would be a life-changing phone call.

TOURING WITH HIS HEROES

'Raheem, can I have a quick word?' Rodolfo Borrell, the youth team coach, asked at the end of training on a hot June day. Raheem nodded and waited behind as all the other players headed into the changing room. His legs were aching and he just wanted to get into the shower. He hoped that whatever Rodolfo had to tell him would be worth the wait.

'Frank McParland came down to have a look at you a month ago,' the coach said, 'and he told Roy Hodgson to come and take a look too. Roy was impressed and he wants to take you on the summer tour. It's a really good chance for the youngsters to see what playing with the first team is like.

Switzerland and Germany – three games in two weeks. How does that sound?'

'Amazing!' Raheem replied with a massive smile. His heart skipped a beat and he started to imagine the exciting moments that lay ahead. He'd be travelling with senior players like Jamie Carragher, Joe Cole and, of course, Steven Gerrard. He might not play for many minutes, but it would be an amazing opportunity to train with them and learn from them. And impress them with his talent. He couldn't wait to share the big news.

'Mum, I'm going on the Liverpool summer tour! Roy Hodgson's been watching me play and he wants me to go with all of the top players!'

'Raheem, that's brilliant! They must be very impressed with you. Can you believe how far you've come in the last few years?! Where is the tour going?'

'Switzerland and Germany. It's only two weeks.'

'OK, well, promise me you'll behave yourself.'

'Yes, Mum!' he said, rolling his eyes.

It was a great experience travelling with the

senior team. Once they'd seen Raheem in action, the players quickly welcomed him into the group. 'Playing against you makes me want to retire!' Jamie Carragher joked, as he stood panting, after chasing him down the wing.

When Raheem got a bit too cheeky with his dribbling in practice, Jamie and Steven Gerrard stopped him with strong tackles. He was playing with the big boys now and they didn't want to be shown up by the new wonderkid. Raheem learnt to keep things simple, and never complained. After all, he wasn't a star yet.

Raheem saw how good the top professionals were up close, how hard they all worked in training and how much effort he would need to put in to get to that level. 'Every training session is at such a high level,' he told his mum on the phone one night. 'The other players hardly ever make mistakes, but that's just pushing me to get better. I want to show that I belong at this level.'

Getting into the Liverpool first team squad was his next aim and he wanted to get there as soon

as possible. But there were lots of really good
youngsters like Tom Ince, Jay Spearing and Jonjo
Shelvey who were ahead of him in the queue. He'd
have to wait his turn. He had to watch from the
sidelines as Liverpool drew against Grasshopper
Club Zürich in Switzerland, and then lost against
Kaiserslautern in Germany.

'Be patient, kid. I remember being your age and
itching to get out on that pitch,' Glen Johnson told
Raheem after the second match of the tour. He could
see that he was disappointed to have been left on
the bench. 'Keep impressing in the youth teams and
the reserves and I think you'll be playing with us
regularly before you know it.'

In the third and final match, against Borussia
Mönchengladbach, and with about five minutes to
go, Raheem finally got his opportunity. Liverpool
were losing 1-0 but there was enough time left for
him to try to make his mark. As he ran on to replace
Jonjo, he puffed out his chest and prepared to do
what he did best: attack. He did well during his brief
performance but the team couldn't find an equaliser.

As he left the pitch, he was sad to lose but pleased with his personal progress. Sometimes he had to remind himself that he was still only fifteen.

Raheem had enjoyed his glimpse of playing at the top level and he was hungry for more. As the squad boarded the plane to return home, he was already thinking about the months ahead. He couldn't wait for the youth team season to start so he could prove that he deserved to move up to the first team on a permanent basis.

CHAPTER 17

YOUTH TEAM SUPERSTAR

'So how was it?' That was the question all Raheem's teammates were asking when he got back to training. One local lad who asked him was Conor Coady, who dreamed of playing for Liverpool in the Premier League. Conor was already England's Under-19s captain, so it was only a matter of time, but he was still pretty jealous that his mate had gone on the tour without him.

'It was brilliant,' Raheem replied. 'Those players are so good! I was a bit scared at first and they teased me a bit about being so young, but they're really nice guys and were really helpful. I can't wait to play in the first team!'

'Me neither!' Conor agreed.

'But for now, we've got the Premier Academy
League and the Youth Cup to win!' Raheem said
loudly, so that everyone else in the changing room
could hear. 'Yeah!' was the response from his
teammates around him. They were a good group
of players and there was a strong team spirit. With
Conor in midfield, Raheem on the wing and Michael
Ngoo and Adam Morgan up front, they had a good
chance of winning lots of matches.

The Liverpool Academy Under-18s were unbeaten
until their sixth match of the season. Raheem found
it so much fun playing in such an exciting team
where everyone worked really well together. The
team was scoring two or three goals in every game,
and Raheem was at the heart of all the attacking play.
In the game against Leeds United, he managed to
score both of the goals himself.

His reward was a call-up to the England Under-17s
for matches against Sweden, Georgia and Poland.

'I'm off to Georgia, Mum! I'm not even sure
where that is,' Raheem told Nadine on the phone.

'You'll have to send me a postcard! You're really travelling the world these days!'

Raheem knew a lot of the other players from his time with the Under-16s, plus Adam Morgan would be going with him from Liverpool. It would be a fun trip and it was a real honour to be selected. Raheem started all three games and while he didn't score, he was happy with his performances. Just as at club level, he was getting closer to the big time with every game.

But it was time to get back to Liverpool. After a couple of defeats in the academy league, they had thumped Bolton 6-0, and now had a big Merseyside derby looming in a few days.

'We're doing well but we've got to beat Everton!' Conor said as they looked at the academy league table.

'Don't worry – we'll thrash them!' Raheem said with a big smile on his face.

In the end, though, it was a tense draw that left the two sides neck and neck at the top of Group C.

Liverpool and Raheem started 2011 in incredible form. He scored one goal against Manchester City and then, in one of his best ever games, achieved five against Southend in a 9-0 FA Youth Cup victory. He was simply unstoppable. For the first of his five, he used his pace to chase down a long goal-kick and shoot past the goalkeeper. For the next, he dribbled in from the left wing, past defender after defender, before smashing the ball into the top corner. To complete his hat-trick, he cut in onto his right foot in the penalty area and found the corner again.

'Man, when did your shooting get so good?' Conor shouted as they celebrated the goal.

'Practice makes perfect. Oh, and God-given talent, of course!' Raheem joked back.

In the second half, he did it all over again. Every time he got the ball, Southend's right-back looked terrified, flapping his arms desperately for others to help. Raheem ran between two defenders like they weren't even there, then past another one, before finding the bottom corner with a brilliant shot. He raced over to the touchline to celebrate and showed off with a little dance that his teammates copied.

And there was still time for one more goal. This

time, Raheem got the ball on the right wing and terrorised Southend's left-back for a change. He twisted one way and then the other, and found the far corner perfectly. Everything he kicked seemed to be hitting the back of the net.

Raheem made the sign of the cross, then kissed his hand and pointed towards to the skies. He had to thank God for performances like that.

'My five goal hero!' Nadine called out as she ran to greet her son after the game.

'Mum! Don't embarrass me in front of my mates,' Raheem replied, looking quickly over his shoulder. But he couldn't be angry on a day like this. He would never forget the day he scored five goals.

Word spread at Liverpool about Raheem's man of the match display. He was already the next big thing at Anfield but now he was the next *really* big thing. 'I think they'll want you in the first team soon,' Conor said, patting Raheem on the back. Raheem knew how competitive youth teams could be with so many boys fighting to keep their places, but he knew Conor was genuinely happy for him.

And Conor was right about the first team call-up. Liverpool manager Kenny Dalglish included Raheem in his twenty-three-man squad for Liverpool's Europa League match in February 2011 against AC Sparta Prague.

'Mum, I'm off to the Czech Republic with the senior squad!'

'Wow! Another country to add to your collection. But wait, what about school?'

'It's half-term, so there's no problem!' he replied quickly. Not that it really mattered. Deep down, he knew that school or no school, nothing would have stopped him going.

In the end, Raheem didn't make the bench for the match but it was a great experience to be around the senior players again. Step by step, he was working his way towards the Premier League.

When Raheem returned to the youth team, coach Rodolfo Borrell took care to make sure the promising player kept his feet on the ground. 'Seeing as you've had a little holiday, you can set out the cones for training.' Rodolfo had seen so many players get too confident about success at a young age. He didn't want that to happen to Raheem; he had so much potential and he wanted to protect that.

'Raheem, you've got to work harder there,' he shouted from the sidelines during the practice game. 'Just because you're an attacker, doesn't mean you don't have to defend!'

Raheem was angry at first. 'Why is he picking on me?' he asked Conor. But he soon understood what his coach was trying to do. There was plenty of hard work still to be done before he became a star. He showed his focus was still in the right place by scoring two more goals against Stoke City and then another against Huddersfield.

All in all, February 2011 had been a massive month for Raheem, and Rodolfo was the first to congratulate him. 'I'm really impressed by the way you've handled these last few weeks. You haven't let the talk go to your head. Well done, lad.'

CHAPTER 18

ENGLAND YOUNG GUN

The 2010–11 academy season was over and the Liverpool Under-18s had finished second in their league, just one point behind local rivals Everton. It had been a frustrating end to the season, so the boys really needed some good news, and as they arrived for a training session, Adam revealed what all the boys needed to hear. 'Raheem, we're in!' he shouted. 'We're all off to Mexico!'

In total, Liverpool had six players in the England squad for the FIFA Under-17 World Cup. Raheem couldn't wait – what an adventure it would be and what a chance to make a name for himself. At the 2009 tournament, Isco and Mario Götze had been

among the star players; back in 2007, it was Toni
Kroos and Danny Welbeck. Could it be Raheem in
2011?

'The pressure is on now, boys,' the head coach,
John Peacock, told them all when they arrived at the
training camp. From the very start, he wanted his
players to know that this was no holiday. 'We're one
of the favourites to win this. Last year, the England
Under-17s won the European Championships. I
know most of you weren't in the squad back then,
but we're still the best team in Europe. So don't let
me down.'

Raheem was ready to take this tournament very
seriously. In the group stages, England would play
Uruguay, Canada and Rwanda. England were
expected to beat all of these teams but in the
summer heat it would be tricky. Raheem knew his
speed would be a key weapon.

In the first match against Rwanda, it took
England nearly seventy minutes to take the lead.
Then, with only a few minutes left in the game,
Raheem got the ball on the left. He was still a

long way away from goal but he was never short of confidence when it came to shooting. Plus, everyone was expecting him to dribble… With a defender coming towards him, Raheem curled the ball up, up and over the goalkeeper and into the top corner. What a goal! It was definitely one of the best that he'd ever scored. Raheem celebrated by performing the dance that he had practised with teammate Nathaniel Chalobah.

'What a strike!' Kenny Swain, England's assistant coach, said at the final whistle. He had always predicted that Raheem would be one of their stars. Defenders just didn't know what he'd do next.

After a disappointing 2-2 draw with Canada, Raheem was rested for the final group match against Uruguay. He was desperate to play but he knew it was only fair to give all of the squad some game time. His teammates won 2-0 without him to set up a tie with England's arch enemies Argentina in the next round. There was no way Raheem was sitting on the bench for that one.

In the event, Argentina took an early lead but

England were always still in the game, especially with Raheem on the wing. With the first half coming to an end, he got the ball on the left. With a burst of speed he cut inside and fired it low and hard towards the far corner of the goal. It was a perfect shot that went beyond the goalkeeper's fingertips and into the bottom corner. 'Raheem to the rescue again!' Kenny shouted from the touchline as they celebrated. In the end the match went to penalties, and Raheem watched nervously as his teammates won 4-2.

'That's revenge for the shoot-out we lost to them at World Cup 1998!' Nathaniel joked after scoring the winning penalty.

In the quarter-finals, Raheem and his teammates faced England's other arch enemies, Germany. 'It's time for revenge for Euro 1996 now!' captain Nathaniel had told them before the game.

'Most of us weren't even two years old when that happened!' Raheem replied with a smile.

In the end, though, Germany were the better side and won 3-2, despite a good second-half fightback from England. It had been a good tournament for Raheem and he was proud of what he had achieved – two goals and some impressive performances. Now, he needed to carry on his good work back at Liverpool.

CHAPTER 19

THE NEXTGEN SERIES

Raheem was confused. 'What's this NextGen Series?' he asked Conor one day as they looked at the fixture list for the new season.

'It's a new tournament,' his mate replied. 'They say it's like the Champions League but for the youth teams. Barcelona, Ajax and Inter Milan have all got teams involved.'

Raheem liked the sound of that; he loved watching the Champions League, with the brilliant theme tune and the amazing players on display. The best against the best – that was the kind of tournament he wanted to play in. It was all about challenging himself.

'Great! Hopefully we can get out of our group,'

Raheem said, already thinking ahead. 'I know the Portuguese youth teams are always really good but we should beat Molde and Wolfsburg.'

'Yeah, Sporting Lisbon will be really tough. That's where Cristiano Ronaldo played!'

Raheem's ears always pricked up when someone talked about his idol. He didn't think he'd ever be able to hit powerful free-kicks like Cristiano but he was working hard on improving his weaker left foot. Raheem loved the way the Portugal star was just as comfortable on both sides – it made it so much harder to defend against him.

Their first game took place in August 2011 at Anfield. Up against Sporting Lisbon, Liverpool put out a strong team but they were no match for the Portuguese side. Raheem was the bright spark and nearly scored a couple of times but in the end it just wasn't their day and they lost 3-0. Even so, Raheem was really impressed by the style and technique of the Portuguese players – they made everything look so easy.

'Wow, this tournament is going to be a real

learning curve for us,' Raheem said to Adam afterwards. 'This isn't Southend United anymore!' He had a bag of ice strapped to each of his calves – it had been a very physical game for him. Every time Raheem ran with the ball, the defenders kicked and pushed him. Sporting Lisbon had obviously marked him out as Liverpool's most dangerous player, and did everything they could to keep him quiet.

'Well played today, Raheem,' Rodolfo told him as they left the stadium, but he could tell that he wasn't happy about losing like that. 'This tournament is going to be exactly what you need – a real challenge! You're as good as these kids if not better. Keep playing like that, and the whole world will start noticing.'

Raheem couldn't wait for his next chance to shine in Europe: against the Norwegian side Molde three weeks later. He nearly scored after just a few minutes but the goalkeeper managed to tip his dipping shot over the bar. Raheem was everywhere all game long, setting up goals, hitting the post and then finally he was rewarded: he scored Liverpool's fourth with a nice side-foot finish, having sprinted past his marker to get into the box.

'That's more like it, boys!' Conor told his teammates at the final whistle. They all looked exhausted as they had a gentle jog to warm down before leaving the pitch. Even Raheem had to admit that he was tired. But it didn't last long.

'Apparently King Kenny's coming to the game tonight!' The dressing room was suddenly full of energy, with loud conversations about who he would be there to watch.

'Toni Silva and Adam have been doing well but I think it's Raheem they're most interested in. They've been watching him for months,' Conor said and most seemed to agree.

Raheem really hoped his captain was right. Either way, it was a great opportunity for him to play well in front of the Liverpool first-team manager.

'If I hear one more word about Kenny Dalglish,' Rodolfo began his pre-match team-talk, 'then I'm going to start dropping players to the bench. He's been here plenty of times before and you just haven't

noticed. It doesn't make a difference – stay focused
and play your normal game. You never know,
he might be here to watch one of the opposition
players!'

Despite his coach's wise words, Raheem still felt
a little nervous as he went out on to the pitch. He
tried to forget about Kenny being in the crowd but it
wasn't working.

He had a golden chance to score the opening goal
but he hit it straight at the goalkeeper's legs. He
stood there with his hands on his head cursing his
luck – and Kenny wouldn't be impressed by that.

Raheem fared no better in the rest of the game.
His touch was poor, his passing wasn't accurate
enough and the right back was blocking his attacking
runs every time. Then Adam came off the bench and
scored two goals to win the match – right in front of
Kenny Dalglish.

Rodolfo could tell that Raheem wasn't happy. He
hadn't said a word in the changing room after the
game and he was still sitting there staring at the floor.
'Chin up, lad!' the coach said. 'It wasn't your best

day today, but it's never about one game is it? It's about performing at the highest level over the course of a whole season and then a whole career. I know you can do that and I know I'm not the only one telling Kenny that you can do that. Learn from today and be ready for the next one. Trust me – you'll have plenty more chances to impress.'

In the NextGen quarter-finals, Liverpool were drawn against Tottenham. Raheem had wanted to play against Barcelona or Ajax but they would just have to beat their English rivals first.

Yet Raheem shone in the Tottenham game. From the first whistle to the last, he was always on the ball and did brilliant things with it. Again and again, he dribbled past two or three Spurs defenders and crossed the ball into the box, but somehow Liverpool couldn't score. It was so frustrating but Raheem never gave up.

'We're playing so well!' he told Conor at half-time. 'It's just a matter of time before we score one and once we've scored one, we'll go on and score four or five.'

Raheem's prediction turned out to be wrong; in

the second-half, Tottenham took the lead. Raheem couldn't believe it – it was so unfair. He attacked again and again but it was like there was a curse on Liverpool's shooting. When the final whistle went, he felt sick. He couldn't have done any more – how had they not won the game? It was a cruel way to learn the importance of taking your goal-scoring chances.

A few days later, though, Raheem and his teammates were smiling again. They were back in contention, as Tottenham had to drop out for fielding two underage players.

'It's great that we're back in the tournament,' Raheem said to Adam as they trained for their semi-final against Ajax. 'But it doesn't feel quite right, does it?'

In the end, the game against Ajax taught Raheem and his teammates another valuable football lesson: the power of 'total football'. The Dutch side's flowing style of passing may have been a joy to watch, but it was a nightmare to play against. Liverpool lost 6-0.

'That's not how I wanted us to go out of the tournament,' Rodolfo told them afterwards, 'but they were a very, very good side. There's plenty that we can take away from that game and work on. Boys, well done this season – I think we'll be better next time!'

Raheem had really enjoyed the NextGen series. He loved testing himself against the best young players in Europe. There was still work to be done on his strength and shooting but he'd played well in almost every game.

'I think I'm ready for the step-up now,' he told his mum as they relaxed in the garden over the summer. 'The youth team's been great but I want first team games now. I just hope Liverpool are willing to take a chance on me.'

Nadine smiled. It felt like only yesterday that they were living on the estate and Raheem was a little boy running from room to room. 'Be patient, son! You've only just turned seventeen. They'll play you when they think you're ready. You can't rush these things.'

Luckily, Raheem wouldn't have to wait long at all.

CHAPTER 20

BURSTING ONTO
THE SCENE

'Raheem, I've got some news you might want to hear,' Rodolfo shouted across the football pitch. His young star was still practising his shooting nearly an hour after the end of training. The goal was full of his successful shots from every angle. When he heard his coach calling his name, Raheem jogged over.

'How are you feeling?' Rodolfo asked him.

'Great thanks, coach. I'm feeling fit and healthy.'

'That's good because Kenny Dalglish called. He's named you in his squad for Saturday's game against Wigan.'

Raheem couldn't believe his dream was coming true. 'In the Premier League?'

'No, in the Rugby World Cup… Yes of course in the Premier League!'

Raheem felt dizzy. There were so many emotions. He was happy, excited, shocked and nervous all at the same time. His hard work over the last few years was really paying off. Many people had doubted that he had the right attitude to make it at football's highest level – but now he would prove them wrong. His number one fan was the first to hear the news.

'Wooooooooooooooo!' Nadine cheered, almost dropping the phone as she jumped up and down. 'My son, the Liverpool star! I could get used to telling people that! You need to get me a ticket so that I can be there to cheer you on.'

Raheem would never forget the day of his Liverpool debut: 24 March 2012. Entering the dressing room and seeing his shirt up there alongside all of the others gave him goosebumps: '31 Sterling'. He took a photo on his phone and sent it to all of his friends and family. He was happy with his squad number but he would have played in a '999' shirt if they had asked him to.

'Enjoy this moment, lad,' Steven Gerrard told him as they prepared for the game. The excitement on Raheem's face had got Stevie thinking about when he'd made his debut back in 1998. Back then, Raheem wasn't even four years old. 'You've earned your place here,' Stevie went on, 'so now show us what you've got. We've all seen and heard really good things. Don't rush things but don't be afraid to run at their defenders either.'

Raheem nodded and thanked Stevie for his advice. He was ready to prove to everyone that he was good enough to play in the Liverpool first team, even at the young age of seventeen.

Warming up before the game, he was the first out on the pitch. He had never felt so nervous or excited – he couldn't wait to play. The noise of the Anfield crowd was the loudest thing he'd ever heard and there was a sea of red everywhere he looked. He just hoped that he could make them happy with his performance on the pitch. He loved to entertain – that's what he did best. As he ran towards the famous Kop End of the stadium for the warm-up, the

Liverpool fans cheered his name. They knew who he was – and what an amazing feeling that was.

Walk on, walk on with hope in your heart
And you'll never walk alone
You'll never walk alone

Hearing the whole crowd sing the classic Liverpool anthem was even better. Raheem felt the hairs on his neck and arms stand on end, and a little shiver went through his body. Stevie had been right; they really were the best fans in the world. For some reason, his thoughts turned to Maverley and his friends back in Jamaica. He wondered what Christopher and Leon were doing now and whether they would believe how his life had turned out since he moved to England.

At the start of the Wigan game, Raheem was only on the bench but it was still amazing to be a part of the squad for a Premiership game. He was sharing a dressing room with Pepe Reina, Jamie Carragher, Steven Gerrard, Dirk Kuyt and Luis Suárez. They were his heroes and some of the best players in the world. And if he was lucky, maybe he would come on and play in the same team as them.

With only five minutes plus stoppage time to go, Liverpool were losing 2-1. It would be a very bad game for them to lose, especially against a team that would probably be relegated. Andy Carroll had come on at half-time to improve the attack but they needed more flair, especially from the wings, if they were to score a second.

'Raheem, get ready! You're coming on,' Steve Clarke, the assistant manager, called to him.

Raheem had never felt his heart beat so fast. This was it – his Premier League debut. He took deep breaths to keep himself as calm as possible. As he waited on the touchline, wearing the famous red Liverpool shirt, Raheem felt on top of the world. It was his time to shine. He just wanted to get on the ball. At the age of seventeen years and 107 days, he was Liverpool's second youngest ever player, even younger than Anfield legend Michael Owen.

Dirk Kuyt gave him a low-five as he came off the field. 'Good luck!' he shouted over the noise of the cheering fans.

Raheem ran on slowly, taking his time. 'Remember

to keep things simple and controlled' – that's what Rodolfo had told him. He couldn't be greedy at this level. The first time he got the ball, he intended to dribble down the left wing but when he saw there were defenders ready to tackle him, he played the easy pass into the centre of midfield. Then he sprinted as fast as he could towards goal and nearly beat the goalkeeper to the ball over the top of the defence. Pace and skill – these were Raheem's key weapons, particularly against a tired defence.

A minute later, Raheem decided it was time to attack the right-back. He ran at him, did four stepovers and took the ball into the penalty area. He found Martin Škrtel but he couldn't get his shot on target.

But Raheem was pleased with his bright start – he was causing problems and creating chances. This was where he belonged. As he was Liverpool's biggest threat on the left, his teammates ensured they were getting the ball to him every time.

As he cut inside and ran towards the box, a Wigan midfielder flew in and brought him down. It was the only way they could handle his speed. But Raheem picked himself up and didn't complain.

Even though Liverpool lost, Raheem's exciting performance gave the fans something positive to talk about as they left Anfield. And there were similar conversations in the Liverpool dressing room that afternoon.

'Welcome to the Premier League!' Jamie Carragher said to Raheem with a smile.

'You looked like you'd been playing out there for years!' Stevie told him.

'As soon as you came on,' added Pepe with a wink, 'those Wigan players couldn't wait for the match to be over!'

As Raheem was leaving the dressing room, Kenny Dalglish approached him. 'Kid, that was one of the best ten-minute displays I've seen in years. If you can do that over a full ninety minutes, you've got a really bright future ahead of you. You'll be getting more opportunities soon.'

Raheem grinned and his legs suddenly felt like jelly – he couldn't help it. It was all happening so fast. It meant so much to hear Kenny praising his performance. Despite the nerves, it had been an unforgettable day. He loved the atmosphere and the challenge of playing in such big games with millions of people watching. His mind was still buzzing and the smile wouldn't leave his face for days. He was already thinking ahead to his next aim: starting a Premier League match for the first time.

CHAPTER 21

FIGHTING FOR MORE OPPORTUNITIES

After such a promising debut against Wigan, Raheem had hoped to at least be on the Liverpool bench again for the next match against Newcastle. But with Craig Bellamy and Maxi Rodriguez back in the squad, there was no space for him anywhere. After a brief taste of the Premier League, it was back to youth team football.

'Don't worry, this is what usually happens with young talent,' Tom Walley told him on the phone. Raheem sounded very upset and frustrated about not being in the senior squad. Tom really admired the kid's ambition. 'They don't want to rush you, that's all. You're their new star and they're just looking at the big picture. They'll bring you on in a few games over the next couple of months. Then next season, you'll be playing a lot more.'

Tom had worked with lots of youngsters over the years, so Raheem was sure that his mentor knew what he was talking about. He knew that patience was not one of his strengths but he'd have to work on it, just like he'd worked on his shooting and defending.

It was over a month after the Wigan match when he next got the call.

'Raheem, you're in the senior squad for Tuesday's game against Fulham,' Rodolfo told him at training. 'Congratulations, Kenny clearly liked what he saw last time!'

Second time around, Raheem wasn't as nervous as he took his place in the Liverpool dressing room. The senior players were all really friendly and welcomed him back into the squad. They knew they'd be seeing a lot of him over the next few years.

After an early own goal, Liverpool were heading for another bad defeat. On the bench, Raheem couldn't sit still. He was chewing gum nervously and drinking from his water bottle every couple of minutes. He wanted to be out there playing and the minutes were ticking by.

'Take it easy!' Jamie Carragher said to him. 'You'll be on soon – you're our only attacking option left.'

As Raheem warmed up along the touchline, the Anfield crowd chanted his name. It was a clear sign that he was already a favourite with the fans; they wanted him out there on the pitch. After seventy-five minutes, Raheem finally came on, once again for Dirk Kuyt, and the crowd responded by giving him the loudest cheer of the day.

He did well on the wing, dribbling past defenders and crossing the ball for the strikers, but Liverpool lost again. It was two games and two defeats for Raheem; he wasn't used to being on the losing side and he hated it.

'Well played again today,' Kenny told him afterwards. He could tell that the youngster was disappointed. 'It wasn't your fault at all; it just wasn't our day.'

Raheem wasn't in the Liverpool squad for the
FA Cup Final defeat to Chelsea in May 2012 but
he faced them just three days later, for the Premier
League match against John Terry and the Blues three
days later. 'Lads, we need revenge today,' Jamie told
them in the dressing room before the game to get
them in the mood. 'They beat us in the cup, now we
beat them in the league!'

With Liverpool 4-1 up, Raheem was desperate to
join the party. Finally, with ten minutes to go, Kenny
brought him on. It was too late to really do much
but it was nice to be a part of such a massive victory.
'Next season, you'll be in the team every week,'
Jonjo told him as the crowd clapped the Liverpool
fans after the game. 'There's no way they can leave
you in the youth team!'

Over the summer of 2012, Raheem worked harder
than ever on his strength. His size had always been
his biggest problem but he was determined to make
sure that didn't stop him. If he was stronger, it would
be harder for bigger defenders to knock him off the
ball. He had a new Liverpool manager to impress,

too; after a brilliant spell in charge at Swansea City, Brendan Rodgers had replaced Kenny Dalglish.

'They say he learnt everything he knows from Mourinho at Chelsea,' Jonjo said as they discussed the news.

'His teams always play really nice, attacking football so I'm excited!' Raheem replied. At Swansea, Rodgers had played with small, quick wingers; surely he'd want to do the same at Liverpool?

In summer training, the players would often have a laugh as they got themselves ready for the season ahead. They'd see who could hit the crossbar from the halfway line, and goalkeepers would take shots at strikers. But from the beginning, Brendan wanted them to get serious.

'Last season, we finished eighth,' he said. 'With the players we have and the money we've spent, that's just not good enough. Things are going to change around here. If you're not interested in working hard and getting better, then you can leave right now. The aim this season is to finish in the top four so that we're back in the Champions League where we belong. To do that, I'm going to need you all at your best.'

Raheem liked the sound of Brendan's plan. He was training with the first team all the time now and one day the manager came over to speak to him one on one. 'You're young and you've got a lot of talent. I'm looking to play better football this season – more passing, faster attacking. You're exactly the kind of player we'll need for that. Stay focused and you'll play a lot of football for me.'

Of course Raheem nodded – that encouragement just made him work even harder. But sometimes he couldn't help acting like the teenager that he still was. At training one day, Brendan caught him messing around. When Raheem tried to defend himself, the Liverpool manager was furious.

'Sterling, you know what I think of your football skills but you have got to have the right attitude for this. If you don't, you won't make the most of that potential and you won't be in my team. If I tell you to do something, you do it. You don't act the fool and you certainly don't argue with me. OK?'

Raheem was really annoyed at himself. It was hard to always stay focused at seventeen, when you just wanted to have fun and enjoy your football. But he knew what he wanted: to be the best player in the world and to win lots of trophies. In order to do that, he needed to get serious. This was his opportunity to play in the Premier League and he wasn't going to ruin that.

CHAPTER 22

SEIZING HIS CHANCE

'Mum, I'm in the starting eleven for tomorrow's game!'

It was August 2012, and only the second game of the new season; Raheem really hadn't expected Brendan to pick him so soon. And especially not in such a big game – against Premier League champions Manchester City. He'd be playing on the left, with new signing Fabio Borini on the right and Luis Suárez up front. He was playing ahead of £20 million signing Stewart Downing. Wow, the pressure was really on now.

'Son, that's brilliant news!' said Nadine. 'I'm so proud of you.'

'Well, I'm going to make you even prouder tomorrow. This is my chance. I have to play so well that Brendan can't even think about leaving me out again.'

Raheem was so excited that night that he couldn't fall asleep. He kept picturing the game, with him scoring the winning goal. In the end, he turned on the light and read one of his magazines as a distraction. Eventually, he fell asleep.

The next day, he raced down the stairs. The nerves were building and he could feel the butterflies in his stomach. He managed to eat two slices of toast, then he rushed to the front door to check his bag for the tenth time. His mum tried to tell him a story she had heard from one of the neighbours but Raheem wasn't listening. The only thing on his mind was the game that afternoon.

His mum drove him to Anfield. Raheem sat next to her in the front of the car but they didn't talk. He had his headphones on, with loud music helping to pump him up. Traffic was light so the journey took no time. As he stepped out of the car and walked towards the players' entrance, Raheem could already hear Liverpool fans chanting.

City had the best defence in the league: England goalkeeper Joe Hart, Pablo Zabaleta, Kolo Touré and club captain Vincent Kompany. It would be Raheem's biggest test yet. In previous games, he'd been given ten minutes to impress but now he had to do it for a full ninety minutes.

'You'll be great, mate,' Jonjo told him as they warmed up. He wasn't used to Raheem looking nervous; he was normally such a cool character. 'They'll try to scare you with some big tackles early on but Stevie will be there to protect you.'

Raheem played football without fear – that was one of the things that made him so good. He just had to believe in himself as much as everyone else did. It felt extra special walking out onto the Anfield pitch as part of the starting line-up with the crowd going wild. This was the big time and he was going to enjoy every minute of it.

His first touch came wide on the left wing. Raheem ran at Kolo Touré, dazzled him with some stepovers and then delivered a great cross into the box. Borini was on the run and Raheem found him perfectly but he hit it just wide. What a start. 'Great ball, Raheem!' Stevie shouted to encourage him.

Minutes later, Škrtel scored with a powerful header. Raheem ran over to celebrate with the team; he was one of the boys now and he was playing his part. 'Get in!' he screamed. In the second half, City got better and Raheem had to work hard in defence as well as attack. Carlos Tevez twice beat him with some great skill but Raheem kept going. Yaya Touré (brother of Kolo) equalised but then Suárez scored a brilliant free-kick to put Liverpool in front again.

The game ended 2-2 and Raheem had played every minute of it. It had been a brilliant game, performed at a really fast pace. By the time the final whistle went, he was exhausted. As they left the pitch, Tevez came over and asked to swap shirts with him. Raheem couldn't believe it – did Tevez really know who he was? It was yet another moment that he would never forget. 'We should get that framed,' his mum said when her son brought the shirt home.

Raheem was pleased with his first Premier League
start. He hadn't scored, or set up a goal, but he had
done everything right and he had never panicked. He
had given Kolo Touré a difficult match with his speed
and direct dribbling, and he had helped the team out
in defence.

'Raheem, that was a great first game,' Brendan
Rodgers said in the dressing room after the game.
He was very proud of the way his young star had
handled the big occasion. 'That's the attitude I'm
looking for from you – you gave 110 per cent for
the whole match. You did everything I asked of you
and more.'

The young player was so pleased to hear that from
his manager. A lot of the players also came over to
say 'Well done'. They seemed really happy to have
him in the squad and could see how he would
help the team. Raheem had taken a big step on his
journey to the top. If he kept playing like that, he
would become a first team regular. His mum had
tears in her eyes when Raheem saw her after the
game. It was a day she would never forget either.

The newspapers the next day were full of praise for him. One had the headline: '*Liverpool get a glimpse of their future in fearless Raheem Sterling*'. 'Cut that one out,' he urged his mum. 'I'm going to need a bigger scrapbook to save all of these!' Suddenly, everyone was talking about Raheem. People were even discussing whether he would play for England or Jamaica at international level. It was crazy after only one full game for Liverpool. Luckily, there was no way that Brendan would let the fame go to Raheem's head.

'Sterling, focus!' the manager shouted the next day at training as the youth joked around. 'You think because you played one good game, you can just do what you want? Stevie's played hundreds of good games and he still listens, so get your act together.' The message was simple: he still had plenty of work to do.

CHAPTER 23

TAKING THE BIG GAMES IN HIS STRIDE

There was no way that Raheem was going to give up his first-team place now that he had earned it. 'I may be young but I've got the desire and I know I'm good enough to play every week,' he told his sister Lakima as they sat watching TV.

'I have no idea but Kingston thinks you're the best!' she replied. Their little brother was now four years old and he was already showing signs that he would follow in Raheem's footsteps. Raheem loved watching Kingston practising his tricks in the garden. 'He wears his little Liverpool shirt with "Sterling" on the back every day,' she said. 'He won't let Mum wash it!'

Raheem laughed. It was nice to have his family

around him, especially now that everything was going so well for him. It had taken him a while to settle in Liverpool after growing up on a busy London estate, but life here felt pretty normal now.

Liverpool's next game was another big encounter – Arsenal at Anfield. Raheem was desperate to play and he was over the moon when he saw his name in the starting eleven again. Brendan was showing real faith in him.

Raheem played well again against the London club but Liverpool lost 2-0. It was a disappointing start to the season but they were starting to play some really nice attacking football. Raheem was working well with Luis Suárez. It would just take a bit of time for them to adapt to the new manager's plans.

'Keep your heads up, guys,' Brendan told them in the dressing room afterwards. 'This is just the start.'

Against Sunderland a couple of weeks later, Raheem got his third start in a row. 'This is what I need,' he told his mum, as they finished dinner the night before the game. 'With a run of games, I can really develop.'

Sunderland took the lead but Liverpool always looked likely to score, especially with Raheem running at the defence. When Stewart Downing came on, Raheem moved over to the right wing. He was happy playing anywhere across the attack. From the left, he could cut inside but on the right he could run down the line and put crosses in.

Raheem knew he had the skill to beat their left-back Danny Rose every time. Sunderland were starting to mark him with an extra defender but Raheem dribbled past one and then inside past Rose. It was a magical move and he made it look so easy. The Liverpool fans were going wild with excitement. Raheem passed to Luis but his shot was blocked. Liverpool were getting closer and closer to scoring.

Moments later, Raheem was at it again. He got the ball and beat Rose with a lovely double stepover. With great composure he looked up and saw Luis in the penalty area. His cross reached Luis perfectly. The goalkeeper saved his first shot but he scored the rebound. Luis and Raheem celebrated the goal together; they were developing a really exciting partnership.

'Raheem, that was brilliant play!' Stevie said as he ran over to join the celebrations. As Liverpool captain, he was always looking out for Raheem, helping him when he needed it and praising him whenever he did something great. He was really pleased to see the youngster getting better and better with each game.

And Raheem was named man of the match. He was delighted with his progress and thanked his teammates and his manager for all their support. He proudly put the bottle of champagne next to his bag but he didn't open it. He knew his mum would want to add it to her collection of special awards from his career so far.

'Raheem, if you keep playing like that, there isn't a defender in the world that can stop you,' Brendan told him, giving him a big hug.

'Now all I want is a win and maybe a first goal!' Raheem told Jonjo as they got on the team coach to head back to Liverpool.

CHAPTER 24

ON THE SCORESHEET

Playing with Luis Suárez was a dream come true for Raheem. Suárez made brilliant runs in behind the defence and he was always where Raheem wanted him to be when he was crossing the ball. The Uruguayan's goal-scoring form in the 2012–13 season was just incredible. Away at Norwich City, the Liverpool players could only watch and admire as Luis scored four in a 5-2 win. Raheem played his part in a couple of the goals but Luis was in a league of his own.

'That guy can win games by himself!' Raheem joked with his mum later that night.

'He's very good but he needs you to run forward

with the ball and play it to him at just the right
moment,' she replied. 'Otherwise he doesn't score!
Talking of goals, I think you need to score one
soon...'

'OK Mum, I'm trying!' Raheem could remember
the days when his mum used to hate football. But
when she realised it was something that her son was
very good at, suddenly she started taking an interest.
And now she watched every game Raheem played
and gave him advice as if she was José Mourinho! It
always made him laugh.

She was right, though. For the Liverpool youth
teams, he had scored lots of goals. It wasn't that long
ago that he had scored five in just one match, against
Southend United. Goals in the Premier League were
much more difficult to score but as one of the team's
three main attackers, he would need to start helping
Luis out. Raheem knew his shooting was good but he
just needed to work hard and take his chances when
they came.

Raheem's first goal for Liverpool finally happened
against Reading in mid-October 2012. And not only

did he score, but he also played probably his best match for the club so far. With his new 'Mohawk' hairstyle, he tormented the Reading defenders from start to finish. They just couldn't deal with the movement of Raheem and his left-side partner Glen Johnson. Again and again, they found each other in space down the wing.

Raheem's first and second shots were blocked, and his third was comfortably saved by the goalkeeper. But he refused to give up and when Luis played him in on goal after half an hour, he knew it was his golden opportunity. Raheem sprinted on to the ball, took two touches to control it and then, just as the defender arrived to tackle him, he hit it sweetly into the bottom corner of the net.

GOOOOOOOOOOOOOOOOOAAAAAAAAAAAA AAALLLLLLLLLLLLLLL! It was a perfect finish that Luis would have been very proud of himself.

Raheem slid towards the corner flag on his knees. The Liverpool fans were chanting his name louder than ever. This was the greatest moment of his career so far. Luis ran over to celebrate with him and they

hugged: 'You did it – your first Premier League goal!'
Only Michael Owen had scored for Liverpool at a
younger age. It was another achievement for Raheem
to cross off his list.

It turned out to be the winning goal and Raheem
played the rest of the game with a massive smile on
his face and his confidence sky high. It was tiring just
watching him as he ran down the wing again and
again, creating chances for his teammates. With his
pace, he only had to knock the ball past a defender
and he was in the clear. Even when the defenders
fouled him, he just carried on trying to get a second
goal to seal the win. 'That's the big game I've been
waiting for,' he told Glen as they clapped the fans at
the end of the match.

'Raheem, those Reading defenders will have
nightmares about that match!' Stevie said at the final
whistle as he high-fived Raheem. 'That's one of the
best attacking performances I've ever seen in the
Premier League.' To hear that from his captain meant
the world to him.

In less than two months, Raheem had gone

from a little-known youngster to one of the most exciting players in the league. It was an incredible achievement for someone so young, but he already felt like he'd been playing at this level for years. He'd come a long way from the day that he'd been asked to leave primary school. There was a lot to be proud of.

After the match, manager Brendan was full of praise for Raheem. 'He is a terrific talent but he has a good head on young shoulders,' he told the news reporters. 'We have been doing a lot of work on the training field, but all credit to him.'

Despite this, Raheem could hear Brendan in his head, reminding him to stay focused. It would be so easy to relax and get too comfortable having made such a brilliant start to his football career. But Raheem had big plans to go to the very top and there was no time to stop and congratulate himself. The football world was waiting to see what he would do next.

CHAPTER 25

THREE LIONS ON THE SHIRT

'They're saying that Roy Hodgson is ready to give you your senior debut!' Jonjo Shelvey said at training one day. 'He wants to make sure that you pick England over Jamaica.'

He had only been playing in the Premier League for a few months, but Raheem was a man in great demand. In September 2012, he had been called up to the national squad at the last minute for England's World Cup qualifier against Ukraine but in the end he didn't get off the bench. Until he made his England debut, Raheem could still decide to play for Jamaica instead.

He loved his homeland and he was proud of his

cultural background. He often went back for holidays to visit his friends and family there. However, when it came to football, England had always been his home. It was in London and then Liverpool where Raheem had received his football education. He had already played for England Under-16s, Under-17s and Under-21s – wouldn't it be strange to change his mind now?

Raheem talked it through with his mum.

'It's your choice, Raheem,' Nadine told him. 'I don't want you to ever forget your Jamaican roots but this is about football. When I chose to bring you here as a five-year-old, I knew that you would grow up thinking of yourself as English. So don't worry, I won't be mad whichever country you decide to play for.'

Raheem was glad to hear that; he really didn't want to let his mum down. And she was right – this was about football and it was England that had helped to develop his talent. It would be an amazing feeling to play for them if they picked him.

Back at club level, Raheem was playing every

minute of every game for Liverpool. He was relishing the challenge of the big games – first a Merseyside derby against Everton, then two weeks later a trip to Chelsea. Sometimes Raheem had to pinch himself to make sure that his dream had actually come true.

'How are you feeling, kid?' the physio asked as he did his tests at the Melwood training facility. 'You must be exhausted – playing so many top-level games is hard on a seventeen-year-old body.' Liverpool really wanted to protect their wonderkid from injuries.

'I feel great!' Raheem replied instantly. 'I don't need a rest. I'll be ready for the next game.'

In mid-November, Raheem got what he wanted more than anything: his debut appearance for England. It wasn't at Wembley as he had hoped, but that didn't matter. What mattered was stepping out with the three lions on his shirt alongside ten of England's best players. These included Joe Hart, Leighton Baines, Steven Gerrard and Danny Welbeck. It was a true honour to play with them and it was a match that Raheem would never forget.

Sweden's Zlatan Ibrahimović stole the headlines

but Raheem was pleased with his first international performance. He had been lively throughout and had proved that he was good enough for the biggest stage. 'Great work, lad!' Stevie congratulated him in the dressing room afterwards. 'You looked really comfortable out there tonight.'

What a year 2012 was proving to be, and it got even better for Raheem when Liverpool offered him a new five-year contract in December. It was the perfect reward for his impressive form so far in the season. Raheem was no longer a youth team player; he was now a first-team star for one of the Premier League's biggest clubs. He couldn't be happier with how far he'd come. 'It's every eighteen-year-old's dream,' Raheem told the media. 'I'm just really grateful to be at such a big club like this.'

With Brendan Rodgers's help, Raheem was determined to keep his feet on the ground. Yes, he was now earning a lot of money, but he was not a superstar yet. 'There's a lot more to be done,' he told the Liverpool website. 'As the manager has said, I haven't begun yet.'

Raheem was keen to start 2013 where he'd left off in 2012. Twenty minutes into the first game of the New Year, Luis played a great ball over the top of the Sunderland defence. Raheem was on to it in a flash and as the goalkeeper came out to close him down, he lifted it beautifully over him and into the back of the net.

GOOOOOOOOOOOOOAAAAAAAAAAAAAAALLL LLLLLLLLLLLLLLLL!!!

With over 40,000 Liverpool fans cheering his name, Raheem ran towards Luis and they celebrated together. Their partnership was developing into something very special. 'This is just the start,' Raheem told himself once again. 'I'm here to stay!'

CHAPTER 26

MOVING TO MANCHESTER CITY

Yet after five amazing years at Anfield, Raheem was feeling restless. He really wanted to win a top trophy with Liverpool but when would that happen? He couldn't wait forever.

The Reds had come so close to winning the Premier League title in 2014, but right at the end, they let it slip away into Manchester City's hands.

'That should have been ours!' Raheem couldn't stop thinking.

It was so frustrating but maybe Liverpool would get another chance? No, because Luis joined Barcelona and without their star striker, it just wasn't the same. Raheem got eleven goals and Stevie got thirteen but that was nowhere near enough to win the league.

'Luis scored thirty-one last season!' Raheem moaned.

Was it time for a fresh start somewhere else? Although Raheem was still only twenty years old, his 'wonderkid' years were over. He was now an experienced first-team star with big dreams to achieve.

But how could he become one of the best players in the world at Liverpool when they weren't even playing in the Champions League anymore? His manager Brendan Rodgers tried to persuade him to stay but Raheem had made up his mind.

And so had Manchester City. They were looking to add more speed and skill to their attack and they saw Raheem as the perfect man for the job. Raheem was in demand, but the club was so rich that money didn't matter. All that mattered was success and trophies.

'Great, let's do this!' Raheem told his agent.

It was sad saying goodbye to everyone at

Liverpool, but at the same time, he couldn't wait to play alongside world-class players like Sergio Agüero and David Silva. At Manchester City, he would be learning from the very best.

In July 2015, the deal was done for a whopping £49 million. Raheem was now the most expensive English player *ever*.

'Sterling is one of the best attacking players in world football,' his new manager, Manuel Pellegrini, told the media.

Wow, the pressure was really on now! Luckily, it didn't take Raheem long to find his feet in Manchester. With City playing awesome attacking football, he scored his first-ever professional hat-trick against Bournemouth.

'Get in!' he shouted up at the sky, as his teammates raced over to congratulate him.

Suddenly, Raheem was firing in goals, left, right and centre – in the Premier League, the Champions League *and* the League Cup.

'This is so much fun!' he screamed with a big smile on his face.

Moving to Manchester City was working out brilliantly for Raheem. Soon, he was back at his beloved Wembley stadium to play in his first big final. City's opponents in the League Cup final? His old club, Liverpool...

'We did it, we did it!' Raheem shouted, hugging Sergio tightly after a tense penalty shoot-out.

At last, he had his first top trophy! Raheem was buzzing with pride as he bounced up and down on the stage with his winners' medal around his neck.

Unfortunately, that was City's only success of the season. They lost to Real Madrid in the semi-finals of the Champions League and finished fourth in the Premier League, 15 points behind Leicester City.

'We've got to do better than that!' City's captain Vincent Kompany demanded.

City's new superstar manager, Pep Guardiola, said exactly the same thing. He quickly signed three new attackers: Nolito, Leroy Sané and Gabriel Jesus. But what about Raheem?

'I know you're a good player and you are a big part of my plans,' Guardiola told him.

Phew! With his manager's support, he started the new season brilliantly. Raheem on the right, Leroy on the left and Sergio through the middle – City's attack was simply unstoppable! Raheem even won the Premier League Player of the Month award for August. Guardiola was really getting the best out of his talent.

'Don't worry if you miss a few chances,' his manager reassured him. 'Just keep taking more shots until you score!'

'Sure thing, boss!' Raheem replied happily. He was getting lots of the ball, thanks to all the perfect passes from David, Fernandinho and Kevin De Bruyne.

'If you can improve your finishing,' Guardiola explained, 'you'll be one of the best in the world.'

Raheem had the speed and he had the skill. Now all he needed was that killer final touch.

It was going to take lots of time and training, though. Raheem finished the 2016-17 season with ten goals and zero trophies. He had hoped for a lot

more than that but he didn't let that get him down.
Guardiola believed in him, so he had to believe in
himself too.

'Next year, I'll get there,' Raheem told the
newspapers, 'One hundred per cent!'

Being a world-class attacker wasn't just about
scoring goals, though; it was about scoring *important*
goals. Lionel Messi and Cristiano Ronaldo scored
crucial goals at crucial moments: opening goals,
equalising goals, winning goals. That was the next
step on Raheem's journey to the top.

City were losing 1–0 to Everton with ten minutes
to go. The ball fell to Raheem near the penalty
spot and he volleyed it into the bottom corner.
IMPORTANT GOAL!

City were drawing 1–1 with Bournemouth with
seconds to go. Danilo crossed and Raheem's shot
deflected up off a defender and over the goalkeeper's
head. *IMPORTANT GOAL!*

'What a hero!' David cried out as the whole team
celebrated with the fans.

In the Champions League, Raheem scored against

Shakhtar Donetsk, Feyenoord and twice against Napoli.

'Watch out, Sergio,' Vincent joked. 'We've got another fantastic finisher now!'

Back in the Premier League, City were drawing 1–1 with Huddersfield with ten minutes to go. What did you think happened next? Yes, that's right – Raheem scored *ANOTHER IMPORTANT GOAL!*

And in the next game against Southampton, he was at it again. In the very last minute of injury time, Raheem played a one-two with Kevin on the edge of the penalty area. Should he shoot? Why not – he was scoring all the time now! Raheem curled the ball over the goalkeeper's outstretched arm and into the top corner.

Goooooooooooooooooooooooooooooaaaaaaaaaaaaaa aaaaaaaaallllllllllllllllllllllllllllllllll!!!!!!!!!!!!!!!!!!!!!!!!

What a season he was having! Raheem ran towards the supporters, punching the air with glee. Important goals like that won Premier League titles – everyone knew that. At Christmas, City were 13 points clear at the top of the league and Raheem was already on 16 goals, his best-ever total.

'I'm aiming for thirty now!' he told his mum excitedly.

16 soon became 17, then 18…In the second-half against West Brom, Raheem had a great chance to make it 19 but he curled the ball just round the post. So close! As he ran back to defend, Guardiola called him over to the touchline.

'Oh no!' Raheem thought to himself. 'He's going to tell me off.'

But instead, his manager gave him a kiss on the cheek. 'Keep going!' he urged.

Raheem did just that. He didn't score himself but he set up goals for Kevin and Sergio instead. Whether it was goals or assists, Raheem so often saved the day.

City made it all the way to Wembley again, for the 2018 League Cup final against Arsenal. Raheem was desperate to play a big part but unfortunately, he had a hamstring injury and it just wouldn't heal in time.

'Don't worry, I'll come celebrate with you guys afterwards!' he promised Kyle Walker confidently.

When City won 3–0, Raheem joined his teammates on the pitch, but he didn't have the same winning feeling as before.

'The Premier League title – that's what I want!' he told himself.

City were getting closer and closer to achieving that dream, and Raheem was smashing his own records along the way.

He scored against Everton, Tottenham and Swansea City – twenty-three goals for the season!

Against West Ham, Raheem set up a Leroy wonderstrike. *1–0!*

Then he spotted Gabriel's run and played the perfect pass. *3–1!*

Finally, he picked out Fernandinho with a clever cross. *4–1!*

Thirteen assists for the season! Fernandinho lifted him high into the air. 'What a genius!' he cried out.

Manchester City were 2017-18 Premier League champions and Premier League record-breakers too. They finished with the most points, the most wins and the most goals in English history. That was beyond Raheem's wildest dreams.

The players walked out onto the pitch at the Etihad one by one, wearing '18 CHAMPIONS' on the backs of their shirts.

'...*AND NUMBER SEVEN, RAHEEM STERLING!*'

As the crowd cheered loudly for him, Raheem collected his winners' medal and then joined the others on the stage. It was party time!

Campeones, Campeones,

Olé! Olé! Olé!

What a winning feeling! Raheem had been looking forward to this moment since he was a young kid. Finally, it was his turn to kiss and lift the big, shiny trophy. Now it all felt real; Raheem was a Premier League champion.

CHAPTER 27

ENGLAND ADVENTURES

'We've got to keep this winning feeling going with England!' Raheem told Kyle, John Stones and Fabian Delph on that amazing afternoon at the Etihad. In a few weeks, the four Manchester City players would travel to Russia together for the 2018 World Cup.

Raheem was desperate to carry on his incredible club form for his country, but it was never that easy. In thirty-seven international games, he had only scored two international goals, and they had both come at Wembley way back in 2015.

What was so different about playing for England? Was it the pressure? Or the tactics? Or the teammates? Raheem wasn't sure, but he was sure about one thing:

'We can't let our country down again!'

The 2014 World Cup had been a proud time for Raheem but a disaster for England. They finished bottom of the group after losing against Italy and Uruguay, and drawing 0–0 with Costa Rica.

Euro 2016 had been even worse, especially for Raheem. Roy Hodgson took him off at half-time against Wales and then after sixty minutes against Iceland in the Round of Sixteen. That embarrassing defeat still haunted Raheem. He had to make things right.

Were England ready to shine in Russia? Their new manager Gareth Southgate believed so. He was building an exciting team for the future. With Jesse Lingard and Dele Alli in midfield, and Raheem and Harry Kane in attack, they had speed and skill.

Was Raheem ready to shine in Russia? He was very resilient but all the negative comments were starting to get him down.

'Does Sterling deserve to start at the World Cup?' the newspapers asked.

'No, he's rubbish for England!' some fans argued.

'Marcus Rashford should start instead!' they said

when he scored a wondergoal against Costa Rica.

Thankfully, Gareth Southgate believed in Raheem just as much as Guardiola did.

'Don't listen to all the talk. I know you and I know what you're capable of. You're a really important part of this team.'

Alright! With Gareth at his back, Raheem was determined to prove his doubters wrong on the world stage. The England team spirit was higher than ever. Now, he just needed to find his own Manchester City confidence...

In the second minute of their first match against Tunisia, Dele crossed to Raheem in the six-yard box. As he pulled his leg back to shoot, a defender poked the ball away. So close to a dream start!

Raheem kept running and battling until Southgate took him off after sixty-eight minutes.

'Great work,' his manager congratulated him. 'Your movement, your touch – that was exactly what I was looking for!'

The praise was nice to hear but Raheem couldn't help feeling disappointed. After all, it was yet another international game without a goal. That was what *he* was looking for! As he sat on the bench, he kept thinking about that early chance to score. If only...

'Hey, forget it,' Jesse told him afterwards. Thanks to Harry's last-minute header, England were the winners and that was all that mattered. 'You'll get more chances against Panama!'

After thirty-five minutes, the Three Lions were 2–0 up and counting. Jesse passed to Raheem and then kept running towards the box for the one-two. Raheem had three defenders around him but he calmly turned and flicked the ball back to Jesse, who curled a shot right into the top corner. *3–0!*

Once Jesse had finished doing his Fortnite dance, he gave Raheem a big hug. 'That pass was perfect!'

Could Raheem now go on and get a goal of his own? When England won a free-kick, the players decided that it was time to try out one of their new training ground routines.

Kieran Trippier passed to Jordan Henderson, who chipped it to Harry at the back post. He headed the ball across to Raheem, who was waiting in the six-yard box, with just the goalkeeper to beat...*SAVED*!

Luckily, John was there to score the rebound. 4–0! Raheem raced over to celebrate with his Manchester City teammate but in the back of his mind, he was thinking, 'If only...'

No, Raheem just had to stay positive, and there was plenty to be positive about because England were through to the World Cup Round of Sixteen.

'What a team performance,' he tweeted. 'Let's continue to build on this. Come on!!'

Next up for the Three Lions was a tough test against Colombia. Harry had already scored five goals in Russia. Surely, it was Raheem's turn to be the national hero?

He ran on to Kieran's pass and fired the ball... BLOCKED!

A clearance fell to him on the edge of the area and he struck a shot...BLOCKED AGAIN!

'When is my bad luck going to change?' Raheem asked himself.

In the end, it was Harry who came to England's rescue again with another penalty. When Raheem came off, they were seconds away from victory. In injury time, however, Colombia equalised.

Thirty long minutes of extra-time and then penalties – it was unbearable to watch. England had never won a World Cup shoot-out before, but this time, they did it! When Eric Dier scored, Raheem raced on to the field to join the big team bundle.

England were through to the quarter-finals! If the whole country wasn't World Cup crazy already, it certainly was now.

'It's coming home, it's coming home,
It's coming, FOOTBALL'S COMING HOME!'

The players had to take it one step at a time, though, starting with Sweden. Their defenders were strong and smart but they lacked one thing that Raheem had lots of – pace. Was this going to be the day he scored? Again and again, he ran through, causing all kinds of trouble.

He controlled a long ball beautifully and tried to dribble around the keeper...SAVED!

He got to the rebound first, tried to pass to Harry, and then took the shot himself instead...BLOCKED!

'It just won't go in for Sterling,' said the TV commentator, as he stood there with his head in his hands.

Raheem hadn't scored but he had played brilliantly. With a 2–0 victory, England were into the World Cup semi-finals! Was football really coming home in 2018?

Despite all the excitement, it wasn't to be. England went 1–0 up thanks to Kieran's fantastic free-kick, but Croatia fought back to win 2–1 in extra-time. Their World Cup was over.

England's players, however, were returning home as heroes. For the first time in years, the team had made their country proud. As he stood there on the pitch, clapping the fans, Raheem felt very proud of what he and his teammates had achieved in Russia. It was the start of great things to come.

'The future is bright,' Raheem tweeted afterwards.

Even though he hadn't scored, his second World Cup had been a whole lot better than his first. Would Raheem's third World Cup in 2022 be even better? He couldn't wait to find out.

RAHEEM STERLING HONOURS

Individual

🏆 Liverpool Young Player of the Year Award:
2013–14, 2014–15

🏆 Golden Boy Award: 2014

Manchester City

🏆 Premier League: 2017–18

STERLING

(7) **THE FACTS**

NAME: Raheem Shaquille Sterling

DATE OF BIRTH: 8 December 1994

AGE: 23

PLACE OF BIRTH: Kingston, Jamaica

NATIONALITY: England

BEST FRIEND: His mum Nadine

CURRENT CLUB: Manchester City

POSITION: LM

THE STATS

Height (cm):	170
Club appearances:	223
Club goals:	49
Club trophies:	1
International appearances:	44
International goals:	2
International trophies:	0
Ballon d'Ors:	0

★ ★ ★ **HERO RATING: 84** ★ ★ ★

GREATEST MOMENTS

Type and search the web links to see the magic for yourself!

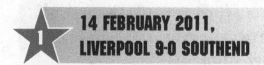

1 14 FEBRUARY 2011, LIVERPOOL 9-0 SOUTHEND

https://www.youtube.com/watch?v=KVVB9nngJZc
Everyone was already talking about Raheem's talent but this FA Youth Cup got people screaming. Southend's defence just could not cope with his speed and dribbling. Every time he got the ball, Raheem looked dangerous. He scored five goals but it could have been even more! It wasn't long before Raheem made his first-team debut.

30 JUNE 2011, ENGLAND 1-1 ARGENTINA (4-2 ON PENALTIES)

https://www.youtube.com/watch?v=qS9rLLvGJ8U

England lost to Germany in the quarter-finals of the 2011 Under-17 World Cup but this Round of 16 victory over Argentina was a great achievement. Raheem was England's hero with a stunning goal to keep his team in the game. He dribbled in from the left wing and curled a perfect shot into the bottom corner.

24 MARCH 2012, LIVERPOOL 1-2 WIGAN ATHLETIC

https://www.youtube.comwatch?v=onNP7xd893g&t=34s

Raheem only played the last ten minutes and Liverpool lost the match, but this was a debut to remember. Still only seventeen, Raheem stayed calm and showed off his pace, skill and intelligence. The Liverpool fans couldn't wait to see their new young superstar in action again.

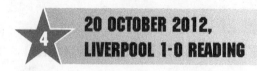

20 OCTOBER 2012,
LIVERPOOL 1-0 READING

https://www.youtube.com/watch?v=AgoEWtB3fA0
This was Raheem's first goal for Liverpool and one of his best performances. He combined brilliantly with Glen Johnson down the left wing and when Luis Suárez put him through, he shot powerfully into the bottom corner. Raheem was delighted to finally get on the scoresheet in the Premier League.

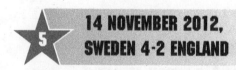

14 NOVEMBER 2012,
SWEDEN 4-2 ENGLAND

https://www.youtube.com/watch?v=Pq9CoZCJH3I
This international friendly will be remembered for Zlatan Ibrahimović's four amazing goals, but it was also Raheem's England debut. He played 85 minutes and he helped to set up Danny Welbeck's goal. It was a bright start to Raheem's England career and a great way to end his fairy-tale year.

PLAY LIKE YOUR HEROES

THE RAHEEM STERLING DRIBBLE

SEE IT HERE You**Tube**

https://www.youtube.com/watch?v=g_AojzNeEg0

STEP 1: Dribble up the pitch, pushing the ball forward with your instep.

STEP 2: Go fast but make sure you always have the ball under control.

STEP 3: Eye up the defender in front of you. Can you beat him for pace?

STEP 4: If so, pretend to cut inside but then use a quick burst of speed to carry on down the wing.

STEP 5: If the defender is quick, use your skill instead. As you dribble forward, bring your weight down to the left. Keep your right leg in the air with the knee turned in.

STEP 6: As the defender moves across, bring your right foot down and drag the ball to the right with the outside of the foot. Cut inside past the tackle, and shoot to score!

TEST YOUR KNOWLEDGE

QUESTIONS

1. What is the name of the style of football that Raheem played when he was young in Jamaica?

2. How old was Raheem when he moved to England?

3. Who taught Raheem some important lessons at Vernon House Special School?

4. Who were Raheem's two football heroes?

5. What nickname did Raheem's friends give him?

6. How old was Raheem when he started playing for QPR?

7. Who was the Liverpool scout who fought to sign Raheem?

8. Which two Liverpool legends did Raheem meet when he first went to the club's training ground?

9. What shirt number did Raheem wear on his Liverpool debut?

10. Raheem became Liverpool's 2nd youngest ever scorer. Who was their youngest ever?

11. Which England manager gave Raheem his international debut?

Answers below. . . No cheating!

1. 'Scrimmage 2. 53. Chris Beschi 4. Ronaldinho and Cristiano Ronaldo 5. Heemio 6. 97. Mark Anderson 8. Steven Gerrard and Fernando Torres 9. 31 10. Michael Owen 11. Roy Hodgson

HAVE YOU GOT THEM ALL?

ULTIMATE FOOTBALL HEROES

MATT AND TOM OLDFIELD

ULTIMATE
FOOTBALL HEROES

MAGUIRE

FROM THE PLAYGROUND
TO THE PITCH

DINO

Published by Dino Books,
an imprint of John Blake Publishing,
2.25, The Plaza,
535 Kings Road,
Chelsea Harbour,
London SW10 0SZ

www.johnblakebooks.com

www.facebook.com/johnblakebooks
twitter.com/jblakebooks

First published in paperback in 2018

ISBN: 978 1 78946 047 6

British Library Cataloguing-in-Publication Data:

A catalogue record for this book is available from the British Library.

Design by www.envydesign.co.uk

Printed and bound in Great Britain by Clays Ltd, Elcograf S.p.A.

5 7 9 10 8 6

John Blake Publishing is an imprint of Bonnier Books UK
www.bonnierbooks.co.uk

For all readers,
young and old(er)

Matt Oldfield is an accomplished writer and the editor-in-chief
of football review site *Of Pitch & Page*. Tom Oldfield is a freelance
sports writer and the author of biographies on Cristiano Ronaldo,
Arsène Wenger and Rafael Nadal.

Cover illustration by Dan Leydon.
To learn more about Dan visit danleydon.com
To purchase his artwork visit etsy.com/shop/footynews
Or just follow him on Twitter @danleydon

TABLE OF CONTENTS

ACKNOWLEDGEMENTS

First of all, I'd like to thank John Blake Publishing –
and particularly my editor James Hodgkinson – for
giving me the opportunity to work on these books
and for supporting me throughout. Writing stories for
the next generation of football fans is both an honour
and a pleasure.

I wouldn't be doing this if it wasn't for my brother
Tom. I owe him so much and I'm very grateful for
his belief in me as an author. I feel like Robin setting
out on a solo career after a great partnership with
Batman. I hope I do him (Tom, not Batman) justice
with these new books.

Next up, I want to thank my friends for keeping

me sane during long hours in front of the laptop. Pang, Will, Mills, Doug, John, Charlie – the laughs and the cups of coffee are always appreciated.

I've already thanked my brother but I'm also very grateful to the rest of my family, especially Melissa, Noah and of course Mum and Dad. To my parents, I owe my biggest passions: football and books. They're a real inspiration for everything I do.

Finally, I couldn't have done this without Iona's encouragement and understanding during long, work-filled weekends. Much love to you.

CHAPTER 1

"SLABHEAD" SAVES THE DAY!

Cosmos Arena, Samara, 7 July 2018

What a massive moment it was for Gareth Southgate's young England team – they were about to play in the 2018 World Cup quarter-finals! As the players arrived at the Cosmos Arena, however, they looked happy and relaxed. Harry Maguire had a particularly big smile on his face. Why not? He was in fantasy land!

In Summer 2014, Harry had just finished seventh in League One with his hometown club, Sheffield United.

In Summer 2015, he had just been relegated from the Championship, while on loan at Wigan Athletic.

In Summer 2017, he had just been relegated from the Premier League with Hull City.

But now, in Summer 2018, Harry was an international footballer, starring for England at the World Cup!

The tournament had already been a big success for the team. They had beaten Tunisia, they had thrashed Panama and best of all, they had finally won a World Cup penalty shoot-out, against Colombia. Could they now go all the way and win the trophy? The players believed, and the fans believed too. England had gone football crazy once again!

It's coming home, it's coming home,
It's coming, FOOTBALL'S COMING HOME!

Every player was now a national hero, from goalkeeper Jordan Pickford all the way through to goal machine Harry Kane.

But perhaps the biggest heroes of all were Southgate's all-Yorkshire back three. Harry Maguire and Kyle Walker were both from Sheffield, while John Stones was born nearby in Barnsley. Kyle brought the speed, John brought the brains, and Harry brought the strength.

Each of them brought their own skill. Together, they formed a deadly defensive team. They were brilliant at the back, but also awesome in attack!

Harry was absolutely buzzing by the time the players arrived in the dressing room. After all, it wasn't every day that he got to play in a World Cup quarter-final! Sweden would be tough opponents but the new England were fearless. If they played well, they could beat anyone.

But wait, there was a problem! As Harry pulled on his red '6 MAGUIRE' shirt, it didn't fit. At six feet four, he was a big guy who needed a big shirt.

'Especially with that Slabhead of yours!' his England and Leicester teammate, Jamie Vardy, was always joking.

'Cheers, Vards!' Unfortunately for Harry, that nickname stuck. Now, lots of his teammates called him 'Slabhead' too.

With minutes to go before kick-off, the England's kit man, Pat, rushed off to print his name and number on a bigger shirt.

Some players might have panicked in that nerve-wracking situation, but not Harry. That wasn't his style. He was a laid-back lad, both on and off the pitch. He could handle the big-game pressure. In fact, he loved it. It was what being a professional footballer was all about.

'Thanks, Pat!' Harry shouted, quickly pulling on his new shirt. 'Right, let's win this, lads!'

It was still only his tenth cap but he was already one of the team leaders.

As usual, Harry started calmly, passing the ball around the defence, to Kyle and John, and to his left wing-back, Ashley. Southgate wanted his team to play out confidently from the back – that's why Harry was in the team!

For a big man, Harry was so comfortable on the ball. Whenever he spotted some space in front of him, he dribbled forward on the attack. With his skill and strength, it was so hard to stop him.

In the thirtieth minute, England won a corner-kick.

'Come on!' their fans cheered loudly in the stands. 'This is it!'

After lots of work in training, Southgate's side were now set-piece specialists. Every time the ball came into the box, they looked like they were going to score.

The deliveries were always dangerous, from Ashley on the left and Kieran Trippier on the right.

And the headers were always heroic, from John and from the two Harrys.

Earlier in the World Cup, in the last minute against Tunisia, Maguire had won the first header and Kane had scored the second. What could they do now against Sweden in the quarter-final?

As Ashley crossed from the left, Harry Maguire made his move towards the penalty spot. This ball was his, and no-one was going to stop him! He muscled his way past the Sweden defenders and powered a thumping header into the bottom corner.

Goooooooooooooooooooooaaaaaaaaaaaaaaaalllllllllllll llllllllllllll!!!!!!!!!!!!!!!!!!!

What a time to score his first-ever international goal! Harry raced towards the fans, pumping his fists and roaring like a lion. Playing for his country meant so much to him. Since his childhood, he had always been England's biggest fan. Now, he was England's goalscoring hero.

Down by the corner flag, Harry slid across the grass on his knees and his teammates piled on top of him.

'Yes, Slabhead!' John cheered.

'Slabhead, you beauty!' Kieran screamed.

As he got back to his feet, Harry looked up and listened. The delighted England fans were singing his song:

Harry Maguire, your defence is terrified!
Harry Maguire, na na na na na na na na na na!

What a feeling! Harry knew that his family would be singing along proudly. They were all there in Russia to cheer him on – his parents, Alan and Zoe, his brothers, Joe and Laurence, his sister Daisy, and his girlfriend, Fern. Without them, Harry's journey might never have happened.

And what a journey it had been! Harry had travelled with Joe and Laurence to watch England at Euro 2016. Just two years later, he was scoring in a World Cup quarter-final.

Harry couldn't get carried away, though.

'Focus!' Southgate shouted from the sidelines.

England had defending to do. Harry won header after header, and tackle after tackle. He certainly wasn't going to ruin his big match by making a big mistake.

In the second half, Jesse Lingard crossed to Dele Alli – 2–0 to England!

When the referee blew the final whistle, John jumped up into Harry's arms.

'We did it, Big Man – we're in the World Cup semi-finals!'

The England celebrations went on and on at the Cosmos Arena. The players partied on the pitch, right in front of their loyal fans. They were all staying in Russia, but as for football itself:

It's coming home, it's coming home,
It's coming, FOOTBALL'S COMING HOME!

'Slabhead saves the day!' Jamie cheered, giving
Harry a big hug. He was so pleased for his friend and
teammate.

'Cheers, Vards. I wouldn't be here if it wasn't for
your annoying banter!'

It took a little while for the importance of their
victory to sink in. England hadn't reached the World
Cup semi-finals since 1990. That was twenty-eight
years ago!

It wasn't just that, though. With their spirit
and style, the players had made their country so
proud. Back at the base camp, Harry watched all
the amazing videos of the celebrations at home in
England.

'Wow, look how happy we've made everyone!' he
thought to himself.

Harry's face was all over the Internet, and it was
even tattooed on a fan's chest!

At the age of twenty-five, Harry had already

achieved his childhood dreams and more. Not only had he become a top Premier League player, but now he was also an England World Cup hero. 'England World Cup hero' – would he ever get used to the sound of those words?

It hadn't been an easy road to glory, however. Harry had worked his way up, step by step, level by level, game after game.

It had taken years of dedication, determination, and brotherly battles.

It had taken years of support from family, friends and coaches.

But boy, had it all been worth it!

CHAPTER 2

BROTHERLY BATTLES

Growing up, Joe and Harry were as inseparable as brothers can be. Where one young Maguire went, the other one almost always followed. Joe was older by eighteen months but that never stopped Harry. Anything his brother could do, he could do too – walking, reading, riding a bike and, of course, playing football.

Their dad, Alan, had been a good player when he was younger. He was now a coach at the local club in Sheffield, Brunsmeer Athletic, and he got his sons kicking as soon as he could.

'That's it!' Alan shouted as Joe booted the ball towards goal. With a dramatic dive, he let his son's shot roll right past him and into the net. *GOAL!*

'Yes!' Joe cheered, lifting his shirt over his head just like he'd seen the superstars do on TV.

'Right, your turn, Harry.'

Anything his brother could do, he could do too, only better! Harry was so determined. As he stood there between the goalposts, Alan could see a very serious look on his younger son's little face.

Harry took a really long run-up, swung his right leg back as far as it would go, and then *Bang!* He booted the ball into the air and it landed perfectly in the bottom corner. *GOAL!*

'What a strike!' his dad cried out with a shocked look on his face. He hadn't even bothered with his usual dramatic dive. How had Harry done that? He was still only four years old!

'Yes!' Harry cheered, sliding across the mud on his knees.

Joe watched on with a sulky frown. He wasn't going to let his younger brother take all the glory. 'Right, it's my turn again!' he said sternly.

Hours later, Alan was still standing there between

the goalposts as his sons took shots at goal, over and over again.

As they got older, the Maguire brothers became more and more competitive. They battled over school reports, pocket money, TV shows and, of course, football.

'Boys, that's enough!' their mum, Zoe, would shout whenever they dared to play one vs one in the living room. 'You know the rules – go outside if you want to do that!'

In their back garden, Joe and Harry didn't have to worry about breaking vases, or tripping over table legs. They were free to play, and play hard.

'Let the battle begin!' Joe said, grinning like an evil villain.

He was bigger and stronger than Harry, and he often used that to his advantage. Fouls? In their back-garden games, there was no such thing! They could do as many pushes, pulls, shoulder barges and sliding tackles as they liked.

After all, there were no referees in their brotherly battles – just parents ready to step in if they really started fighting.

'Play nicely out there, okay?'

'Yes, Mum!'

Harry loved every minute of it. Yes, he was smaller, but he was more skilful than his brother. He was a natural with the ball at his feet. He knew that he could dribble past Joe, and if only he could dodge his angry arms and long legs, then... *GOAL!*

Harry was also braver. He hated losing, and especially losing to his elder brother. That was the worst thing in the world! Joe would boast about it for days. So, Harry always did everything he could to make sure that didn't happen.

He chased, he challenged,

He barged, he blocked.

Their battles were always close and always fierce. They couldn't help it; they were competitive kids who loved football.

'Sorry!' they called out when they smashed a kitchen window.

'Sorry!' they called out when they turned the garden into a mud-bath and their dad had to lay down new grass.

21

Sometimes, their battles went on all day long and then carried on the next morning too. However long it took, they always ended with red faces, red knees and sweaty shirts.

'Well played,' Harry said, shaking Joe's hand. He was tired but happy because he had another victory to add to his list. 'Another battle tomorrow?'

'Of course,' his brother replied immediately. 'I want revenge!'

Harry and Joe's one vs one battles later turned into two vs two. Laurence wanted to do everything his older brothers did, and so did their sister, Daisy. With double the players, there was double the trouble.

It was total mayhem in the Maguire back garden, with tackles flying in everywhere. Their dad's freshly-laid grass didn't stand a chance.

'Why are our kids so competitive?' Zoe asked, as she kept watch from the window. 'I don't know where they get it from!'

Alan smiled fondly. 'Oh, I think I know. Sorry!'

CHAPTER 3

BRUNSMEER ATHLETIC

As much as Harry loved his brotherly battles with
Joe, they did get a little boring after a while. It was
the same challenge, every time! There were so many
other opponents out there for Harry to compete
with. Plus, how fun would it be to finally play *with*
Joe, rather than against him?

'Dad, when can I come and play for Brunsmeer?'
Harry begged. 'Please!'

When he was younger, Alan had been Brunsmeer
Athletic's big, powerful centre-back, but now he
was their Under-11s coach. Joe was already in the
team and when Harry turned eight years old, he
was finally allowed to join him. He was at least a

year younger than everyone else, but that never stopped Harry. Anything his brother could do, he could do too.

Joe was a strong defender, just like his dad. Harry, however, was a different type of player. He wasn't as big as the rest of his family and he was more comfortable on the ball. He loved dribbling and passing his way towards goal.

'Right, we'll play you in centre midfield,' Alan decided before he had even trained with the team.

Harry would have played anywhere, but centre midfield was the best position on the pitch. He still got to battle bravely for the ball, just like he did in the back garden at home. But on top of that, he also got to rush forward and use his skills to attack.

'It's the best of both worlds!' he told Joe happily.

Harry loved wearing Brunsmeer's red and black stripes. Every Sunday morning, he woke up bright and early, buzzing for the match ahead. The weather, the pitch, the opponents – none of that really mattered to him. Harry just wanted to play

and have fun. When it came to football, he was
totally fearless.

'Bring it on!' he shouted in wind, rain or sunshine.

Harry was like a busy bee, buzzing all over the
pitch. He treated every match like a brotherly battle
that he could not lose. *Tackle! Block! Header!
Interception!*

'Great work, bro!' Joe called out again and again.

But once Harry was on the ball, everything slowed
down. Now that he had it, he didn't want to waste it. If
he could see a teammate in space, he played the simple
pass, but if not, he held on to it and dribbled forward.
He made it look so easy. He wasn't the quickest player
around but it was so hard to get the ball off him.

'The Maguire Boys' were soon the talk of the
Sheffield youth leagues. With Joe controlling the
back and Harry bossing the midfield, Brunsmeer
were unbeatable.

Harry and Joe were the deadliest duo around.
When they played together for their primary school
team, the game was over before it even started. Their
opponents didn't stand a chance!

Parents would ask:

'How did you get on?'

'We lost 12–0!'

'12–0? Who were we playing against?'

'Immaculate Conception.'

'Were the Maguire Boys playing?'

'Yes, both of them.'

'That explains it then!'

Alan was very proud of his sons but he never gave them special star treatment. In fact, quite the opposite – as they got older, he expected more from them than from anyone else in the team.

'You're a lot better than that,' he would tell Harry whenever he had a poor game. 'Your passing was sloppy today and you were totally off the pace!'

At first, the criticism hurt but Harry knew that his dad was just trying to help him improve as a footballer. Everyone made mistakes; everyone had a bad day every now and again. He just had to believe in himself and keep getting better.

'If you keep learning and working hard, you could all be professional footballers one day,' Alan said to his three sons. The youngest, Laurence, was now following in his brothers' footsteps. He believed in them.

'A professional footballer!' Harry repeated to himself excitedly. That was his dream, but could it *really* be more than just a dream? With lots of hard work, he hoped so.

CHAPTER 4

WORLD CUP 2002

'Morning, Harry!' Mrs Emmot, the Immaculate Conception Primary Headmistress called out as she walked past the assembly hall.

Harry tore his eyes away from the big screen for long enough to turn and reply politely, 'Morning, Miss!'

'So, are England finally going to win the World Cup again?' she asked.

'Of course, Miss!' he nodded eagerly.

Harry had only been five years old for the 1998 tournament, so 2002 was his first proper World Cup, and he was loving it! Every day, there were more exciting international football matches to watch –

France vs Senegal, Brazil vs China, Cameroon vs Germany, Mexico vs Italy...

'This is the best thing ever!' Harry cheered. It was a non-stop football fiesta.

The 2002 World Cup was taking place in Japan and South Korea. They were eight hours ahead of English time, which meant that the 3.30pm kick-offs were shown at 7.30am for Harry in Chesterfield. Perfect – he could watch the matches on a big screen in the assembly hall before the school day started!

Harry watched, Harry learned and Harry dreamed. How amazing would it be to become one of the best players on the planet! 'The Maguire Boys' were the stars of the local school tournaments but one day, they could be World Cup stars. Anything was possible!

Although Harry watched as many World Cup matches as he could, the team he was really supporting was England. The nation had high hopes for Sven-Göran Eriksson's team. With Michael Owen up front, David Beckham in midfield, and Sol Campbell in defence, why couldn't the Three Lions go all the way?

Harry was still playing in central midfield for his club and for his school, but his favourite England player was the young centre-back, Rio Ferdinand.

Ferdinand was a cool new kind of defender. He was still awesome at tackling, heading and marking strikers, but he was also awesome at passing. When he got the ball in defence, he didn't panic and hoof the ball up the pitch like some centre-backs. Instead, Ferdinand was calm, classy and confident.

'Apparently, he was an attacker when he was younger,' Harry's dad told him.

Of course! That made total sense to Harry. Hopefully, if he grew big and tall, he could be the next Rio Ferdinand…

Against England's old rivals Argentina, it was Beckham who stepped up and scored a penalty under so much pressure. 1–0!

In the second half, however, it was Ferdinand's turn to be the hero. As hard as Argentina's star striker Gabriel Batistuta tried, he just couldn't get through! In the Immaculate Conception assembly hall, Harry cheered every block and every clearance.

When the final whistle blew, he punched the air.

'What a win!'

Harry got even more excited during England's Round of 16 match against Denmark. In the fifth minute, Beckham curled a corner to the back-post and Ferdinand headed the ball over the goal line. 1–0! While Rio danced on the pitch in Japan, Harry danced at his school in Chesterfield.

'England! England!' he chanted with his friends.

Owen made it 2–0 and Emile Heskey made it 3–0. The Three Lions were through to the World Cup quarter-finals!

At 7.30am on Friday, 21 June, the Immaculate Conception assembly hall was packed for the massive match against Brazil. Harry was England's biggest fan and he wanted them to win so badly. He was too nervous to even eat.

'You do know you're not playing in the game, right?' Joe joked.

Very funny! Harry rolled his eyes at his brother but in his head, he was thinking, 'How amazing would it be if I *was* playing in a World Cup quarter-final?'

That dream would have to wait. For now, he was cheering on Ferdinand, Beckham and co. When Owen scored, Harry jumped for joy. 1–0 – England were beating Brazil!

Sadly, it couldn't last. Just before half-time, Ronaldinho dribbled through the defence and passed to Rivaldo. 1–1!

'Come on, England!' Harry shouted up at the screen.

Early in the second half, Brazil won a free kick way out on the right wing. Ronaldinho placed the ball down and looked up at the England goal.

'No way, he can't shoot from there!' Harry said to his friends. 'He's going to cross it.'

But the ball sailed over David Seaman's arm and into the top corner. 2–1!

Harry's young heart sank. What a disaster! The England players kept going but they couldn't grab a second goal. Their World Cup was over.

'What a fluke!' Harry muttered moodily. 'There's no way Ronaldinho meant to do that.'

After a few days of disappointment, Harry went

back to watching the semi-finals on the big screen at school. Even though his favourite player and favourite team were out, he could still learn lots from players like Ronaldo and Germany's Michael Ballack.

Harry would never forget the 2002 World Cup. By the end of that special month, he knew what his life-long dream would be – to one day play for England at a major international tournament.

CHAPTER 5

THE BOY'S A BLADE!

In Sheffield, there are two big football teams:
Sheffield Wednesday and Sheffield United. The clubs
are fierce rivals, so it's important to choose your
colours carefully – blue and white for Wednesday, or
red and white for United.

Harry had a very difficult decision to make. His
dad was a Wednesday fan but his mum supported
United! Which team would Harry pick? Would he
become an Owl or a Blade?

Alan did his best to persuade his son. He took
Harry to matches at Wednesday's big Hillsborough
stadium.

'See?' his dad turned to him as the crowd clapped

and cheered loudly. 'This is the team to support, son!'

Harry loved the loud atmosphere at Hillsborough but the football was hard to watch. Wednesday seemed to lose every single match they played! When Harry was ten years old, in 2003, they got relegated from the First Division to the Second Division.

'You should have seen us back in 1997,' his dad said, trying to stay positive. 'Wednesday finished seventh in the Premier League! We'll be back there soon, I'm sure.'

United, meanwhile, were flying high. With Rob Page in defence, Michael Brown in midfield and Carl Asaba and Paul Peschisolido in attack, the Blades finished third in the First Division. That was a massive nineteen places higher than Wednesday! United were even one match away from promotion to the Premier League but they sadly they lost to Wolves in the play-off final.

'Never mind,' his mum sighed. 'There's always next year!'

Despite that disappointment, Harry decided that supporting United looked a lot more fun than supporting Wednesday. Plus, by the age of eleven, he had another very special reason for wearing red and white. After a year at Barnsley, Harry had been scouted by the Sheffield United youth academy.

'Sorry, Dad, I'm a Blade now!' he announced proudly. He had the club kit to prove it.

It didn't take long for Alan to also become a Blades fan. If he wanted to support his son, what else could he do?

Life at Sheffield United was a dream come true for Harry. It was exactly the kind of challenge he had been looking for. He loved competing with top players and training under top coaches.

'I'm learning so much!' Harry told his dad happily at dinner.

'Hey, what are you saying about my sessions at Brunsmeer?' Alan joked.

Wearing his team tracksuit, Harry couldn't help dreaming of the future. In five years' time, he could be playing for the Under-18s, then the reserves, then the Sheffield United first team. In ten years' time, he could be a Bramall Lane hero!

'One step at a time,' he had to keep reminding himself.

Unfortunately, Harry's next step wasn't becoming Sheffield United's first-ever twelve-year-old wonderkid. Instead, he became one of the club's ball boys at Bramall Lane.

'Ball boy? What a boring job!' his younger brother, Laurence, argued but Harry loved it, even on the wettest, coldest winter nights.

At every Sheffield United home game, Harry got to watch the senior players in action, right from the side of the pitch. They were so close that he could reach out and touch them! Sometimes, he *did* touch them when he handed them the ball for a throw-in.

'Keith Gillespie smiled at me,' Harry told Laurence, 'and he even said thanks!'

Suddenly, ball boy sounded like a pretty awesome job, in fact.

Harry's stool next to the pitch was one of the best seats in the whole Bramall Lane stadium, especially during the 2006–07 season, because The Blades were playing in the Premier League!

So, Harry could not only watch Sheffield United stars Phil Jagielka and Rob Hulse, but also:

Chelsea's John Terry and Didier Drogba...

...Manchester United's Rio Ferdinand and Cristiano Ronaldo...

...Liverpool's Xabi Alonso and Steven Gerrard...

...and Arsenal's Cesc Fàbregas and Thierry Henry.

Harry was in fantasy land! It was an amazing opportunity to study superstar footballers up close. Their decision-making, their movement, their vision, their teamwork. Harry tried to take in as much as he could. He wanted every game to go on forever.

Even after Sheffield United were relegated back to the First Division, Harry carried on being a ball boy in the Championship. There was still plenty for him to watch and learn from players like Ryan Shawcross at Stoke City and Kevin Phillips at West Brom.

It was those Premier League glory days, however, that made Harry more determined than ever. He had a new target to aim for. With hard work and self-belief, Harry would lead The Blades back to the big-time.

CHAPTER 6

MR SPORTY

Although football was Harry's favourite thing in the world, he loved playing all sports. Anything that involved running and competing, he would say 'I'm in!' immediately. He always wanted to win, even if there was no trophy.

When he enrolled at St Mary's Roman Catholic High School, he had a wide range of options. Harry quickly showed his new PE teacher, Mr McKee, that he was an excellent all-round sportsman.

Harry ran the 800 metres,

he threw the heavy discus,

he joined the school's successful cross-country team,

he played golf,

he played tennis,

he played badminton,

he played rugby,

he played hockey...

The list went on and on and on.

'Is there any sport that you're not good at?' Mr McKee joked.

Harry smiled cheekily. 'I'm not much of a gymnast, Sir. I can barely do a forward roll!'

'Well, we'll see about that, Maguire!'

When Harry decided that he wanted to achieve something, he worked really, really hard until he achieved it. He took that same can-do attitude with his school subjects too.

'Your determination will get you far in life!' his deputy headteacher told him when he got his GCSE results aged sixteen. He had got 3 A*s, 4 As and a B. His parents were delighted and so were his brothers, although they didn't always show it.

'What happened with that B, clever clogs?' Joe teased.

'Shhh you!' their mum laughed. 'We're so proud of you, son! What's next – college?'

Harry's parents had always let him play as much sport as he wanted, just as long as it didn't get in the way of his schoolwork. Education was very important for them, and for Harry's future.

'You've got to keep concentrating on your studies,' his mum told him when he was fourteen. 'There are hundreds of young players there at the academy, and most of them are not going to make it as professional footballers. You're a bright boy, so make sure you've got a Plan B!'

Harry had listened to his parents. He had the good grades he needed to go to college, but he was still playing for the Sheffield United youth team and hoping to have a long career at the club. He liked Maths but he *loved* football!

In between all the other sports, Harry had still found time to shine for the St Mary's football team. He was their midfield maestro, controlling games with his passing and dribbling. Once the battle started, no opponent could stop him.

'Once you get out on the pitch, it's like you double in size or something,' his best friend Danny joked. 'Maybe you're a superhero!'

Harry had proved that he was an excellent all-round sportsman, but football was his natural talent. With his perfect mix of passion and technique, he made the beautiful game look so easy.

'You've got what it takes to get to the top,' his PE teacher Mr McKee told him again and again. 'Whatever you do, don't give up on your dream!'

Mr McKee didn't really need to tell him, though. No-one was more determined than Harry. It was time to focus fully on football. Some of his friends thought he should have done that a lot earlier, but Harry disagreed. Over time, he had learned different skills from each of his different sports:

Cross-country gave him the stamina to run for even longer on the football pitch.

Rugby improved his bravery, and his dribbling skills too. If he could weave through tackles with a ball in his hand, he could do it with a ball at his feet too!

Hockey helped to develop his passing abilities and his vision on the ball. That was really important in football as well.

'See? It's all part of my training!' Harry argued.

Now, though, it was time for Mr Sporty to become Mr Football.

CHAPTER 7

THE PERFECT POSITION

By the time he turned sixteen, Harry knew that
he was going to become a professional footballer.
His family knew it, his friends knew it – even the
Sheffield United youth coaches knew it. There
were two important questions, however, that still
needed to be answered:

1) Was Harry good enough to play for Sheffield
   United? And...

2) What position would Harry play?

The first question could wait but the second
couldn't because all of a sudden, Harry was growing
taller and taller each day. He shot up into the sky –

six feet tall, six feet one, six feet two. . . all the way up to six feet four!

'Blimey, kid, what have you been eating lately?' the Sheffield United youth coaches asked in awe as they looked up at him.

Since his very first game for Brunsmeer, Harry had been a busy central midfielder, full of energy and skill. But now that he was a giant, could he still play that role? He wasn't so quick and nimble anymore. With longer legs, he felt so clumsy on the ball.

'Where do you want to be in three years' time?' the academy manager, John Pemberton, asked him during an important meeting in his office.

Harry knew the answer to that one. 'I want to be playing for the first team,' he replied confidently.

'Well, I'm sorry but I don't think you'll make it in midfield,' Pemberton told him. He had a plan, though: 'Let's see what you can do in defence instead.'

If it would help the team, Harry was happy to try anything. Just as long as he played professional football, he didn't mind *where* he played on the pitch.

'Welcome to the family position!' Joe chuckled. He

was a centre-back, their dad was a centre-back, their brother Laurence was a centre-back, and now Harry was too.

'Thanks,' Harry replied. 'I think I'm going to need your help!'

Zonal marking, offside traps, clever strikers – it was a whole new world for Harry to get used to. Fortunately, he was a fast learner and he had great teammates and coaches to help him.

'That's it – show them who's boss!' the academy manager shouted as Harry jumped highest to win a header. He was so competitive that he hated losing a single battle.

The ball flew through the air, over the halfway line, and landed at the feet of United's striker.

'Blimey, that big head of yours is more powerful than your boot!' Harry's centre-back partner, Terry Kennedy, laughed.

Pemberton was delighted with the youngster's progress. Harry could read the game so well for a young player and get himself into the right positions to deal with any danger. He was starting to look like he'd been a defender all his life. It was time for Stage Two of the master plan.

'Maguire, go short for the pass!' Pemberton called out as the goalkeeper got ready to kick the ball downfield.

Harry had the height and strength of a centre-back but he could pass and dribble like a midfielder. That made him a very rare talent and Pemberton wanted to make the most of him.

When the goalkeeper rolled it to him, Harry just hoofed the ball long straight away. He couldn't take risks so close to his own goal. He was a defender now! His coach, however, had other ideas.

'Take your time on the ball,' Pemberton urged. 'Play like you used to play in midfield. Don't worry if you make a few mistakes.'

At first, Harry made lots of mistakes.

Sometimes, when the strikers pressed him, he panicked and played a bad pass, either too short or too heavy. *GOAL!*

'Sorry!'

Sometimes, he tried to dribble past one opponent too many and got tackled. *GOAL!*

'Sorry!'

Whatever the reason, Pemberton always said the same thing. 'Head up, keep going!'

Harry hated giving away goals. It left a horrible sinking feeling in his stomach. His teammates didn't say anything but they didn't have to. Harry knew that it was all his fault. He was letting his team down badly.

'But I'm just doing what I'm told!' he argued with himself. His manager had told him to be bold on the ball.

Harry had to persevere and he had to improve. Thanks to lots of hard work in training, he soon looked his usual, comfortable self again. And Harry's skills became Sheffield United's secret weapon.

Under pressure in their own half? No problem! Harry would bring the ball out of defence, weaving his way up the pitch and then picking out a pass.

1–0 down, with a few minutes to go? No problem! Harry moved forward confidently, looking for the chance to shoot.

'Congratulations, kid,' Pemberton smiled. 'You've found your perfect position!'

CHAPTER 8

FA YOUTH CUP

There was no stopping Harry, now that he had found his perfect position. He couldn't wait to test himself against England's best young strikers in the 2011 FA Youth Cup.

'Let the battles begin!' Harry and Terry cheered together.

Could anyone defeat Yorkshire's deadliest defensive duo? It didn't seem so:

Cheltenham Town 1–4 Sheffield United
Sheffield United 3–0 Millwall
Sheffield United 3–1 Blackpool
Leicester City 1–2 Sheffield United

With four wins in a row, the young Blades were through to the semi-finals.

'Great work, lads,' Pemberton cheered proudly. 'Two more performances like that and we'll be in the final!'

Sheffield United had never got that far in the sixty years of the FA Youth Cup. Could these kids make history? The club's fans were delighted to have something to cheer about. Their senior team was struggling down at the bottom of the First Division.

United! United! United!

Mark Smith, the Reserves coach, gave Harry some very good news. 'Speedo is really impressed with you. Keep it up, kid!'

Gary Speed, the Sheffield United manager, had watched him play? Wow, Harry was now even more determined to dazzle in defence!

A few days after his eighteenth birthday, he travelled to Villa Park to take on Aston Villa. Ahead of the biggest game of his football career, Harry felt more excited than nervous. Harry believed in himself and he believed in all of his brilliant teammates.

Together, they could handle the pressure and win yet another battle.

'Let's keep it tight tonight,' Pemberton told them in the dressing room before kick-off. 'Remember, we've got the home leg back at Bramall Lane still to come.'

The young Blades wanted to win both games, though. Harry and Terry at the back were stopping every Villa attack. What could Sheffield United do on the counter-attack? Just before half-time, Jordan Slew dribbled into the Villa box and cut the ball back for Joe Ironside to score. 1–0!

Watching from the halfway line, Harry punched the air with joy. Now, he had more defending to do.

A long ball over the top… no problem! Harry calmly let it run through to his goalkeeper.

A cross into the box… no problem! With his big head, Harry cleared the danger.

A long-range shot… no problem! Harry bravely blocked it with his body.

When the final whistle blew, he punched the air again, this time with both fists. A win *and* a cleansheet – what a perfect late birthday present!

'We're halfway there, lads,' Pemberton said, patting them all on the back.

In the second leg, Sheffield United scored, again just before half-time. This time, though, the goal was created by their dazzling defenders. Harry crossed from the left to Terry at the back post. He headed it down for Elliott Whitehouse to tap in. 2–0 on aggregate!

Harry joined in the team celebrations and then ran back to his own half. He had more defending to do.

A Villa shot from the edge of the area… no problem! Harry blocked it with his long legs.

Another long-range Villa shot… no problem! Harry headed the ball away.

What a hero! At the final whistle, he threw his arms up above his head and hugged Terry. Two big games, two big clean sheets.

'We did it!' Harry shouted. 'We're in the final!'

It was already one of Sheffield United's greatest ever achievements, but could the young Blades go all the way and win the trophy? It wasn't going to be easy. Their final opponents would be Premier League giants, Manchester United. The club had already won the FA Youth Cup nine times, most famously with their Class of 1992, featuring David Beckham, Ryan Giggs, Paul Scholes, Gary Neville, Phil Neville and Nicky Butt.

Nineteen years on, their Class of 2011 was packed with future superstars too, including a young midfield maestro called Paul Pogba.

'We've got nothing to be scared of tonight,' Pemberton told his players before the first leg at Bramall Lane. 'We deserve to be here, so let's show them what we can do!'

It was going to be Harry's biggest test yet. Jesse Lingard, Ravel Morrison and Will Keane were all excellent and promising young attackers at Manchester United with lots of speed, skill and clever movement.

'Come on, this is going to have to be our best game ever!' Harry told Terry as they took up their positions on the pitch.

Unfortunately, with 30,000 fans watching, Harry's night quickly became a nightmare.

As Pogba crossed from the right wing, Lingard slipped away from Harry and got to the ball first. His shot deflected up off the goalkeeper and struck the crossbar. As it bounced down, Harry tried to clear it but instead, he could only head the ball into his own net. 1–0 to Manchester United!

What a disaster! Harry had that horrible sinking feeling in his stomach again. He had let his team down. He wanted to hide away but he couldn't.

'Head up, keep going!' – that's what his coach always told him. Harry stayed strong and fought until the final whistle.

'Well done, kid,' Pemberton said, putting an arm around Harry's broad shoulders. With a 2–2 draw, Sheffield United's FA Youth Cup dream was still alive. 'You showed real guts out there.'

In the second leg at Old Trafford, the young Blades did their best, but ultimately Manchester United were just too good. Morrison and Keane scored two goals each in a 4–1 thrashing.

No, Sheffield United hadn't won, but Harry was still really proud of his runners-up medal. The FA Youth Cup final had taught him some tough lessons about football at the highest level. Harry still had a long way to go and lots to learn, but he was on the right track.

CHAPTER 9

FIRST GAME FOR THE FIRST TEAM

By April 2011, the Sheffield United manager, Micky Adams, was under real pressure. The Blades were about to get relegated down to League One, and the fans were furious. They booed the team's most experienced players, shouting,

'Get them off, they don't deserve to wear the shirt!'

What did the fans want Adams to do instead?

'Give the kids a chance!' they demanded.

The juniors had just reached the FA Youth Cup final, after all. They couldn't do any worse than the seniors.

Who should Adams choose? Elliott? Joe? Jordan?

Terry? No, Harry was the team's stand-out player and not just because of his height. He also had that amazing mix of passion and talent. It was time to see if he was ready for the Championship challenge.

When Harry first started training with the first team, some of the senior players were shocked. They took one look at him and thought, 'No way, that kid's too big to be a good footballer!'

That all changed, though, when Harry got the ball. With a neat first touch, he dribbled forward from the back, gliding past one player and then another. With great composure, he looked up and played a clever pass through to the striker. Wow! Sheffield United's senior players were *really* shocked now!

'Ok, that kid can *play*!' they said, having all changed their minds.

Harry didn't play in the home game against Leeds United but he was there on the subs bench just in case. It was like the good old days of being a ball boy at Bramall Lane. From up close, he could watch Sheffield United's centre-back Nyron Nosworthy really carefully.

How tightly did he mark the Leeds strikers? How often did he talk to the other defenders?

Harry was always looking to learn. He had come a long way since those ball boy days and he was now so close to achieving his childhood dream. So close that he could almost reach out and touch it.

Harry's whole family was there at the stadium, hoping to see him make his debut.

'You'll get your chance soon,' his mum reassured him after the match.

She was right. Harry was back on the bench for the home game against Cardiff City and this time, he didn't stay there.

Sheffield United were heading towards another disastrous defeat. They were losing 1–0 early in the second half, when not one but two defenders got injured! First Nyron hobbled off, and then Joe Mattock. Nick Montgomery came on for Nyron, but who would Adams bring on to replace Joe? Harry's heart was beating extra fast on the bench.

'Maguire, you ready?' one of the coaches called out.

Harry nodded eagerly. Of course, he was ready!
He jumped up out of his seat and tucked in his red
and white shirt on the touchline. '40 MAGUIRE,'
the back of it read. This was it – his first game for the
Sheffield United first team.

'Just take your time and keep it simple,' his
manager Micky Adams told him. 'Good luck!'

The Sheffield United fans clapped and cheered as
Harry ran onto the field. Finally, Adams was listening
to them, and giving the kids a chance. The mood
lifted around Bramall Lane.

'They reckon this guy's going to be the next John
Terry!'

'He's a future England captain, I heard, and he's a
local lad too.'

Harry was determined to make a good first
impression and live up to those great expectations.
He was playing against Craig Bellamy, one of the best
and smartest strikers in the league. The Welshman
had scored eighty-one Premier League goals for clubs
like Manchester City and Liverpool.

What a big first test for Harry! As he took a deep

breath, the words of his youth coach flashed through his head – 'Show them who's boss!'

He was ready for battle. When the first pass arrived at Bellamy's feet, BOOM! Harry won the ball with a tough tackle that sent Bellamy flying through the air.

'That's more like it!' The Sheffield United supporters rose to their feet to clap and cheer their new young star. 'I love him already!'

Slowly, Bellamy got back to his feet. He accepted Harry's handshake and smiled. 'Boy, you're a big lad! Is that why they brought you on?'

After that very strong start, however, Harry nearly went from hero to villain. United passed the ball across the defence, just like Pemberton had always encouraged the youth team to do. That style was perfect for Harry but just as it came to him, he slipped and fell. *GASP!* The fans feared the worst but fortunately, Cardiff didn't score a second goal.

Phew! Harry breathed a sigh of relief.

'Forget that, keep going!' Neill Collins, his centre-back partner, told him.

Harry focused on his task and fought hard until the final whistle. The match ended in another defeat for Sheffield United but at least the game had brought one bright light at the end of the dark tunnel: Harry.

He walked all the way around the stadium, thanking the fans for their amazing support. He wanted to stay on the pitch and keep playing.

'Great performance, kid,' Adams said as Harry finally made his way down the tunnel to the dressing room.

Upstairs in the players' lounge, his family was waiting to congratulate him too.

'Well done, I'm so proud of you!' his mum said, hugging him tightly.

'Yes but we lost,' Harry reminded her. 'Again.'

'You played so brilliantly, though. Could you hear everyone cheering when you made that big tackle?'

'Could you hear everyone groaning when you nearly gave away that goal?' his brother Laurence added cheekily.

Sheffield United only had five games left in the Championship season. Harry started four of them and even won the man of the match award against Preston. He would have started the other game too, if he hadn't been suspended.

The suspension happened in a game against Bristol City, Nick tried to pass the ball back to Harry but instead, it fell to the striker. Harry panicked and brought him down. *Foul!* The referee gave Bristol City a penalty and sent Harry off.

'Nooooo! Why did I dive in like that?' he groaned as he slowly jogged off the pitch. The horrible sinking feeling was back.

That red card helped to keep Harry's feet firmly on the ground. He couldn't get too big for his big boots. Yes, he was now a Sheffield United first-team star and a fans' favourite, but he still had lots more to learn.

CHAPTER 10

LIFE IN LEAGUE ONE

And what better place to learn than in League One?
That's where Sheffield United would be playing for the
2011–12 season. During the summer, Harry's centre-
back partner, Neill, passed on some helpful advice.

'Look, I know you like to get the ball down and
pass it around, but you're playing a different kind
of football now. In League One, it's much more
physical. Teams are going to hoof long balls up to
their big, strong strikers, who will to try to push you
around. Just be ready for that.'

'Thanks, I will be!'

Harry didn't mind playing dirty if he had to. He
was six feet four, after all!

On the opening day of the season, Sheffield United

travelled to Oldham Athletic. Their striker, Matt Smith, was even taller than Harry – he was six feet six!

'See!' Neill said with a smile. 'Welcome to League One!'

Luckily, Harry loved nothing more than a challenge. He didn't win every header but he did keep Smith quiet.

Early in the second half, Harry went forward for a corner-kick. The penalty area was like a wrestling ring, with lots of pushing and shoving everywhere. But when the cross came in, Harry outmuscled and then outjumped his marker to power a header into the top corner.

Goooooooooooooooooooooaaaaaaaaaaaaaaaaallllllllllll llllllllllllllll!!!!!!!!!!!!!!!!!!!

It was the moment Harry had dreamt about since he was eleven years old – his first goal for Sheffield United! He watched the ball land in the back of the net and then ran over to the away fans to celebrate. He lept high into the air and then dropped to his knees. It was the greatest feeling ever.

Neill was one of the first teammates to hug Harry.

'Ok fine, you're ready for League One!' he joked.

Sheffield United started the season well with four wins out of five, and three clean sheets. Thanks to Harry, they had the best defence in the division.

The team's new manager, Danny Wilson, was delighted. Young players usually made a few mistakes, especially centre-backs. But at the age of eighteen, Harry already looked just as calm and consistent as an experienced pro like Neill.

But would Sheffield United be able to hold on to their star centre-back for long? Hopefully, for as long as the club got promoted back up to the Championship.

The Blades spent the whole season in the top six but in the end, they finished third, three points behind their bitter rivals, Sheffield Wednesday.

'Hey, it's not over yet,' Wilson told his disappointed players. 'We just have to win the play-offs now!'

There was good news to help cheer Harry up. He was one of three United players named in the League One Team of the Year. Not bad for a nineteen-year-old playing in League One for the first time! It was a

very proud moment but Harry kept his eyes on the
prize – promotion through the play-offs.

With a tense 1–0 win over Stevenage, Sheffield
United were through to the final. As a local lad,
Harry was especially excited. Two years earlier, he
had been a youth player and a ball boy. Now, he
was about to play in a final at Wembley Stadium.
Everything was happening so fast but somehow,
Harry stayed as calm as ever.

'We know Huddersfield will be a tough team,' he
told the media, 'but we have always believed that we
will be in the Championship next season.'

As Harry walked out onto the pitch, he looked up
at the 52,000 cheering fans. The atmosphere was
amazing and the game hadn't even kicked off yet.

'I could get used to playing in front of a crowd like
this!' he chuckled to himself.

Pressure? Harry loved pressure! It was what
being a top professional footballer was all about. He
couldn't wait for the biggest battle of his life to begin.

'Come on, let's do this!' he cheered.

Sadly, it wasn't the fun final that both sets of fans

were hoping for. Instead, it was tight and tense. Neither team was brave enough to take a risk, in case they made a mistake. After 120 minutes without a goal, the match went all the way to penalties.

'At least that's another clean sheet for us!' Harry joked, trying to lighten the mood. Neill was taking one of Sheffield's five penalties and he looked nervous.

Both teams hugged their goalkeepers and wished them luck. Who would be the hero? United's Steve Simonsen, or Huddersfield's Alex Smithies?

After ten penalties, the score was 2–2. The shoot-out went to sudden death, and even Harry was starting to feel a little anxious. One miss and it would be all over.

3–2 to Huddersfield, 3–3, 4–3 to Huddersfield…

It was Harry's turn to take a penalty. 'You've got this!' Neill shouted to him as he made the long walk from the halfway line to the penalty area. So many of Harry's friends and family were there at Wembley to watch him win. He couldn't let them down.

Harry placed the ball down on the spot and took a few steps backwards. He looked down at the ball and then up at the target. 'You've got this!' he told himself as he started his run-up. The keeper dived to his left and Harry smashed his shot straight down the middle.

Goooooooooooooooooooaaaaaaaaaaaaaaaalllllllllll lllllllllllllll!!!!!!!!!!!!!!!!!!!!

Harry didn't show any emotion. He just picked the ball out of the net, put it back on the spot, and walked back to his teammates.

The penalty shoot-out went all the way to the eleventh men. It was goalkeeper vs goalkeeper! Smithies went first... and scored.

It was all down to Simonsen now. He stepped up... and blasted the ball over the bar!

Sheffield United would not be playing in the Championship next season. As the Huddersfield players celebrated, Harry stood there, frozen in a daze of despair. It was the most painful moment he had ever experienced. That horrible sinking feeling was nothing compared to this.

'Head up, kid,' Wilson said as he walked over to give Harry a reassuring hug. 'You should be so proud of what you've achieved this season. Unbelievable! You'll be back – *we'll* be back.'

CHAPTER 11

GAME AFTER GAME

After Harry's fantastic breakthrough season in
2011–12, lots of clubs wanted to sign him. The list
even included Premier League teams like Newcastle
United. Was it time to move on to bigger things?

A few Sheffield United players did move on.
Right-back Matthew Lowton joined Aston Villa, and
midfielder Stephen Quinn joined Hull City. Harry,
however, chose to stay at the club.

'I don't want to go somewhere else and sit on the
bench,' he decided. 'I want to keep playing game
after game!'

Week in week out, Harry was the star of the
Blades' defence. He was already the Bramall Lane
hero that he had hoped to be. During the 2011–12

season, he had played in fifty-six matches. That was a massive number for a teenager!

'At a Premier League club, I might not even play ten proper matches,' Harry argued. 'No thanks!'

First-team experience was so important, no matter which division it was in. Harry needed to be playing under pressure, in matches that really mattered. How else was he going to learn and improve as a centre-back? With Neill by his side, Harry was getting a great football education at Sheffield United.

'If you can defend well in League One, you can defend well in the Premier League,' his manager Danny Wilson assured him. 'Trust me, you've got what it takes!'

Plus, Harry couldn't walk away from his local club without having another go at achieving his number one aim – promotion to the Championship.

In the 2012–13 season, Harry's consistency continued. He wore the Number 5 shirt now and he only missed two of United's forty-six league matches.

Game after game, he battled bravely against big, strong strikers.

'No-one's getting past Maguire today!'

Game after game, he used his body to block powerful shots.

'That's heroic defending there from Maguire!'

Game after game, he jumped highest to win headers.

'A towering leap from Maguire!'

Game after game, he stopped goals with his crunching, sliding tackles.

'Maguire with a crucial challenge!'

Game after game, he brought the ball forward out of defence to set up attacks.

'What a run this is from Maguire. Will he go all the way?'

Not only was Harry becoming a brilliant centre-back, but he was also a local lad. The Sheffield United fans loved him even more for that.

Harry, Harry Harry, Harry, Harry, Harry Harry, HARRY MAGUIRE!!

One day, they knew, he would move on to bigger and better things, but they wanted to keep him for as long as possible.

Don't leave us, Harry, we love you!

In February 2013, he made his 100th senior start for Sheffield United, and he was still not quite twenty years old. He felt like an experienced professional now, even if he didn't look like one.

'Sometimes, I forget how young you are,' Neill joked, 'but then I look at your awful clothes and your scruffy haircut, and I remember!'

What did Harry wish for on his twentieth birthday? Promotion to the Championship, of course.

'Come on, we can do it!' he told his teammates.

Again, Sheffield United were in the top six all season but again, they finished in the play-off places. Last year's Wembley defeat to Huddersfield still haunted them but Harry stayed positive. He was desperate to play at a higher level.

'This is our year, lads!'

The Blades beat Yeovil Town 1–0 in the first leg at Bramall Lane and the team travelled to Huish Park feeling confident. The sun was shining and United were wearing their black and red away kit, the colours of Harry's childhood club, Brunsmeer Athletic. It was going to be a good day.

In the first few minutes, however, Yeovil scored. It was now 1–1 on aggregate. Harry kicked the air in frustration. What a terrible start!

Sheffield United didn't give up, though. They fought back and nearly grabbed the goal they needed. Jamie Murphy's curling shot crashed against the crossbar. So close!

'Unlucky, keep going!' Harry called out.

In the last few minutes, Yeovil crossed a hopeful ball into the box. It flew over Harry's head and fell to their striker, Ed Upson. Harry watched in horror as Upson's header whizzed towards the top corner.

No, no, NO! Harry turned away in disgust. He couldn't bear to see the ball land in the back of the net. There would be no return trip to Wembley Stadium. Their season was over.

Nothing could ease Harry's pain – not even another Sheffield United Player of the Year award, and not even a spot in the League One Team of the Year for the second year in a row.

Yes, he was Mr Consistent, but would Harry ever be able to lift his team out of the lower leagues?

CHAPTER 12

ENGLAND CALLING = PART ONE

The older Harry got, the more he thought back to his childhood dreams. He had achieved so many of them already. He was a professional footballer, and a very successful one too. He was playing for his favourite club, Sheffield United, and the fans loved him. He had scored goals at Bramall Lane and he had even played at Wembley. What else was left?

International football! Ever since World Cup 2002, Harry had been England's biggest fan. For the most important matches, the Maguire family liked to throw massive parties at their house. Wearing his white England shirt, Harry watched and hoped.

His heroes were the two centre-backs: Rio

Ferdinand and John Terry. They were the best in the business – calm, quick, strong, and classy on the ball.

'With those guys at the back, we can't lose!' Harry thought, but sadly, he thought wrong.

He was miserable when England lost on penalties to Portugal at Euro 2004.

'We were robbed!'

He was devastated when the same thing happened again at the 2006 World Cup.

'How could Cristiano Ronaldo get Wayne Rooney sent off like that? They play together at Manchester United!'

He was heartbroken when England didn't even qualify for Euro 2008.

'Who am I going to support now?'

England fared a little better in the 2010 World Cup but Harry was still disappointed when they got thrashed by their old rivals Germany. Then at Euro 2012, they lost on penalties… AGAIN!

'We're cursed!' Harry told his best friend, Danny.

For years, Harry only thought about supporting England – on TV and at Wembley. The idea of actually *playing* for England seemed impossible!

Once he became a Sheffield United's best centre-back, however, people started talking about a call-up to the Under-21s. He didn't want to get his hopes up, though.

'They hardly ever give League One players a chance,' he reminded his brothers.

In November 2012, that all changed. The England Under-21s were about to play a friendly match against Northern Ireland but they were struggling for numbers. Jason Lowe and Sammy Ameobi were both injured and Wilfried Zaha had been called up to the senior squad.

'Is it too late to call up a few extras?' the Under-21s manager Stuart Pearce asked his coaches.

No, it wasn't, because the match was nearby – at Blackpool's Bloomfield Road stadium. The first player they asked was Leicester City striker Martyn Waghorn. And the second? Harry, of course!

At first, he didn't believe it. Was it Danny playing a prank on him? No, it really was Stuart Pearce on the phone, calling him up to the England Under-21s.

'Wow, thanks, it's a real honour!' Harry replied, trying not to sound too much like a star-struck kid.

But that was exactly how he felt at first. He was the only League One player in the squad and many of his new teammates were already Premier League stars. Harry watched them on *Match of the Day* every Saturday night.

Connor Wickham played for Sunderland, Andros Townsend played for Tottenham, and Nick Powell played for Manchester United. Captain Jordan Henderson had signed for Liverpool for nearly £20million!

'Welcome to the team!' Jordan said with a smile.

Harry had no idea if he would get to play in the match but it was a great experience to train with such brilliant players and coaches. Was he good enough to compete at this level? Of course, he was. He just had to believe in himself.

'Blimey, you're a beast!' Connor told him after receiving one of his trademark tackles.

At Bloomfield Road, Harry watched the first half from the subs bench. The England Under-21s had won all of their matches in 2012 and Northern Ireland were no match for them. Harry was impressed by his team's flowing, passing football. He couldn't wait to join in if he got the opportunity…

Jordan and Josh McEachran created chance after chance and eventually, Connor headed home. 1–0!

England were winning but Pearce wanted more. After sixty minutes, he made a triple substitution. Benik Afobe came on for Andros in attack, Nathaniel Clyne came on for Adam Smith at right-back, and Harry came on for Andre Wisdom at centre-back.

Wearing the white Number 15 shirt, Harry jogged out onto the pitch. The 9,000 supporters in the stadium clapped quietly. It was a cold Tuesday night in Blackpool, rather than a sell-out at Wembley, but Harry didn't care about that. He was an England international now! The last of his childhood dreams was coming true.

'Right, focus!' Harry told himself.

He could enjoy his proud moment with his family. For now, he had some defending to do. If he played well, maybe Pearce would call him up again.

The last thirty minutes flew by in a flash. What could Harry do to leave his mark on the match? He did his best to show off his heading and his passing, as the Three Lions cruised to victory. There were no goals or heroic blocks, but he was pleased with his debut, and so was his manager.

'Well done, you looked really comfortable out there!' Pearce said at the final whistle, shaking his hand.

Harry was still buzzing when he returned to Sheffield United.

'Oh, here comes our England star,' his teammates teased. 'We better roll out the red carpet!'

Harry laughed along but that taste of international football had made him more focused than ever. Now, he knew that he could do it – he was good enough to reach the highest level. With hard work and determination, he could one day play in the Premier League, and perhaps even play for his country at a major tournament.

Although that turned out to be Harry's one and only appearance for the Under-21s, his England days were far from over.

CHAPTER 13

GOAL MACHINE!

Neill and the new Sheffield United manager Chris Morgan were always reminding Harry about the rules of being a centre-back:

'Defend first, and attack second.'

'If in doubt, get it out!'

'Safety first!'

Harry knew the rules but every now and then, he couldn't help breaking them.

'If I see space ahead of me, why shouldn't I dribble forward?' he thought. That was his old mid-fielder brain talking. Sometimes it was a little risky but most of the time, it really helped the team to attack.

Harry could weave his way through tackles, he

could play perfect long passes, and he could score goals too.

In the Football League Trophy second round against Notts County in October 2012, Harry chased after a clearance. From way out on the right wing, he calmly curled the ball over the goalkeeper's outstretched arm and in off the post.

Goooooooooooooaaaaaaaaaallllllllllllllllllllllll!!!!!!!!!!!

'Extraordinary!' the TV commentator cried out, as Harry celebrated with his teammates.

'Was it a shot, or was it a cross?' they asked.

'Of course it was a shot!' he told them confidently.

If Ronaldinho could claim that goal against England in the 2002 World Cup, then Harry was definitely claiming this one.

During the 2012–13 League One season, he scored once with his right foot and twice with his powerful head.

'That nearly burst the net!' his teammate Nick Blackman cheered, giving him a big high-five.

As a defender, Harry loved keeping clean sheets and making important tackles, but scoring goals was also really fun. It was an amazing feeling to hear the fans at Bramall Lane cheering his name.

Harry, Harry Harry, Harry, Harry, Harry Harry, HARRY MAGUIRE!!

Harry was always looking for ways to improve – more tackles, more passes, more dribbles, and more goals.

On the first day of the 2013–14 season, Sheffield United were once again playing Notts County, this time at home. They were drawing 1–1, but that really wasn't the result that the Blades wanted – they wanted to win!

Stephen McGinn curled a free-kick all the way to Harry at the back post. He watched the ball carefully as it dropped down towards him. He was unmarked, but it was going to take a brilliant header to beat the keeper from there. BOOM! Like a bullet, the ball flew into the top corner of the net.

Goooooooooooooaaaaaaaaaalllllllllllllllllllllll!!!!!!!!!!!!

Harry ran over to the Sheffield United fans with his arms in the air and a massive smile on his face. It was the winning goal and he was the hero.

Two weeks later, the Blades were losing 1–0 to Colchester United. Febian Brandy passed a quick free kick to Harry near the halfway line.

'Shoot! Shoot!' the fans urged.

Why not? Harry dribbled forward and hit a swerving, long-range right foot rocket. It wasn't his best strike ever but it caught the goalkeeper by surprise. He spilled the ball into his own net!

Goooooooooooooaaaaaaaaaalllllllllllllllllllllllll!!!!!!!!!!!!

Harry pointed up at his family in the stands and punched the air. Two goals in three games – what a start to the season!

'What would we do without you?' his manager asked.

Two months later, Harry was still Sheffield United's joint top scorer with two goals. The Blades were bottom of the league. What a disaster! They needed a hero more than ever.

Against Crewe Alexandra, a cross bounced across the penalty area, and Harry reacted quicker than any of the defenders around him. With a clever header, he steered the ball low into the bottom corner. 1–0!

'Get in!' Harry roared but he wasn't done yet. Ten minutes later, he scored another header to make it 2–0.

Goooooooooooooaaaaaaaaaalllllllllllllllllllllll!!!!!!!!!!!

Harry was definitely his team's top scorer now! Those goals gave Sheffield United the confidence to climb back up the table. By the end of 2013, they were out of the relegation zone but Harry was still their top scorer.

'Maybe I should play up front instead!' he joked.

From corners and free kicks, Harry was simply unstoppable in the air.

Step One: He used his strength to outmuscle his marker.

Step Two: He used his height to win the header. *BOOM!*

Step Three: He used his power and technique to find the back of the net. *GOAL!*

Eventually, Chris Porter took over as United's top scorer, but Harry only finished two goals behind him. He was becoming an amazing all-round player – defender *and* attacker.

CHAPTER 14

BATTLING WITH THE BIG BOYS

Sheffield United didn't quite make it to the League One play-offs in 2014, but the season was still a big success.

The Blades hadn't got past the fifth round of the FA Cup in years but suddenly, they were beating everybody: Colchester United, Cambridge United... even Aston Villa!

Against Villa, it was Harry vs Christian Benteke, their big Belgian target man. Some young players would have been nervous but Harry couldn't wait to test himself against one of the Premier League's strongest strikers.

'Let the battle begin!' Harry told Neill.

Wherever Benteke went, Harry was always right behind him. He was a big centre-back but he was also quick and clever, and the Belgian couldn't escape from him.

With every header and block, Harry grew in confidence. He felt ten feet tall! He couldn't get carried away, though. This was top-level football. Everything could change in a second. Harry had to stay focused until the final whistle.

FWEEEEEEEEEEEEEEET!

It was over – Aston Villa 1 Sheffield United 2. The players ran around hugging each other as if they had just won the FA Cup. It was a proud day that Harry would never forget. He had won his biggest battle yet!

'See, you're Premier League quality, big man!' Neill told him, feeling like a proud parent.

Could the Blades pull off another cup upset against Fulham? Yes!

Harry got the ball near the halfway line and dribbled forward at speed.

'Keep going!' the Bramall Lane crowd screamed. They were up on their feet, waiting, hoping…

On the edge of the penalty area, Harry shrugged off a tackle and crossed the ball to Chris. 1–0 to Sheffield United!

Harry punched the air. He was helping his team at both ends of the pitch.

When their captain, Michael Doyle got sent off, it was Harry who took the armband. He was still only twenty years old but he was a born leader.

'Stay strong, we can do this!' he called out to his nine teammates. He was always talking, always organising the defence.

In the seventy-fifth minute, Fulham's Hugo Rodallega got the ball on the edge of the box. Harry threw himself to the floor to try and block the shot but it flew past him and into the bottom corner. 1–1!

'No!' Harry lay on the grass with his head in his hands for a few seconds, but then he got back up and carried on. He had to. Sheffield United needed to hold on for a draw and a replay.

At Craven Cottage, United won a corner in the very last minute. This was their last chance to score, before the match went to penalties.

Harry stood near the back post, waving his arms in the air. 'On my head!' he called out to Jose Baxter. The cross was brilliant and so was Harry's header back across goal to Shaun Miller. 2–1 – they were through to the FA Cup Fifth Round!

Again, the players celebrated like they had just won the whole competition. It was such an exciting time to be a Sheffield United player or supporter. Harry was both, so it was doubly exciting for him.

'United! United!' he cheered.

The Blades were on a roll. They beat Nottingham Forest 3–1 and then Charlton Athletic 2–0 to make it through to the FA Cup semi-finals. It was a fantastic achievement for a team in League One.

'Wembley, here we come!' Harry yelled at the top of his voice. He couldn't wait to return to the Home of Football, and win this time.

The fans couldn't wait either. Thousands of them travelled down to London for the game against Hull City. One more win and Sheffield United would be in the final for the first time since 1936.

At half-time, they were 2–1 up and halfway there.

'Just keep going lads,' their manager encouraged them. 'You're all heroes already but if we win this, you'll be legends!'

In the second half, however, Hull fought back with two quick goals. There was nothing that Harry could do to stop them. Sheffield United were in shock and they fell apart. It was game over, and the end of their incredible cup run.

'What a nightmare!' Harry muttered to himself at the final whistle. In his head, he kept replaying all five of Hull's goals. 'We let in FIVE - what was I doing out there today?'

'Don't be so hard on yourself, you played well,' Neill said, putting an arm around his shoulder. 'Without you, there's no way we would have got this far. No way!'

Once his disappointment faded, Harry looked back happily on his FA Cup adventure. He was particularly proud of his performances against the Premier League clubs, Aston Villa and Fulham. He had battled against the big boys, and won both times. Harry now felt ready to do that week in week out, game after game.

CHAPTER 15

HEADING FOR HULL

By the end of the 2013–14 season, Harry was one
of the highest-rated youngsters in English football. If
scouts hadn't already known about him, they certainly
did after Sheffield United's incredible cup run.

'He's got great feet for a big centre-back!'

'Look at that composure on the ball – he can
really play!'

Scouts from Manchester United, Chelsea and
Tottenham came and went. Arsenal sent their old
defender Martin Keown to Bramall Lane.

'Maguire's very good,' Keown reported back,
'but I'm not sure he's quick enough for the Premier
League.'

It was Championship club Wolves who made the first bid of £1 million for Harry.

'No way!' Sheffield United said firmly.

Wolves came back with a second bid: £1.5 million.

'No way!' Sheffield United said firmly again. 'Harry's worth a lot more than that.'

Soon, they received a higher bid from Hull City. Harry couldn't believe it. 'They still want to buy me after the FA Cup semi-final?'

Yes! The Tigers had been watching Harry for years in League One. Eventually, their main scout, Stan Ternent, decided to speak to the manager, Steve Bruce.

'There's a young defender at Sheffield United that I think you should take a look at.'

'Okay, what's his name?'

'Harry Maguire. He's only twenty-one but he's already played 150 games for them! He's tall, he's strong, and he's talented with the ball too. He's been in the League One Team of the Year for the last two years. I think he's ready for the next step but see what you think.'

'Thanks for the recommendation, Stan. I'll go and watch him play.'

Bruce was very impressed by Harry's stats but what about his actual skills? The Hull manager was very impressed by those as well.

At first, he just looked like another big, beefy centre-back, who wrestled with strikers and won lots of headers.

'No, we won't need one of those in the Premier League,' Bruce muttered to himself.

But then Harry got the ball down and started to play. He passed and moved up the pitch, turning defence into attack. He had the confidence to take players on and dribble straight past them.

'Wow!' The Hull manager was blown away by Harry's composure. '*That* is exactly what we need in the Premier League!'

When the Tigers played Sheffield United in the FA Cup semi-final in April 2014, Bruce got another chance to see Harry in action. Harry didn't have his best game in defence but he still created lots of chances in attack when he brought the ball

forward. The Hull midfielders couldn't cope with his
confident, powerful runs.

'He looks like he's been playing at this level for
years,' Bruce told his assistant, Steve Agnew. 'We
have to sign him, before someone else does!'

Sheffield United rejected Hull's first offer of
£2 million but the second was too good to turn
down: £2.5 million was a lot of money for a League
One club.

'We really want you to stay here,' the Blades
manager, Nigel Clough, told his star player, 'but it's
your choice now. Have a think about it.'

The more Harry thought about it, the more
excited he became. If he signed for Hull City, he
would finally get to play in the Premier League, and
the Europa League too! That had been his dream for
years. He would get to play alongside experienced
stars like Curtis Davies, Michael Dawson and Tom
Huddlestone. Harry knew that he could learn so
much from Hull's players, and also from Hull's
manager.

Bruce had been a brilliant centre-back for

Manchester United in the 1990s, winning three Premier League titles alongside legends like Ryan Giggs, David Beckham and Eric Cantona. Harry was sure that he would have lots of great advice for a young defender with big ambition.

'It's time for a new challenge,' he told his parents. 'I'm ready!'

'Of course you are,' they reassured him. 'We believe in you!'

It would be sad to say goodbye to Sheffield United after so many happy years, but what if Harry never got another opportunity like this? If he didn't take it, he might regret it forever.

It also helped that Hull was only an hour's drive away from Sheffield. Harry wasn't yet ready to leave his family, and Yorkshire, behind.

'I'm sorry but I can't stay another season,' he told Clough. 'This is my chance to play in the Premier League.'

His manager understood. 'Good luck, you're going to be great!'

After passing the medical and signing the contract,

it was photo time. Harry was a Hull player now! He stood in the stands of the KC Stadium, wearing the orange-and-black-striped shirt and holding up an orange-and-black-striped scarf. There was a big smile stretched across his face.

'I can't wait to get started!' Harry told the club's website.

At least he wasn't starting his scary new adventure alone. On the very same day, Hull also signed a Scottish left-back. His name was Andrew Robertson and they quickly became good friends.

'Dundee United? Never heard of them!' Harry liked to tease Andrew about his former club. 'I thought there was only one decent team these days – Celtic.'

'Hey, the Scottish Premier League is still a lot better than English League One, Big Man!'

Harry was a year older than Andrew but they got on really well. They were both young players who had just made the big move to the best league in the world. Together, they coped with the challenges of being the new kids at the club. Before the opening match of the season, they each had to sing a song in front of the entire Hull squad. Andrew went first.

'Excellent, Andy!' the audience cheered and sang along.

'Right, your turn, H!'

Harry was as calm as ever as he stood up on a chair in the middle of the dressing room. The pressure was on. It was time to get the party started:

'Come on, let's twist again!' he sang, shaking his hips from side to side.

The other players were soon rolling on the floor with laughter. What a performance! Somehow, Harry managed to keep his balance and not fall off the chair. When he finished, he got a standing ovation.

'With moves like that, you're going to be a big hit here at Hull!' Curtis predicted.

CHAPTER 16

SLOW START AT HULL

Harry played for Hull in the Europa League and the League Cup, but he had to wait a long time for his Premier League debut. Often, he wasn't even on the bench.

'I don't get it. What am I doing wrong?' Harry asked his family.

'Just keep working hard and be patient,' they replied.

Harry wasn't used to being patient. He wanted to keep playing game after game, just like he had at Sheffield United. The Hull coaches, however, didn't think he was ready for that.

'We need to get you fitter first,' they told him.

That was one of the biggest differences between League One and the Premier League. In order to compete against teams like Chelsea and Manchester City, Harry needed to be a lean, mean running machine! Otherwise, strikers like Diego Costa and Sergio Agüero would destroy him again and again.

'They'll turn you inside out if you're not careful!' Curtis and Michael warned him.

Harry was a big, strong centre-back but he needed to be agile too. In the top division, teams attacked with so much skill and speed. How would he cope with that? It was time for Harry to get serious about his lifestyle. He needed to start eating better and sleeping better.

'I'll do anything to play in the Premier League!' he told his coaches at Hull.

With that positive, can-do attitude, Harry got fitter and fitter. Andrew was playing week in week out at left wing-back, and that spurred him on. Soon, that would be him! Curtis and Michael were playing brilliantly, and so was James Chester. Harry was the fourth-choice centre-back but at some point, he would get his chance to shine.

In the meantime, he kept smiling and joined in with all the dressing room jokes. Many of them were about the size of Harry's head.

'Is it hard to find hats that fit?' Tom teased.

He always had a comeback ready. 'Is it hard to find clothes that awful?'

In December 2014, Harry's big moment finally arrived. With fifteen minutes to go against Swansea City, Hull were losing 1–0 and Curtis was injured. Bruce looked at his bench and decided to give Harry an early Christmas present.

'Get forward as much as you can!' the manager told him.

Sure thing! Harry ran onto the pitch, proudly wearing the Number 12 shirt. He could now call himself a Premier League player.

'Go on, Big Man!' Andrew called to him.

Harry was desperate to become Hull's new hero. This was it – his chance to shine. Unfortunately, there was no time for him to attack. Instead, Harry had defending to do. He batted bravely in the air against Wilfried Bony and Marvin Emnes.

Before Harry knew it, the match was over. His Premier League debut had ended in defeat. Hull were now deep in the relegation zone. If only he could help…

But no, Harry was back on the bench in the Hull games against Sunderland and Leicester City. Had that been his one and only chance?

Against Everton, Harry came on with thirty minutes to go. Hull were winning 2–0.

'Just keep things tight,' Bruce told him.

Sure thing! Harry stayed focused until the final whistle. There was no way he was going to let Romelu Lukaku or Arouna Koné score.

'Well played, H!' Curtis cheered as they celebrated a very important victory.

Was this Harry's big breakthrough? He hoped so but no, he was back on the bench again for the next game.

Against West Ham, Harry came on at half-time. The score was still 0–0 – what a chance for him to shine! He couldn't wait to play a whole forty-five minutes of football.

Oh dear! Thirty minutes later, Hull were losing badly. When Alex Song played a defence-splitting pass, Harry couldn't keep up with Stewart Downing. 3–0! That horrible sinking feeling was back.

'I just need more game-time!' he groaned.

The only answer was to go out on loan. Harry joined Wigan Athletic and stayed until the end of the season. It felt weird wearing blue and white, like United's Sheffield rivals, Wednesday, but he was willing to do anything for game-time.

Playing in the Championship, Harry's confidence came back quickly. In his first game against Reading, in February 2015, Wigan kept a cleansheet and won for the first time in months.

'Thank goodness you're here!' his new manager Malky Mackay said.

Harry was just happy to be playing game after game again. He was Mr Consistent at the heart of the Wigan defence, winning headers and crunching tackles.

And he got forward to attack too. Away at Blackpool, a corner-kick came in and he won the header at the back post.

Goooooooooooooooooooooaaaaaaaaaaaaaaaaallllllllllll lllllllllllllll!!!!!!!!!!!!!!!!!!!!

The old Harry was back! He ran over to the fans, shaking his fists in the air. 'Get in!' he roared, with joy rushing through his veins.

Harry did his best to rescue Wigan from relegation. He really didn't want to go back down to League One again. Unfortunately, his efforts were too little, too late.

'I've played every game since I've been here, and I've enjoyed my time here,' Harry told the local newspapers. 'The lads and the staff have been brilliant, it's a great club.'

He was sad to leave Wigan in such a bad state but things weren't much better back at Hull either. They had just been relegated from the Premier League to the Championship.

'Wherever I go, I bring bad luck!' Harry told his brothers, and he was only half-joking.

The news wasn't all negative, though. During the summer of 2015, James Chester joined West Brom for £8 million. When Bristol City then tried to sign Harry, Bruce said no.

Hopefully, that meant that Harry would now get lots more game-time at Hull. After a slow start, it was time for Sheffield's star to shine.

CHAPTER 17

PROMOTION AT LAST!

Again, however, Harry had to be patient. Michael and Curtis started the Championship season as Hull's first-choice centre-backs.

'Don't worry, your time will come,' Bruce promised.

But when? Sometimes, Harry forgot that he was still only twenty-two. While he waited, he tried to learn as much as he could from his experienced teammates. Michael and Curtis were always happy to help whenever he had any questions.

'Communication is key,' Michael told him. 'I know I talk a lot out on the pitch but that's a big part of my job! It keeps the defence alert and organised.'

Of course, Harry really didn't want either of his

teammates to get injured, but how else was he going to get into the team? He was desperate to get back to playing game after game.

'Maybe one of them will get a red card instead!' his mum suggested.

Sometimes, Andrew kept Harry company on the Hull bench. It was nice to have supportive friends by his side.

'One day, we'll be Premier League stars and we'll look back on these bad days and laugh. Trust me!'

Slowly but surely, Harry fought his way into the team. First, he played ten minutes, then twenty, then seventy against Brentford. In a back three with Michael and Curtis, he had the freedom to attack, as well as defend.

'Up you go, Big Man!' Curtis called out whenever Hull won a corner-kick.

Harry was causing all kinds of trouble in the Brentford penalty area. He headed the ball into the danger zone and when it bounced back to him, he pulled his right leg back and BANG! The goalkeeper saved his shot but Sam Clucas was there for the rebound. 2–0! Harry and Sam celebrated by sliding across the grass on their knees.

'Premier League, here we come!' they cheered together.

The Tigers were top of the table and full of confidence. How could Bruce put Harry back on the bench after that? He couldn't!

Harry played instead of Curtis, and Hull beat their promotion rivals Middlesbrough 3–0. It was the best team performance of the season.

'Keep up the good work!' his manager told Harry with a big thumbs-up.

Harry played instead of Michael, and Hull beat Reading 2–1. The more games he played, the better he became. Sometimes, Harry took a few risks but he worked and worked to help his team to win. The fans loved his all-action style.

Against QPR, he beat two opponents to the ball and sent them both flying!

'That's it, Harry!'

Against Cardiff, he went up for a corner and a defender wrestled him to the floor. Penalty!

'They just can't handle him!'

Hull were on a roll. Their deadly defence kept cleansheets against Cardiff City, Charlton Athletic, Fulham, Blackburn Rovers... The list went on and on.

'I told you everything would work out for us!' Andrew reminded Harry.

But just when he was feeling on top of the world, Michael returned from injury – and Harry was back on the bench again.

'But I was playing really well!' he moaned.

It seemed so cruel to just drop him like that. Without Harry, Hull slipped from first place down to fourth.

'Bring back Maguire!' the supporters cried out.

Harry came back with a bang against Brentford. In the thirtieth minute, the Hull goalkeeper rolled the ball out to him in defence. After a few sideways passes, Harry saw the space ahead of him and galloped forward.

As usual, Andrew was making a brilliant run down the left wing. Harry spotted it and his long, diagonal ball was an absolute beauty. It floated just over the right-back's head and dropped down in front of Andrew. His cross was so dangerous that the Brentford centre-back could only kick it into his own net. 1–0!

'Keep Maguire in the team!' the supporters cried out.

Sadly, it was too late for Hull to win the Championship title now. The Tigers would have to win promotion through the play-offs instead.

'Not again!' Harry thought to himself.

Twice, he had got to the League One Play-offs with Sheffield United and twice, they had lost. Was it bad luck or bad mistakes? Harry had been relegated twice, and how many times had he been promoted? Zero!

In the play-offs, Bruce selected Michael and Curtis at the back, and Harry on the bench. Hull beat Derby County 3–2 to reach the final at Wembley.

'Well done, lads!' Harry cheered. Even though he wasn't playing in the team, he was still a great team player. 'We're nearly there!'

The final was one of the tightest and nerviest matches that Harry had ever seen. After all, Hull and Sheffield Wednesday were battling each other for a place in the Premier League. What a prize for the winner!

On the bench, Harry looked up at the 70,000 fans and listened to their non-stop noise. How he wished that he could be out there, playing on the pitch against United's Sheffield rivals. Hull needed a hero...

That hero turned out to be midfielder Mohamed Diamé. With twenty minutes to go, he hit a thirty-yard screamer into the top corner. 1–0!

At that moment, Harry was warming up along the touchline. He stopped to watch the ball fly past the goalkeeper and then raced over to join the big team hug.

'Mo, what a beauty!' he yelled.

In the end, Harry did get to play a part in Hull's big day at Wembley. With five minutes to go, he came on to replace Mohamed. The manager's instructions were simple:

'Just don't let them score!'

Those five minutes were the longest of Harry's life. Wednesday had shot after shot but Hull held on.

'Yes, yes, YES!' Harry screamed at the final whistle. 'We're back in the Premier League!'

He had won promotion at last. Harry was the third player up the stadium steps to shake hands and collect his winners' medal. Once it was placed around his neck, suddenly it all felt real. He turned to his captain, Michael, and grabbed him by the face.

'We did it, Daws!' he grinned. 'We did it!'

The players were bouncing up and down before Michael even lifted the trophy. He passed the big silver cup down the line until, eventually, Harry had it in his hands. He kissed the trophy twice and lifted it above his head. What a feeling, in front of all his friends and family at Wembley!

Back down on the pitch, the Hull players posed for team photos together. Harry was right at the centre, dancing, smiling, and shielding his eyes from the spraying champagne.

'Curtis, stop aiming for me!'

'Sorry, your big head's an easy target!'

The celebrations carried on all afternoon and all night too. Harry couldn't wait to be back in the Premier League. This time, he was going to prove himself at the highest level.

CHAPTER 18

AGAINST THE ODDS

As the 2016–17 Premier League season kicked-off, fans disagreed about which team would finish top:

'I reckon Tottenham can do it. They came so close last season and they've got more experience this time around.'

'No, it's going to be Manchester City's year. They've got Pep Guardiola in charge now, and the guy's a genius!'

'What about José Mourinho at Manchester United? He sure knows how to win the Premier League!'

At the other end of the table, most fans agreed about which team would finish bottom:

'Hull City.'

'Yeah, they're going to get hammered every week!'

'They could be relegated by Christmas!'

It had been a very hard summer for Hull. First, their right-back Moses Odubajo picked up a really bad injury in preseason. Then, their manager Steve Bruce resigned and their captain Michael hurt his knee. Finally, their play-off hero Mohamed signed for Newcastle United. Bit by bit, the club's Premier League excitement was fading away.

'Oh no, this is going to be a disaster!' the Hull fans feared.

The opening game against Leicester City was only weeks away, and the Tigers still only had twelve fit players in their first-team squad.

'Come on, lads, we've got to stick together here!' their new manager, Mike Phelan, told them.

Thankfully, there was a strong team spirit amongst the players. They didn't mind battling against the odds.

Harry certainly wasn't giving up on his Premier League dream. He had spent the summer working really hard on every aspect of his game.

On the training pitch, he focused on his fitness. Thanks to the new sports technology, he could look at lots of running stats every day: distance, average speed, and number of sprints. He challenged himself to get faster and faster.

'Look at that acceleration!' Andrew joked. 'Agüero better watch out!'

Off the training pitch, Harry sat through hours and hours of his own performances on video. He found it really embarrassing to watch, but it was a great way to learn from his mistakes.

'No! What were you doing there?' he shouted at himself on the screen. 'Concentrate!'

Harry preferred watching videos of other defenders in action. Premier League legends like John Terry and Rio Ferdinand hardly ever made wrong decisions. They read the game so well that they saw the danger coming and dealt with it every time. They made it look so simple.

'One day, I'll reach that level,' Harry told himself.

Sometimes, Phelan watched videos with him and gave him extra advice. He had been Sir Alex

Ferguson's assistant at Manchester United and so he had worked closely with Ferdinand. Harry eagerly asked him question after question.

'What do you think Rio would have done there?'

'How did Rio know that the striker was going to do that?'

'Who do you think Rio preferred playing against – Fernando Torres or Didier Drogba?'

Each answer added to Harry's football education. He had to learn from the best in order to compete with the best.

Harry played the last ten minutes against Manchester United and then the last forty-five minutes against Arsenal and Liverpool. Hull lost all three matches but he didn't let that get him down. It was all good experience. By the time Phelan gave Harry his first-ever Premier League start against Bournemouth, he felt 100 per cent ready.

'Let's do this!' Harry cheered, high-fiving Curtis, his centre-back partner.

Unfortunately, those high hopes only lasted five minutes. Junior Stanislas' free kick hit the post and

Charlie Daniels scored the rebound, despite Harry's brave dive to stop it. 1–0! After that, Hull just collapsed.

Steve Cook jumped highest to win a header against Harry. 2–1!

Robert Snodgrass gave away a penalty. 3–1!

Adam Smith crossed and Stanislas scored. 4–1!

Joshua King's cross landed on Callum Wilson's head. 5–1!

Daniels passed to Dan Gosling and he curled the ball into corner of the net. 6–1!

Hull had been absolutely hammered. As he trudged off the pitch, Harry felt so many negative emotions at once – humiliation, disappointment, guilt, frustration, anger. It was the worst defeat of his entire career. The horrible sinking feeling stayed in his stomach for days.

'What if I never get to play Premier League football again?' he groaned. He was dreading his post-match video session. Phelan had every right to be furious with him for his poor performance.

'Look, that defeat wasn't your fault,' his manager told him. 'We win as a team and we lose as a team. Every player has to take responsibility. The important thing is how you recover. Rio had bad games too but he always bounced straight back. Now, you've got to do the same!'

Phelan was right; Harry was a strong character and it was time to show it.

Ten days later, he was playing for Hull in the FA Cup against Bristol City. In the last minute of the first half, Ryan Mason curled a high corner into the box. Harry timed his run perfectly and headed home at the back-post. 1–0!

Goooooooooooaaaaaaaaaalllllllllllllllllllllll!!!!!!!!!!!!!!

Harry punched the air proudly. He had finally scored his first goal for Hull! Michael ran over and gave him a massive hug.

'Nice one, H!' his captain shouted, patting his big head.

Soon, Harry was playing in the Premier League again too. Against Crystal Palace, he chested the ball down near the halfway line and looked up. Andrew was making a great run down the left but it would take an incredible long pass to reach him. Instead, Harry calmly dribbled past one player and then played it to Hull's striker, Adama Diomande, who turned and scored. 2–2!

'Great work, H!' Michael shouted.

Against Everton, Harry did it again. He collected the ball at the back and bravely brought it forward.

'Keep going!' the fans urged him on.

Why not? Harry had put his Bournemouth disaster behind him. He now felt really comfortable playing Premier League football. It was his time to shine.

The Everton midfielders backed away in fear as Harry galloped through the middle like a race horse. Eventually, one of them tried to stop him. Foul – free kick!

'Brilliant run, H!' Curtis called out.

Robert fired the free-kick straight into the top corner. 2–1 to Hull!

Against the odds, the Tigers were no longer bottom of the table. Harry was loving every minute of his Premier League adventure, despite all the ups and downs.

'It's a good thing I love rollercoaster rides!' he said with a big smile on his face.

CHAPTER 19

ATTACK FROM THE BACK

Unfortunately, the chaos continued. In January 2017, Hull sacked Mike Phelan and replaced him with a young Portuguese manager called Marco Silva.

'I know we don't have a lot of time,' he admitted in his first interview, 'but I want the fans to believe, like I believe.'

Could the Tigers really stay up? It was going to take a miracle, especially when the club sold two of their best players, Jake Livermore and Robert Snodgrass.

'Come on, lads, we've got to stick together here!' Harry told his teammates.

He didn't know much about Silva but they got

on really well straight away. The new manager
had big plans for the defence, and for Harry in
particular.

'I want you to be the one who brings the ball
forward,' Silva told him. 'We're going to attack from
the back!'

'No problem!' Harry thought to himself. It was the
role that he was born to play.

Silva's first game was the rematch against
Bournemouth. Harry had been looking forward to it
for months. He was desperate to get revenge for that
awful 6–1 thrashing in his first Premier League start.
the Tigers were a much better team now, and Harry
was a much better player.

It didn't look that way, however, when he gave
away a penalty with a clumsy tackle. Hull were 1–0
down after only three minutes.

'No, no, NO!' he screamed.

Harry didn't panic and give up, though. 'That's
not what Rio would do,' he thought to himself. He
had to stay strong and make things right. He pushed
his team up the pitch with his clever dribbling and

passing, and Hull fought back to win 3–1. Silva was impressed.

'You showed real character today,' he told Harry. 'Keep it up – you've got some big battles ahead of you!'

At Stamford Bridge, Harry fought ferociously against Chelsea's star striker, Diego Costa. Hull lost 2–0 but Harry picked up the man of the match award for his all-action performance. At the back, he made eight tackles, seven clearances and eight interceptions. In attack, he took more shots than any of his teammates.

'Great game,' Cesc Fàbregas said, shaking his hand at the final whistle. 'I love the way you play!'

At Old Trafford, Harry frustrated Manchester United's legendary striker Zlatan Ibrahimović all game long. And when Harry got the ball at the back, he wasn't afraid to take a few risks in attack. He even dribbled past his old FA Youth Cup opponent, Paul Pogba. The fans loved Harry's confidence and character.

Ohhhh, Harry Maguire!

Ohhhh, Harry Maguire!

0–0 – an important point for Hull!

At the KC Stadium, Harry and his new centre-back partner, Andrea Ranocchia, kept out Liverpool's ace attackers Roberto Firmino and Sadio Mané. Then just before half-time, Harry headed a corner towards goal and Alfred N'Diaye bundled it in. 1–0!

'Thanks, H!' Alfred cheered, putting an arm around his broad shoulders.

Silva's coaching was working wonders. The team looked fitter than ever and they were passing the ball around beautifully.

Harry was keeping Hull's survival hopes alive, at both ends of the field. Once the defending was done, he loved to attack from the back. It really helped that Harry had one of the best friends by his side. He was now the left centre-back, with Andrew next to him at left-back. Together, they formed a perfect partnership – strength *and* speed, great passes *and* great crosses.

With eight games to go, Hull were just one point away from safety.

'Come on lads, we can do this!' Harry kept telling his teammates.

Now that Michael and Curtis weren't playing so often, he was their heroic leader at the back. Wearing the captain's armband, Harry was improving game after game.

At the start of April 2017, Hull faced Middlesbrough in an epic relegation battle. After an awful start, the Tigers really came back roaring.

Lazar Marković poked the ball in after a goalmouth scramble. 1–1!

Abel Hernández set up Oumar Niasse. 2–1!

'That's more like it!' Harry shouted, punching the air with joy and relief.

The game, however, was far from over. There were still sixty minutes left to play. Could Hull hold on for that long?

No, Harry had a better idea. He got the ball deep in his own half and decided to attack from the back. As he looked up, he saw Sam Clucas making a great run down the right wing. Harry found him with the perfect pass. He curled the ball just past a

Middlesbrough midfielder's outstretched foot, and then in between two defenders. Sam crossed it first-time to Abel. 3–1!

Abel pointed at Sam to thank him for the assist but Sam pointed to his centre-back. 'H, what a ball that was!' he screamed above the deafening crowd.

Middlesbrough scored again just before half-time but luckily, Harry wasn't finished yet. With twenty anxious minutes ahead, Hull won a free kick. Andrew whipped the ball into the box, knowing exactly where his big friend would be: the back post! Harry was unmarked but he still had plenty of work to do. He headed the ball over the goalkeeper's arms and it looped down into the far corner of the net. 4–2 – game over!

Goooooooooooooooooooooaaaaaaaaaaaaaaaaalllllllllllll llllllllllllll!!!!!!!!!!!!!!!!!!!

What a time for Harry to score his first Premier League goal! The Hull fans went wild as he ran over and jumped into Michael's arms.

Ohhhh, Harry Maguire!
Ohhhh, Harry Maguire!

There was no stopping him now. Away at
Southampton a few weeks later, Harry was Hull's
hero yet again.

Sofiane Boufal dribbled into the penalty area, past
two flying challenges, but he couldn't get past Harry.
TACKLE!

Nathan Redmond crossed to Dušan Tadić but he
couldn't score past Harry. *BLOCK!*

0–0 – another important point for Hull!

He was really making a name for himself now.
Every Premier League club wanted a 'Harry Maguire'
at the heart of their defence.

'He has very good skills,' Silva praised his captain.
'It's clear to me that he will have a big career in the
future.'

That future, however, would not be at Hull.
Despite his best efforts, they lost their big battles
against Sunderland and Crystal Palace. The
rollercoaster ride had come to an end. Harry was
relegated for the third time in his career.

This time, however, he was going down with
his big head held high. In his first full season in the

Premier League, Harry had been Hull's hero, captain, and Player of the Year.

After the last home game of the season, he walked slowly around the pitch, clapping to the tearful fans. Harry had given 100 per cent to help his team, and they loved him for that.

Ohhhh, Harry Maguire!
Ohhhh, Harry Maguire!

Harry would always be grateful for their support, especially during his difficult early days on the bench. Wow, he had come a long way since then! What was next for Harry?

CHAPTER 20

LEICESTER CITY

Harry was trying to relax on his family summer holiday in Majorca, but he had a difficult decision to make. As he lay there by the pool, soaking up the sun, he asked himself,

'Who do I want to play for next season?'

After his big breakthrough year with Hull, lots of top clubs were queuing up to sign him: Tottenham, Leicester City, Stoke City, Everton, Newcastle United, Southampton, West Ham… The list went on and on.

When his agent told him, Harry's first thought was, 'Great, I'll get to stay in the Premier League!'

Now, however, he had to pick which team to play for. What a hard choice!

Tottenham were the Premier League runners-up for two years in a row. They had an amazing manager, Mauricio Pochettino, and amazing players like Harry Kane, Christian Eriksen and Dele Alli.

'Plus, you'd be playing Champions League football next season!' Laurence argued.

The only problem was that they already had a deadly defence. Toby Alderweireld and Jan Vertonghen were two of the best centre-backs in the world, and they had Eric Dier as well!

'No, there's no way that I'm going to play week in week out at Spurs,' Harry decided.

No matter what, he wasn't going back to the bench again. He was twenty-four years old now. Wherever he went, he needed guaranteed game-time.

Harry moved on to his next option, 'Okay, well how about Leicester City, then?'

The Foxes were the 2015–16 Premier League Champions and they still had their world-class forwards, Jamie Vardy and Riyad Mahrez. Harry could start the attacks from the back and they would finish them off. Easy!

'They've got some other promising young English players too,' Joe argued. 'Ben Chilwell's good, and Demarai Gray's rapid!'

But, most importantly, what about their defence? Did they have space for a new centre-back? Yes, they had a big, Harry-shaped gap to fill!

Robert Huth and Wes Morgan were both coming towards the end of their careers and Leicester City didn't really have a back-up option.

'Maguire is our man!' their manager, Craig Shakespeare, decided.

He was so desperate to sign Harry that he flew all the way out to Majorca to meet him.

'I hope you're having a nice summer holiday,' Shakespeare began. 'This shouldn't take long. I'm rebuilding the Leicester defence and I want to rebuild it around you!'

That sounded awesome but Harry didn't want to rush into things. This was the biggest decision of his life, and he had to get it right. He had lots of questions for the Leicester manager:

What formation would the team be playing – 4–4–2 or 3–5–2?

What style of football did he want his team to play?

And what were the club's expectations for the season ahead – Top Four, Top Six or Top Ten?

As he answered each question, Shakespeare grew more and more impressed. Harry was clearly a very clever young man, who studied football closely. It only made the Leicester manager even more determined to sign him.

Harry grew more and more impressed too. Not only had Shakespeare come all the way to a Spanish island to speak to him, but he had big, bold plans for the football club.

'And I want you to be a key part of it!' the manager told him passionately.

Leicester were building towards a brighter future. They were improving their academy, their training ground, and, of course, their squad. The Foxes were on the up and they were aiming for European qualification.

'Perfect, where do I sign?' Harry thought to himself.

He didn't want to join a global giant like Manchester United or Chelsea. That wasn't his style. Leicester was a family club that cared about its local community, just like his home team, Sheffield United. He knew that he would be very happy there.

'I've made up my mind,' Harry told his family at dinner one night. 'I'm going to Leicester!'

It was a sad day when Harry went back to say goodbye to all his friends at Hull. They felt like family.

'Good luck, Big H!' Michael cheered.

'Cheers for everything, Daws. I couldn't have done it without you!'

'I'm going to miss playing with you!' Andrew said as they hugged.

'Me too, mate! Why don't you just come with me?'

Back in 2014, Hull had paid £2.5 million to sign Harry from Sheffield United. Three years later, Leicester were writing a much, much larger cheque.

'£17million for someone who just got relegated?' people on Twitter reacted. 'The world's gone crazy!'

'That Hull defence let in eighty goals last season. Leicester are having a laugh!'

Yes, it was an awful lot of money, but there was only one way that Harry could prove his value – by performing well out on the pitch.

First, however, Leicester's new Number 15 needed to settle in. It didn't take him long to make new friends in the squad. There were lots of big, fun characters at the club.

'Alright mate, is it true that you're an Owls fan like me?' Jamie teased. He was from Sheffield too, and had started out in the Wednesday youth team.

Harry rolled his eyes. 'Stop winding me up, you know I'm a Blade through and through!'

Harry quickly became a popular member of the Leicester dressing room, and a key member of the team. He scored his first goal for his new club in August 2017 against Burton Albion and, for once, it wasn't even a header. As the ball bounced down in the box, he smashed it home with his right foot.

Gooooooooooooooooooooaaaaaaaaaaaaaaaalllllllllllll llllllllllllllll!!!!!!!!!!!!!!!!!!!!!!

It was only a preseason friendly, but Harry meant business. He had new targets for the new year.

'Every player wants to play for their country,' he told the journalists afterwards. 'I felt like this was the club that could help me progress into the England squad.'

Some people laughed at Harry's ambition, but he was being deadly serious. This was going to be *his* season.

With Robert Huth out injured, Harry started alongside Wes Morgan against Arsenal. It wasn't the solid defensive debut that he was hoping for, but he played his part in attack.

In the fifth minute, Harry crept in at the back post, as usual, to head the ball back for Shinji Okazaki. 1–1!

'Thanks, H!' Shinji cheered, giving him a big hug.

A week later against Brighton and Hove Albion, Harry got a cleansheet and a goal. It was a trademark towering header at the back post.

Goooooooooooooooooooooaaaaaaaaaaaaaaaaaallllllllllll llllllllllllllll!!!!!!!!!!!!!!!!!!!!!!

As Harry celebrated in front of the fans, Wilfred Ndidi and Wes jumped up on his back. He was so strong that he could carry them both!

'£17million, eh?' Jamie laughed. 'What a bargain for that big head of yours!'

Suddenly, Harry's dreams of a first England call-up didn't seem so silly at all.

CHAPTER 21

ENGLAND CALLING – PART TWO

Even though he was a Premier League star now, Harry was still England's biggest fan. When his brothers and friends went to France to watch Euro 2016, he decided to join them.

'Three Lions on a shirt!' he sang along with the rest of the supporters in Saint-Étienne. As long as he didn't sing too loudly, or badly, he could blend into the crowd.

The match finished Slovakia 0 England 0. It wasn't the most exciting game of football that Harry had ever seen, but the trip was worth it for the amazing atmosphere alone. The fans showed so much passion, even when their team wasn't playing very well.

'You should be out there playing, H!' his brothers told him.

Harry looked down at the white shirt he was wearing, and the blue Three Lions over his heart. Then he looked up at the players on the pitch. Nathaniel Clyne, Jordan Henderson – he had played with both of them for the Under-21s. In that moment, anything seemed possible.

A year later, after a sensational season at Hull and a big-money move to Leicester, Harry's England dream seemed more than possible. The national team manager Gareth Southgate was watching him closely.

'Every kid wants to play for their country,' Harry told the media. 'I want to play in the World Cup.'

Dele Alli, Raheem Sterling, Harry Kane – Harry Maguire was competing against the best players every week in the Premier League. And then there was Jamie, Harry's Leicester teammate.

'If Vards can play for England, then so can I!' he told himself.

In August 2017, nearly five years after his only

cap for the Under-21s, Harry finally got the call-up he was hoping for. He was named in Southgate's squad for the World Cup qualifiers against Malta and Slovakia.

'I did it!' he told his family on the phone. 'I'm in!'

It was yet another proud moment for all the Maguires.

When Harry joined the squad at St George's Park, he made a bigger entrance than he had expected. While the other England players arrived with their designer clothes and fancy suitcases, he turned up in his Leicester tracksuit, with his boots and shin pads in a black bin bag. The photos were trending on social media in seconds.

'Harry Maguire looks like he's moving into student halls in freshers' week,' someone wrote on Twitter.

When the news reached Harry's mum, she wasn't happy.

'A bin bag?' she told him off via text message. 'What were you thinking? So embarrassing!'

'Sorry, Mum!' Harry replied quickly.

'If I get called up again, I'll treat myself to some

proper luggage!' he joked with the journalists.

Out on the training pitch, however, Harry was 100 per cent focused on football. This was his big chance to impress Southgate. In the squad of twenty-eight players, there were at least other four centre-backs ahead of him: Chelsea's Gary Cahill, Manchester City's John Stones, and Manchester United's Phil Jones and Chris Smalling.

All four were top defenders at Champions League clubs, but Harry was as fearless as ever.

'Let the battles begin!' he told himself.

It was a sharp learning curve for Harry. He was playing at the very highest level now. He listened carefully to all the advice he received, especially from his manager. Southgate had played fifty-seven times for England as a centre-back. He knew what he was talking about when it came to international defending!

In the end, Harry didn't make his debut against Malta or Slovakia. Instead, he watched from the bench as Gary and Phil led England to victory. He wasn't too disappointed, though – he returned to

Leicester feeling more motivated than ever. He was nearly there! One month later, he was called up again.

'Nice new suitcase, H!' Jordan teased. 'They must be paying you well at Leicester!'

Harry Kane's late winner against Slovenia meant that England were through to the World Cup with one game to spare! That was especially good news for Harry because Southgate now had the chance to try something new.

'We're going to play a back three against Lithuania,' his manager explained, 'and I want you to play on the left.'

Harry couldn't believe it – he was in the England starting line-up!

Once he had recovered from the shock, he thanked his three Hull managers: Bruce, Phelan and Silva. They were the ones who had spotted his potential as the ball player in a back three. And, of course, his friend Andrew. Without him at left-back, Harry's job would have been so much harder.

'Good luck, mate!' Andrew messaged back,

followed by a Scottish flag emoji.

The LFF Stadium in Vilnius wasn't exactly Wembley, but Harry didn't care. He would have happily made his England senior debut in front of one man and his dog!

As the match against Lithuania kicked off, he was more excited than nervous. He tried to treat it like any other of the hundreds of games that he had played.

In the fourth minute, he had the perfect chance to make it a dream debut. Aaron Cresswell's cross was perfect, right on his big head. Somehow, however, he missed the ball completely.

'Noooo!' Harry groaned. He was usually so good in the air.

But instead of dwelling on his mistake, he kept going. England were dominating the game, so Harry did what he did best – attack from the back!

In the twenty-sixth minute, he chipped a clever ball through to Jordan, who headed it back into Dele's path. As Dele ran onto it, a defender fouled him. Penalty!

'Great ball, H!' Jordan called out, giving him a big thumbs-up.

Phew! He had made up for his earlier error. England's other Harry – Harry Kane – scored from the spot. 1–0!

That turned out to be the final score. As he shook hands with the Lithuania players, Harry felt happy with his first England performance. One game, one cleansheet! Apart from that missed header, he had looked comfortable and composed throughout. But had he done enough to keep his place against tougher opponents?

Harry would have to wait and see. In the meantime, he enjoyed his big moment. After years of being England's biggest fan, he was now an England player! Once his teammates had signed his shirt, he framed it and hung it proudly on his wall at home.

'You never know – that might be my only cap!' he told his girlfriend, Fern.

It wasn't, though. In November 2017, Harry played ninety minutes against Germany and then ninety minutes against Brazil. Battling with the best

attackers in the world, he was as solid as a rock
in England's back three. Three games, three clean
sheets!

'I just stopped Neymar from scoring!' Harry
laughed.

Sometimes, he had to pinch himself to make sure
that he wasn't dreaming. With the 2018 World Cup
only months away, Harry was now one of England's
first-choice centre-backs. He just had to keep playing
well, and keep believing.

CHAPTER 22

LEICESTER'S NEW LEADER

It was turning into a whirlwind season for Harry. Four days after keeping Neymar quiet at Wembley, he was back in the Premier League, with Leicester, taking on Pep Guardiola's awesome Manchester City attack. For forty-five minutes, Leicester's defence held on.

'Keep concentrating!' Harry shouted to his teammates. He was one of their leaders already.

Raheem Sterling played a one-two with Kevin De Bruyne, and then slipped a pass through to David Silva, who quickly crossed to Gabriel Jesus. 1–0!

As the ball rolled past Kasper Schmeichel, Harry kicked the air in frustration. Leicester had been beaten by a magical City move but it was still disappointing. These days, Harry felt every goal he conceded like a punch in the gut. He wanted to be the best defender in the world!

'Next time,' Harry muttered to himself. That was the good thing about playing game after game. He always had the chance to learn from his mistakes. Ten days later, Leicester beat Tottenham 2–1. In the battle of England's 'Harrys', Maguire defeated Kane.

Leicester changed their manager – Claude Puel replaced Craig Shakespeare – but the team tactics stayed the same. With two defensive midfielders protecting him, Harry had the freedom to attack from the back.

'Go!' Claude Puel told him, pointing towards the opposition half.

Against Southampton, Harry chested the ball down in the penalty area, turned and then fired a dangerous ball across goal. Andy King was there for a tap-in at the back post. 3–1 to Leicester!

'Cheers, H!'

Against Manchester United, Leicester were losing 2–1 with seconds to go. As Marc Albrighton curled one last ball into the box, Harry made his trademark dash towards the back post. His England teammates Phil Jones and Chris Smalling watched the cross sail over their heads and thought it was going out for a goal kick.

How wrong they were! Harry stretched out his long right leg and coolly volleyed the ball past the goalkeeper.

Goooooooooooooooooooaaaaaaaaaaaaaaaalllllllllllll llllllllllllll!!!!!!!!!!!!!!!!!!!!!

Harry was Leicester's last-minute hero! He ran past the club mascot, Filbert Fox, and slid on his knees in front of the delighted fans. There was no better feeling in the whole of football.

Harry Maguire! Harry Maguire!

'What a finish!' Shinji shouted.

Harry was dominating in defence too. Training against Jamie every week was tough, but it made him a better player. As a defender, he faced lots of different challenges. With his height and strength, he could battle with the big boys like Lukaku and Costa all game long.

It was the smaller, speedier strikers that caused him more problems. Jamie was one of the quickest players Harry had ever seen. In order to stop him, Harry had to be alert all the time, looking out for signs of danger. Their battles were fierce and full of banter.

'How many have you scored today, Vards?' he asked.

'Shut up, Slabhead! How many Premier League titles have you won?'

Harry was loving life at Leicester. Robert still wasn't back from injury, so he played game after game, in the Premier League, the League Cup *and* the FA Cup. Harry even played twice against his old club, Sheffield United. It was a nice reminder of how far he had come.

'Don't overdo it!' his mum warned him. 'Remember, you've got the World Cup coming up this summer.'

'I know, I can rest when I've retired!' Harry replied.

He had to keep playing. Every header, block, tackle and interception was taking him one step closer to Southgate's final squad for the tournament in Russia.

Harry started on the bench in England's next friendly against the Netherlands but he didn't stay there long. Joe Gomez got injured in the tenth minute and Harry ran on to replace him.

England had an all-Yorkshire back three now: Kyle Walker on the right, John Stones in the middle and Harry on the left. Kyle was from Sheffield, and he had been a couple of years ahead of Harry at United.

'The Maguire Boys!' he remembered with a grin. 'Yeah, I used to hear lots of good things about you guys!'

John, meanwhile, was born just up the road in Barnsley.

'I started out in the Tykes academy,' Harry explained excitedly. 'Maybe we met when we were younger, Stonesy!'

'I doubt it, mate. I wouldn't forget a big head like yours!'

Between the three of them, Kyle, John and Harry had so much strength, skill and speed. The poor Dutch attackers had no chance.

The match finished England 1 Netherlands 0. Four games, four clean sheets!

Fingers crossed, Harry had done enough to earn a World Cup place. There was no time to worry, though. Four days after returning to Leicester, Harry was too busy beating Brighton.

In the end, the Foxes finished ninth in the Premier League and reached the quarter-finals of both cups. It had been an acceptable campaign for Leicester but an exceptional one for their new young leader at the back.

At the club's end of season ceremony, Harry won both the Players' Player and Player of the Year awards. He'd achieved this at three clubs – first Sheffield United, then Hull City, and now Leicester City!

The audience clapped and cheered as Harry walked onto the stage, dressed in a smart navy suit. It made a change from his usual club tracksuit! Everyone agreed that he was a worthy winner. He had been Leicester's Mr Consistent, playing every single minute of every single Premier League match.

'I'm really honoured to collect these awards,' he said humbly. 'I've been really lucky to come to this club. There's a great bunch of lads here and a great team spirit. The supporters have been brilliant with me ever since I joined. So thank you, and let's hope we can win a few trophies next season!'

Before that, however, Harry was hoping to win a trophy for his country. On 16 May, Southgate announced his England squad for the 2018 World Cup.

The FA released a video where each player's name was revealed one by one. Raheem Sterling was first, then John Stones, then Trent Alexander-Arnold. Eventually, the camera zoomed in on a tall grey tower block where a girl and a boy were holding up a big white banner. They yelled the two words written there at the tops of their voices:

'HARRY MAGUIRE!'

'Yes, Big Man!' Jamie messaged. He was in the squad too. 'Russia, here we come!'

CHAPTER 23

WORLD CUP 2018

Being selected for England's 2018 World Cup squad was a huge achievement for Harry. However, his ambition didn't stop there. He wanted to start every single match for his country, just like he did for his club. Kyle Walker and John Stones were guaranteed to play but Harry was battling with Gary Cahill for that final place in the back three.

'Cahill's won two Premier League titles *and* the Champions League!' his brothers told him, hoping to fire Harry up. The whole Maguire family was heading out to Russia to cheer him on.

Yes, Gary was certainly the more experienced option. He had fifty-nine England caps, whereas

Harry only had four. However, if Southgate wanted someone who could bring the ball out of defence, Harry was his man!

In England's last two warm-up matches, Gary played against Nigeria and then Harry played against Costa Rica. Gary scored in a 2–1 win, and then Harry kept a clean sheet in a 2–0 win. Before the first group game against Tunisia, Southgate had a big decision to make.

In the meantime, the England players settled into their World Cup base camp in Repino. They were miles away from the capital city, Moscow, and Harry was expecting to be really bored. But instead, he had loads of fun!

When training ended, there were lots of different activities for the players to do together: Fortnite, basketball, pool. When Jamie wanted to play table tennis, he knew who to ask.

'Fancy a game, Big H?'

'Sure, Vards, as long as you're ready for another thrashing!'

It all helped to build a really strong team spirit.

During the Premier League season, they competed
against each other for their clubs but this was
different. For the World Cup, they were united,
competing together for their country.

After weeks of watching and thinking, Southgate
picked Harry to play in England's first match
against Tunisia. When he heard the great news, he
wanted to slide across the grass on his knees. Harry
couldn't wait!

The Three Lions started brilliantly. They could have
been 2–0 up after ten minutes! Instead, however, it
was still 0–0 as Harry went forward for the corner.
Ashley Young delivered a deep cross towards
England's big men and John headed it goalwards. The
Tunisia keeper made a super save but Harry Kane was
in the right place for the rebound. 1–0!

All the players piled on top of each other in a
happy team bundle. As a big centre-back, Harry had
to be careful not to hurt anyone.

'Sorry!' he shouted sheepishly to Raheem.

England were in total control until the thirty-fifth
minute. Suddenly, a cross came in and Kyle fouled

the Tunisia striker. Penalty – 1–1!

It was a cruel blow but the England players didn't panic. There was plenty of time left to grab another goal.

Harry did what he did best – attack from the back! In the second half, he played like an extra midfielder. He dribbled forward into space, looking for a killer pass. Harry had more touches on the ball than any of his teammates, but with seconds to go, the score was still 1–1.

Corner-kick! Harry rushed forward to attack Kieran Trippier's cross. It was now or never. *BOOM!* He jumped high to win the header. Harry Kane was in the right place again to steer the ball home. 2–1!

The two Harrys were the England heroes! It was an amazing moment that neither of them would ever forget. In their first-ever World Cup match, with the hopes of a nation resting on their shoulders, they had saved the day.

'Nice one, Slabhead!' Jamie shouted as the whole squad celebrated in front of the relieved and jubilant fans.

It was the start of an exciting new era for England. After years of misery and frustration, the nation had finally found another team of fearless footballers.

Back home, the hope was building but at the England base camp, it was all fun and games. The players relaxed by racing inflatable unicorns in the swimming pool.

'Where's the VAR when you need it?' Kyle joked.

A few days later, Harry was answering questions from the media, when a familiar face snuck into the room.

'It's Jamie Vardy here from Vardy News,' he said, pretending that his fist was a microphone. 'Just how big is the diameter of your head?'

'Good one, Vards!' Harry thought to himself. Now his big head was all anyone wanted to talk about.

England's next match against Panama was a whole lot easier. Thanks to goals from John, Jesse Lingard and Harry Kane, they were 5–0 up by half-time! The Three Lions were through to the Round of 16.

Even a 1–0 loss to Belgium couldn't dampen their spirits. England hadn't won a World Cup knock-out match since 2006, but that was all about to change against Colombia. The whole country believed.

'Three Lions on a shirt!' Joe and Laurence Maguire sang along with the rest of the supporters in Moscow. This time, their brother wasn't with them; Harry was out there playing on the pitch instead!

And what a game he was having. At the heart of the England defence, Harry won header after header. It was an angry, competitive match but there was nothing he liked more than a battle.

When Harry Kane scored a penalty, it looked like they were through to the quarter-finals. In the last minute, however, Yerry Mina equalised for Colombia.

The England fans fell silent. Could their warriors keep fighting, or was it game over? Harry certainly wasn't giving up.

'Come on, lads!' he clapped and cheered. 'We can do this!'

Together, the team held on through the thirty minutes of extra-time. Penalties!

'Oh no!' the fans groaned.

England had never won a World Cup shoot-out. They had lost against West Germany in 1990, against Argentina in 1998, and against Portugal in 2006. On top of all that, there were the losses against Germany in Euro 96, against Portugal in Euro 2004, and against Italy in Euro 2012.

As England's biggest fan, Harry had seen a lot of failure. It was time for them to write a new story of success.

Even when Jordan Henderson's penalty was saved, Harry didn't give up hope.

Mateus Uribe stepped up and… hit the crossbar!

Carlos Bacca ran up and… Jordan Pickford made a super save!

Now, Eric Dier just needed to keep cool and…

Goooooooooooooooooooooaaaaaaaaaaaaaaaaalllllllllll llllllllllllllll!!!!!!!!!!!!!!!!!!!

What a moment – England were through to the World Cup quarter-finals after WINNING ON PENALTIES! Harry was ecstatic as he raced over to join the big team bundle.

In the stands in Russia, and back in England, everyone was singing the same old tune:

It's coming home, it's coming home,
It's coming, FOOTBALL'S COMING HOME!

Was football really coming home? Suddenly, the impossible seemed possible.

'Good luck, Big H!' Andrew messaged him before the quarter-final, followed by a Scottish flag emoji.

His friend had just played in the Champions League final with Liverpool. Hull's two young signings had turned into superstars!

Sweden were the next team standing in England's way. It wouldn't be easy but Harry wasn't leaving the World Cup without an almighty fight.

In the thirtieth minute, Harry's thumping header gave England the lead.

Goooooooooooooooooooooaaaaaaaaaaaaaaaaalllllllllllll llllllllllllll!!!!!!!!!!!!!!!!!!!!

What a time to score his first international goal! Harry raced towards the fans, pumping his fists and roaring like a lion. His country meant so much to him.

Sixty long minutes later, England were through to the World Cup semi-finals! It was an incredible achievement for such a young, inexperienced group of players. Of all the new national heroes, Harry was now the biggest of them all.

First, there was the song:

Harry Maguire, your defence is terrified!
Harry Maguire, na na na na na na na na na na!

Then, there were the memes. A funny photo of Harry talking to Fern after the Colombia match exploded on to the Internet. Everyone was adding their own comedy captions, including Harry himself:

'Can you ask the neighbours to put the bins out on Monday?' he wrote after the Sweden win. 'We're not going home just yet!'

That was one of the many things that the England fans loved about Harry; he was just so normal and down to earth. Despite becoming a World Cup hero, he was keeping his feet firmly on the ground. Ahead of the semi-final, he took part in a fun darts challenge.

'Good luck, Harry!' the fans cheered for their favourite.

He won, of course! Harry was a natural, all-round sportsman. After shaking hands, he went back to focusing on football.

Against Croatia in the semi-final, England got off to an amazing start. In the fifth minute, Kieran curled a free-kick into the top corner. 1–0!

It's coming home, it's coming home,
It's coming, FOOTBALL'S COMING HOME!

No, Harry knew that England weren't in the final yet. There was lots of defending left to do. The back three battled hard, winning headers, tackles and interceptions.

Kyle, John and Harry – they were a brave band of superheroes.

'Nothing's getting past us!'

In the second half, however, Croatia fought back fiercely. They attacked again and again until finally they scored. 1–1!

Could England hold strong? Harry did his best but the whole team was so tired. Deep in extra-time, Mario Mandžuki grabbed the winning goal. As Harry watched the ball cross the line, he had that horrible sinking feeling once again. England were out of the World Cup.

Harry was very disappointed but it wasn't all doom and gloom. No-one had expected them to get so far in the tournament. The players had made their country very proud. Harry and his England teammates stood together on the pitch, thanking the fans with their heads held high.

'This is just the beginning, boys!' Gareth Southgate promised.

Harry hoped so. He really didn't want his amazing football adventure to end. It was hard to believe how far he had come already.

After starting out with Sheffield United, Harry had risen higher and higher, step by step, game after game, through ups and downs, highs and lows. League One, then the Championship, then the Premier League – and now the World Cup.

Through hard work, belief and dedication, Harry and his big head had conquered them all.

Turn the page for a sneak preview of
another brilliant football story by
Matt and Tom Oldfield. . .

KANE

Available now!

CHAPTER 1

ENGLAND HERO

Thursday, 5 October 2017

In the Wembley tunnel, Harry closed his eyes and
soaked up the amazing atmosphere. He was back
at the home of football, the stadium where he had
first achieved his childhood dream of playing for
England. 19 March 2015, England vs Lithuania – he
remembered that game like it was yesterday. He
had scored that day and now, with England facing
Slovenia, he needed to do it again. As England's
captain and Number 9, it was his job to shoot them
to the 2018 World Cup.

'Come on, lads!' Harry called out to his teammates
behind him, friends like Joe Hart, Kyle Walker and

Eric Dier. It was a real honour to be their leader.
With a victory over Slovenia, they would all be on
their way to the biggest tournament of their lives in
Russia.

Harry looked down at the young mascot by his
side and smiled at him. 'Right, let's do this!'

As the two of them led the England team out on to
the pitch, the fans clapped and cheered. Harry didn't
look up at the thousands of faces and flags; instead,
he looked down at the grass in front of him. He was
totally focused on his task: scoring goals and beating
Slovenia.

'If you get a chance, test the keeper,' Harry
said to his partners in attack, Raheem Sterling and
Marcus Rashford, before kick-off. 'I'll be there for the
rebound!'

Harry's new Premiereship season with Tottenham
Hotspur had not begun well in August, but by
September he was back to his lethal best. That
month alone, he scored an incredible 13 goals,
including two goals for England against Malta. He
could score every type of goal – tap-ins, headers, one-

on-ones, long-range shots, penalties, even free kicks. That's what made him such a dangerous striker.

With Slovenia defending well, Harry didn't get many chances in the first half. He got in good positions but the final ball never arrived.

'There's no need to panic yet,' Harry told his teammates in the dressing room. He really didn't want a repeat of England's terrible performance against Iceland at Euro 2016. That match still haunted him. 'We're good enough to win this by playing our natural game. Be patient!'

As Ryan Bertrand dribbled down the left wing, Harry sprinted towards the six-yard box. Ryan's cross didn't reach him but the ball fell to Raheem instead. His shot was going in until a defender deflected it wide.

'Unlucky!' Harry shouted, putting his hands on his head. 'Keep going, we're going to score!'

Without this kind of strong self-belief, Harry would never have made it to the top of European football. There had been lots of setbacks along the way: rejections, disappointments and bad form. But every time, Harry bounced back with crucial goals at crucial moments. That's what made him such a superstar.

A matter of seconds later, a rebound fell to him on the edge of the penalty area. Surely, this was his moment. He pulled back his left foot and curled a powerful shot towards the bottom corner. The fans were already up on their feet, ready to celebrate. Harry never missed… but this time he did. The ball flew just wide of the post. Harry couldn't believe it. He looked up at the sky and sighed.

On the sideline, England manager Gareth Southgate cheered his team on. 'That's much better – the goal is coming, lads!'

But after ninety minutes, the goal still hadn't come. The fourth official raised his board: eight minutes of injury time.

'It's not over yet, boys!' Harry shouted, to inspire his teammates.

The Slovenian goalkeeper tried to throw the ball out to his left-back but Kyle got there first. Straight away, Harry was on the move from the back post to the front post. After playing together for years at Tottenham, they knew how to score great goals.

As Kyle crossed it in, Harry used his burst of speed to get in front of the centre-back. Again, the England supporters stood and waited anxiously. The ball was perfect and Harry stretched out his long right leg to meet it. The keeper got a touch on his shot but he couldn't keep it out.

Goooooooooooooaaaaaaaaaaaaaaaaaaaallllllllllllllllllllll llllllll!!!!!!!!!!!!!!!!!!!!!!

He had done it! Joy, relief, pride – Harry felt every emotion as he ran towards the fans. This time, he hadn't let them down. He held up the Three Lions on his shirt and screamed until his throat got sore.

'Captain to the rescue!' Kyle laughed as they hugged by the corner flag.

'No, it was all thanks to you!' Harry replied.

At the final whistle, he threw his arms up in the air. It was a phenomenal feeling to qualify for the 2018 World Cup. He couldn't wait to lead England to glory.

'We are off to Russia!' a voice shouted over the

loudspeakers and the whole stadium cheered.

It was yet another moment that Harry would never forget. Against the odds, he was making his childhood dreams come true. He was the star striker for Tottenham, the club that he had supported all his life. And now, like his hero David Beckham, he was the captain of England.

Harry had never given up, even when it looked like he wouldn't make it as a professional footballer. With the support of his family and his coaches, and lots of hard work and dedication, he had proved everyone wrong to become a world-class goal machine.

It had been an incredible journey from Walthamstow to Wembley, and Harry was only just getting started.

HARRY MAGUIRE HONOURS

Hull City
🏆 Football League Championship Play-Offs: 2015–16

Individual
🏆 PFA League One Team of the Year: 2011–12, 2012–13, 2013–14
🏆 Sheffield United Player of the Year: 2011–12, 2012–13, 2013–14
🏆 Hull City Fans' Player of the Year: 2016–17
🏆 Hull City Players' Player of the Year: 2016–17
🏆 Leicester City Player of the Season: 2017–18
🏆 Leicester City Players' Player of the Season: 2017–18

MAGUIRE

15 & 6

THE FACTS

NAME: JACOB HARRY MAGUIRE

DATE OF BIRTH: 5 March 1993

AGE: 25

PLACE OF BIRTH: Sheffield

NATIONALITY: England

BEST FRIEND: Jamie Vardy

CURRENT CLUB: Leicester City

POSITION: CB

THE STATS

Height (cm):	**194**
Club appearances:	**301**
Club goals:	**18**
Club trophies:	**1**
International appearances:	**12**
International goals:	**0**
International trophies:	**0**
Ballon d'Ors:	**0**

★ ★ ★ **HERO RATING: 82** ★ ★ ★

GREATEST MOMENTS

Type and search the web links to see the magic for yourself!

4 JANUARY 2014,
ASTON VILLA 1–2 SHEFFIELD UNITED

https://www.youtube.com/watch?v=clGWwAvkiSI

Harry was already playing game after game in League One but this FA Cup run gave him the chance to battle with the big boys. At Villa Park, he took on Christian Benteke, one of the strongest strikers in the Premier League, and won! After that, Harry knew that he could play at the highest level.

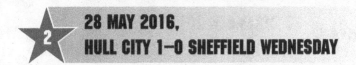

28 MAY 2016,
HULL CITY 1–0 SHEFFIELD WEDNESDAY

https://www.youtube.com/watch?v=qBcqlQ9-TzM

Harry was only on the pitch for the final five minutes of this play-off final but it was still a massive moment for him. After two relegations and two play-off failures, he won promotion at last! Best of all, it gave Harry his second shot at playing in the Premier League.

5 APRIL 2017,
HULL CITY 4–2 MIDDLESBROUGH

https://www.youtube.com/watch?v=FA7n5TRqHwA

Marco Silva almost pulled off the miracle of keeping Hull in the Premier League. Harry was Silva's leader on the pitch and he saved his best performance for this epic relegation battle. First, Harry set up Abel Hernández with a perfect pass and then he scored a goal of his own.

23 DECEMBER 2017,
LEICESTER CITY 2–2 MANCHESTER UNITED

https://www.youtube.com/watch?v=1BwcWeNdnJ4
It didn't take Harry long to become a Leicester leader after his big-money move. The Foxes were losing 2–1 to Manchester United with seconds to go, when up popped Harry, at the back post as usual. He stretched out his long right leg and coolly volleyed the ball past the goalkeeper.

9 JULY 2018,
SWEDEN 0–2 ENGLAND

https://www.youtube.com/watch?v=yMloUtQRHos
Harry was already an England World Cup hero but, in the quarter-final, he became a superhero! In the 30th minute, he muscled his way past the Sweden defenders and powered a thumping header into the bottom corner. 1–0! And England were on their way to the semi-finals!

PLAY LIKE YOUR HEROES

THE HARRY MAGUIRE
THUMPING HEADER

SEE IT HERE YouTube

https://www.youtube.com/watch?v=L7qSFd6YyYo

STEP 1: When your team wins a corner, make your way forward. This is your big moment!

Step 2: Stop on the edge of the penalty area. You can have a little chat with your teammates if you like because...

Step 3: ...You want to leave it as late as possible before making your run. That way, you catch your marker by surprise!

Step 4: Muscle your way through the defence. Don't let anything stop you.

Step 5: Aim for a corner. Top or bottom, left or right – just make your header impossible to save! GOAL!

Step 6: Run towards your fans, roaring like the lion you are.

TEST YOUR KNOWLEDGE

QUESTIONS

1. What was the name of Harry's first football club?

2. What was Harry's first position on the football pitch?

3. Who did Harry's Sheffield United face in the 2011 FA Youth Cup Final?

4. Harry played for the England Under-21s – true or false?

5. How old was Harry when he made his 100th start for Sheffield United?

6. Which other young star joined Hull City on the same day as Harry?

7. Which club did Harry join on loan in 2015?

8. Who did Harry replace in the Leicester City defence?

9. How many games did Harry miss during the 2017-18 Premier League season?

10. Who were England's opponents when Harry made his senior international debut?

11. Who gave Harry the nickname 'Slabhead'?

Answers below. . . No cheating!

1. *Brunsmeer Athletic* 2. *Centre Midfield* 3. *Manchester United* 4. *True - but he only played one match!* 5. *Only 19!* 6. *Andrew Robertson* 7. *Wigan Athletic* 8. *Robert Huth* 9. *Zero!* 10. *Lithuania* 11. *Jamie Vardy*

HAVE YOU GOT THEM ALL?

ULTIMATE FOOTBALL HEROES

MATT AND TOM OLDFIELD

ULTIMATE
FOOTBALL HEROES

KANE

FROM THE PLAYGROUND
TO THE PITCH

DINO

Published by Dino Books,
an imprint of John Blake Publishing,
2.25, The Plaza,
535 Kings Road,
Chelsea Harbour,
London SW10 0SZ

www.johnblakepublishing.co.uk

www.facebook.com/johnblakebooks ￼
twitter.com/jblakebooks ￼

This edition published in 2018

ISBN: 978 1 78606 927 6

British Library Cataloguing-in-Publication Data:

A catalogue record for this book is available from the British Library.

Design by www.envydesign.co.uk

Printed and bound in Great Britain by Clays Ltd, Elcograf S.p.A.

9 10

Papers used by John Blake Publishing are natural, recyclable products made from
wood grown in sustainable forests. The manufacturing processes conform to the
environmental regulations of the country of origin.

Every reasonable effort has been made to trace copyright-holders of material
reproduced in this book, but if any have been inadvertently overlooked the publishers
would be glad to hear from them.

John Blake Publishing is an imprint of Bonnier Books UK
www.bonnierbooks.co.uk

For Noah and Nico,
Southampton's future strikeforce

Matt Oldfield is an accomplished writer and the editor-in-chief of football review site *Of Pitch & Page*. Tom Oldfield is a freelance sports writer and the author of biographies on Cristiano Ronaldo, Arsène Wenger and Rafael Nadal.

Cover illustration by Dan Leydon.
To learn more about Dan visit danleydon.com
To purchase his artwork visit etsy.com/shop/footynews
Or just follow him on Twitter @danleydon

TABLE OF CONTENTS

CHAPTER 1

ENGLAND HERO

Thursday, 5 October 2017

In the Wembley tunnel, Harry closed his eyes and soaked up the amazing atmosphere. He was back at the home of football, the stadium where he had first achieved his childhood dream of playing for England. 19 March 2015, England vs Lithuania – he remembered that game like it was yesterday. He had scored that day and now, with England facing Slovenia, he needed to do it again. As England's captain and Number 9, it was his job to shoot them to the 2018 World Cup.

'Come on, lads!' Harry called out to his teammates behind him: friends like Joe Hart, Kyle Walker and

Eric Dier. It was a real honour to be their leader.
With a victory over Slovenia, they would all be on
their way to the biggest tournament of their lives
in Russia.

Harry looked down at the young mascot by his
side and smiled at him. 'Right, let's do this!'

As the two of them led the England team out onto
the pitch, the fans clapped and cheered. Harry didn't
look up at the thousands of faces and flags; instead,
he looked down at the grass in front of him. He
was totally focused on his task: scoring goals and
beating Slovenia.

'If you get a chance, test the keeper,' Harry said
to his partners in attack, Raheem Sterling and
Marcus Rashford, before kick-off. 'I'll be there for
the rebound!'

Harry's new Premiership season with Tottenham
Hotspur had not begun well in August, but by
September he was back to his lethal best. That
month alone, he scored an incredible thirteen goals,
including two goals for England against Malta. He
could score every type of goal – tap-ins, headers, one-

on-ones, long-range shots, penalties, even free kicks. That's what made him such a dangerous striker.

With Slovenia defending well, Harry didn't get many chances in the first half. He got in good positions but the final ball never arrived.

'There's no need to panic yet,' Harry told his teammates in the dressing room. He really didn't want a repeat of England's terrible performance against Iceland at Euro 2016. That match still haunted him. 'We're good enough to win this by playing our natural game. Be patient!'

As Ryan Bertrand dribbled down the left wing, Harry sprinted towards the six-yard box. Ryan's cross didn't reach him but the ball fell to Raheem instead. His shot was going in until a defender deflected it wide.

'Unlucky!' Harry shouted, putting his hands on his head. 'Keep going, we're going to score!'

Without this kind of strong self-belief, Harry would never have made it to the top of European football. There had been lots of setbacks along the way: rejections, disappointments and bad form. But every time, Harry bounced back with crucial goals at crucial moments. That's what made him such a superstar.

A matter of seconds later, a rebound fell to him on the edge of the penalty area. Surely, this was his moment. He pulled back his left foot and curled a powerful shot towards the bottom corner. The fans were already up on their feet, ready to celebrate. Harry never missed... but this time he did. The ball flew just wide of the post. Harry couldn't believe it. He looked up at the sky and sighed.

On the sideline, England manager Gareth Southgate cheered his team on. 'That's much better – the goal is coming, lads!'

But after ninety minutes, the goal still hadn't come. The fourth official raised his board: eight minutes of injury time.

'It's not over yet, boys!' Harry shouted, to inspire his teammates.

The Slovenian goalkeeper tried to throw the ball out to his left-back but Kyle got there first. Straight away, Harry was on the move from the back post to the front post. After playing together for years at Tottenham, they knew how to score great goals.

As Kyle crossed it in, Harry used his burst of speed to get in front of the centre-back. Again, the England supporters stood and waited anxiously. The ball was perfect and Harry stretched out his long right leg to meet it. The keeper got a touch on his shot but he couldn't keep it out.

Goooooooooooooaaaaaaaaaaaaaaaaaaaalllllllllllllllllllll llllllll!!!!!!!!!!!!!!!!!!!!!!

He had done it! Joy, relief, pride – Harry felt every emotion as he ran towards the fans. This time, he hadn't let them down. He held up the Three Lions on his shirt and screamed until his throat got sore.

'Captain to the rescue!' Kyle laughed as they hugged by the corner flag.

'No, it was all thanks to you!' Harry replied.

At the final whistle, he threw his arms up in the air. It was a phenomenal feeling to qualify for the 2018 World Cup. He couldn't wait to lead England to glory.

'We are off to Russia!' a voice shouted over the loudspeakers and the whole stadium cheered.

It was yet another moment that Harry would never forget. Against the odds, he was making his childhood dreams come true. He was the star striker for Tottenham, the club that he had supported all his life. And now, like his hero David Beckham, he was the captain of England.

Harry had never given up, even when it looked like he wouldn't make it as a professional footballer. With the support of his family and his coaches, and lots of hard work and dedication, he had proved everyone wrong to become a world-class goal machine.

It had been an incredible journey from Walthamstow to Wembley, and Harry was only just getting started.

CHAPTER 2

ALWAYS KICKING

'Mum!' Charlie shouted, stamping his feet.

Kim sighed and put her magazine down. 'What's happened now?'

'I spent ages building a Lego tower and Harry just kicked it over,' her older son answered. 'That was *my* tower!'

'I'm sorry, darling, but I'm sure Harry didn't mean it. Your brother doesn't know what he's doing with his little feet yet.'

Harry was nearly two years old and he was always on the move around their house in Walthamstow, North London. He had a few bumps on his head but it was his legs that caused the most trouble. Everywhere he went, they never stopped kicking.

Kim wasn't surprised, though.

'Do you remember before your brother was born when he was still in my tummy?' she asked Charlie as she lifted Harry up onto the sofa. Charlie didn't reply; he was busy building a new tower. 'He was always kicking, even back then, wasn't he? I didn't get a good night's sleep for months!'

Kim held Harry up in the air to give his legs room to swing. 'No, you don't like letting me sleep, do you?' He smiled and wiggled his hands and feet. 'I knew you'd be a boy; there was no doubt about that. I told your Daddy that you were going to be sporty and do you know what he said? He said, "Great, he'll play for TOTTENHAM!"'

Harry's smile grew wider when he heard the name of their local football club. It was a word that his dad, Pat, said so often that it had become his favourite word. The Kane family lived only five miles away from Tottenham's stadium, White Hart Lane.

'Wow, you really love that idea, don't you!' Kim laughed. 'Well, your Grandad Eric was a good footballer in his day. Maybe you'll get his talent, rather than your Dad's. Bless him, he always says that bad injuries ruined his career but I think it was his bad first touch!'

It was a bright, sunny afternoon and so Kim took her two sons out to the local park. Hopefully, after a few hours of open space and fresh air, Charlie and Harry would sleep well that night, and so would their mum. Once they found a shady spot on the grass, Kim lay down the picnic rug and lifted Harry out of the pushchair.

'Charlie, you've got to stay where I can see you!' she called out as he chased after a squirrel.

After doing a few laps of the rug, Harry sat down and looked around him. He saw leaves and twigs and insects. He saw huge trees above him and patches of blue sky in between. Then his eyes fixed on the exciting scene in front of him. A group of kids were playing football with jumpers for goalposts. That looked like fun. He stood up and went over to explore.

'Harry, stop!' Kim shouted. She chased after her son and scooped him up just before he reached the other kids' football game. In her arms, Harry kept

watching and his legs kept moving. He was desperate
to kick the ball.

'Not today, darling,' his mum said, giving him a
kiss on the cheek. 'But soon, I promise!'

*

'So, how was your day?' Pat asked, as they all
ate dinner together. After a long day's work at the
garage, he loved to come home to his happy family.

Charlie could now feed himself like a grown-
up but Harry still needed a high chair and some
help. Even with Pat holding the spoon, Harry got
strawberry yoghurt all over his hands and face.

'I built an awesome tower but Harry broke it
with his silly little feet,' Charlie told his dad. He was
looking for sympathy, but Pat had other ideas.

'Good, your brother's getting ready for his big
Tottenham career! Football runs in the family, you
know. Just ask your Grandad – I was one of Ireland's
best young players but sadly...'

Kim rolled her eyes. Not again! She decided not
to mention Harry's kicking in the park. It would only
get her husband's hopes up even more.

CHAPTER 3

HEROES AT WHITE HART LANE

'Have you been good boys today?' Pat asked his sons one evening as they all ate dinner together.

Charlie and Harry knew the right answer. 'Yes!'

Their dad smiled and reached into his trouser pocket. He took out three rectangles of white card and placed them down on the table. Then he watched and waited for his sons' reactions.

Harry thought he knew what they were but he didn't want to get his hopes up until he was sure. His dad had promised him that he could go to his first Tottenham game once he turned four. For his birthday, he got a Spurs shirt and a Spurs football, but no Spurs ticket. Charlie had been to White Hart Lane a few times and Harry was desperate to join them. Was his dream finally going to come true? There in the top left corner was the important word, written in navy blue – 'Tottenham'. He was right; they *were* match tickets! Harry jumped for joy.

'Wow, thanks!' he said, running over to give his dad a big hug. 'This is the best gift ever!'

Suddenly, Harry and Charlie weren't interested in eating anymore. Instead, they ran around the living room, waving the tickets in the air and chanting, 'We're going to White Hart Lane! We're going to White Hart Lane!'

Kim laughed. 'You'll need to keep a close eye on them,' she warned her husband. 'This is just the start!'

'Yes, I think I'll look after these,' Pat said, taking the tickets back from his over-excited sons.

It was a three o'clock kick-off on Saturday but Harry and Charlie were sitting in their Tottenham shirts at breakfast. They spent the morning playing football in the garden, pretending to be their heroes.

'David Ginola gets the ball on the left,' Charlie began the commentary, 'he dribbles past one defender and then another. Look at that skill! He's just outside the penalty area now, he looks up and...'

Harry didn't like playing in goal against his brother. He hardly ever made a save because Charlie's shots were too powerful.

...*Goooooooooooooooooooaaaaaaaaaalllllllllllllllllllllll llllllllllllll!!!!!!!!!!!!!!!!!!!!!*

Charlie ran towards the corner of the garden and celebrated by pulling his Spurs shirt over his head.

'Right, my turn!' Harry said, picking up the ball.

His number one hero, Teddy Sheringham, had just left Tottenham to sign for Manchester United. But Harry already had his new favourite – German Jürgen Klinsmann. It was a hard name for a four-year-old to say but Harry did his best.

'Kiman runs towards the penalty area...'

He needed to strike the ball perfectly if he wanted to score past his older brother. Harry looked up at the goal and kicked it as hard as he could. The ball bounced and skipped towards the bottom corner...

...*Goooooooooooooooooooaaaaaaaaaaaaaallllllllllllll llllllllllllll!!!!!!!!!!!!!!!!!!!!!*

Normally, Harry celebrated with the Klinsmann dive but his Spurs shirt was white and he couldn't make his White Hart Lane debut wearing a muddy shirt! So instead, he jumped up and pumped his fist. He could tell that it was going to be a very good day.

After lunch, it was finally time for them to leave.

'Have you got your hats?' Kim asked at the front door.

Harry nodded.

'Gloves?'

Harry nodded.

'Good, stay close to your dad and have a great time!'

They were off! Harry couldn't wait to get to White Hart Lane. On the bus, he imagined the people, the noise, the goals. As they crossed through the Walthamstow reservoirs, Charlie had a thought.

'Dad, have you got the tickets?'

There was panic on Pat's face as he checked all of his pockets, once and then twice. 'Oh dear,' he muttered.

Harry's face dropped with disappointment. How had his dad forgotten the tickets? Why hadn't he checked before they left?

Suddenly, a smile spread across Pat's face, and he held up the tickets. 'Just kidding!' he cheered.

'Dad, don't scare us like that!' Harry shouted. He didn't find the joke funny at all.

When they got off the bus, the stadium was right there in front of them. Harry stood there looking up, his mouth wide open. It was even bigger than he'd expected.

'Come on, let's go in and find our seats!' his dad said. 'Don't let go of my hand, okay? If you get lost, Mum won't ever let us come back.'

Harry held on tightly as they moved through the crowds towards the turnstile, on their way to their seats. There were so many people everywhere and so much to see and hear.

'Get today's match programme here!' the sellers shouted.

Some Tottenham fans talked about their players in between bites of burgers and hot dogs. Other

Tottenham fans were already singing songs even before they entered the stadium. It was all so exciting.

Once they were through the turnstile, Harry could see a square of green in the distance. His eyes lit up – the pitch! As they got closer, he couldn't believe the size of it. How did the players keep running from box to box for ninety minutes? It looked impossible.

'Look, there's Ginola!' Charlie shouted, pointing down at the players warming up. 'And there's Klinsmann!'

Harry stood up on his seat to get a better view. He was in the same stadium as his heroes; it didn't get any better than that.

Tottenham, Tottenham!

As the players ran out of the tunnel for the start of the game, the noise grew even louder. Spurs needed a win to stay out of the relegation zone. After a few minutes, Ginola got the ball on the left wing.

'Come on!' the Tottenham fans cheered, rising to their feet.

Ginola curled a brilliant cross into the penalty area. Harry held his breath as Klinsmann stretched to reach it...

Goooooooooooooooooooooaaaaaaaaaaaaaaaaaaaalllll lllllllllllllllllllllll!!!!!!!!!!!!!!!!!!!!!!!

What a start! Harry and Charlie jumped up and down together, cheering for their heroes.

The rest of the match was very tense but Tottenham held on for the victory. By the final whistle, Harry was exhausted but very happy. He was already looking forward to his next trip to White Hart Lane.

'So, who was man of the match?' Pat asked his sons on the bus home.

'Ginola!' Charlie replied.

'Klinsmann!' Harry replied.

Their dad shook his head. 'If we ever keep a clean sheet, it's always the goalkeeper!'

CHAPTER 4

RIDGEWAY ROVERS

'Why do we have to leave?' Charlie cried out. 'It's not fair. This is our home!'

Their parents had just given them some terrible news; the family was moving from Walthamstow to Chingford. They had never even heard of Chingford.

'We'll have more space there,' Kim replied. 'You'll have bigger bedrooms and a bigger football pitch in the garden too.'

'Look, we're not talking about Australia!' Pat said. 'Chingford is only a few miles away.'

'But all our friends are *here*,' Charlie argued.

As the conversation carried on, Harry had an important question to ask: 'How far is it from White Hart Lane?'

'It's only five miles away, the same distance as now.'

Kim and Pat finally won the family argument
with a killer fact: David Beckham had grown up in
Chingford.

'Really?' Harry asked excitedly. After the 1998
World Cup, Beckham was England's most famous
footballer. Despite his red card versus Argentina,
every kid in the country wanted to look and play
like Becks.

His dad nodded. 'He played for a local team called
Ridgeway Rovers.'

'Cool, can I play for Ridgeway Rovers too?'

'It's a deal!' Kim said, looking relieved.

Harry was determined to become a star striker
for Tottenham and England, especially after visiting
White Hart Lane. He practised all the time, with
whatever he could find. In the garden and the park,
he played with his own real football. It was his
pride and joy, and he looked after it carefully. In the
street, he played with any can or bottle that he
could find. In the house, he swapped his football for
rolled-up socks.

'STOP KICKING THINGS!' Charlie shouted angrily from through his bedroom door.

'Sorry!' Harry replied quickly, running downstairs to help with dinner. He had been using his brother's door as a shooting target again. He knew that it wasn't allowed but he just couldn't help himself.

'Can I join Ridgeway Rovers now?' Harry asked his parents as they sat down to eat. He was desperate to test his talent against real opponents on a real pitch.

Pat knew that his son wasn't going to give up until it was sorted. Fifteen minutes later, he returned to the living room with good news. 'The Ridgeway Rovers trials are coming up in a couple of weeks. I'll take you along.'

'Thanks!' Harry cheered. He couldn't wait to follow in Becks' footsteps. But first, he had lots more practice to do.

'It's great to see so many of you down here,' Dave Bricknell, the Ridgeway Rovers coach, told the eager young faces at Loughton Rugby Club. 'Welcome! Today, we're looking for brilliant new players to join our club, but most importantly, we're going to have some fun, yes?'

'YES!' Harry cheered with the other boys.

As they all practised passing in pairs, Dave walked around the pitch. He was looking for a nice touch, as well as accuracy and power in the pass.

'Very good!' he called out to Harry.

Next up was dribbling. It wasn't Harry's favourite skill but he managed to keep the ball under control as he weaved in and out of the cones. He was relieved when it was over and he had only knocked one over.

'Right, it's the moment you've all been waiting for,' Dave said to the group. 'Shooting! Do we have a goalkeeper here?'

Everyone looked around but no-one stepped forward.

The coach looked surprised. 'Really? Not a single keeper?'

Harry was really looking forward to scoring some goals but he also didn't mind playing in goal, especially if it wasn't Charlie who was shooting at him. Slowly, he raised his arm.

'Great! What's your name?' Dave asked.

'Harry.'

'Thanks, Harry! You'll get a chance to shoot later on, I promise.'

He put on a pair of gloves, walked over to the goal and waited. As the first shot came towards him, he didn't even have to move. He caught the ball and rolled it to the side. The next shot was better and he had to throw himself across the goal to tip it round the post.

'What a save, Harry!' Dave clapped. 'I think we've found our new keeper!'

Harry enjoyed diving around but he didn't want to be Ian Walker or David Seaman. He wanted to be Teddy Sheringham or Jürgen Klinsmann.

'Coach,' he called out after the first round of shots, 'I don't really play in goal. I normally play outfield as a striker.'

'Not again!' Dave thought to himself. Young keepers always got bored and asked to move to attack for the glory. Even so, he made a promise to the boy:

'No problem, I'll put you up front for the match at the end. You're a natural in goal, though!'

Harry waited patiently for his chance to shine. It took a little while, even once the match had started. But finally, his teammate kicked a long pass down the pitch and he was off, sprinting as fast as his little legs could go. He wasn't the fastest but he had a head start because of his clever run.

Harry beat the defender to the ball, took one touch to control it and calmly placed his shot in the bottom corner.

Goooooooooooooooooooaaaaaaaaaaaaaaaaaallllllllllllll llllllllllllllll!!!!!!!!!!!!!!!!!!!

Ten minutes later, Harry had a hat-trick and a place in the Ridgeway Rovers team.

'You're a natural keeper *and* a natural striker,' Dave laughed. 'I guess you're just a natural footballer!'

Harry couldn't wait for the real matches to begin. As he stepped out onto the field for the first time in the blue and white Ridgeway Rovers shirt, he felt unstoppable. This was it. He was ready for the big time, but was the big time ready for him?

When the ball came to him in the penalty area,
Harry took a shot and it deflected off a defender and
out for a corner.

'I'll take it!' Harry shouted, chasing over to the
flag.

It was a long way from the corner to the penalty
area, so he kicked it as hard as he could. The ball
flew over the heads of everyone, including the
goalkeeper. It landed in the back of the net.

*Goooooooooooooaaaaaaaaaaaaaaaalllllllllllllllllllllll
lllllll!!!!!!!!!!!!!!!!!!!!*

Harry punched the air with joy – he was off the
mark on his debut! It was a lucky strike but that
didn't matter. Would he ever get tired of scoring
goals? He really didn't think so.

CHAPTER 5

FOOTBALL, FOOTBALL, FOOTBALL

'That's it! Keep your head steady and lean over the ball as you kick it.'

At the weekends, Harry's dad often helped him with extra training in the back garden. There was so much that he wanted to improve, especially his shooting. He couldn't relax if he wanted to keep his place as Ridgeway Rovers' number one striker.

'Right, I think that's enough,' Pat said after an hour. 'You've got a game later today and you'll be too tired to score.'

'Okay, just three more shots,' Harry begged.

If his dad was busy, he went to the park with Charlie. When Harry was younger, his older brother used to make him stand between two trees and try to save his powerful shots for hours. That wasn't much fun but now that he was eight, Charlie let him join in properly. If there were other kids around, they'd play a big match but if it was just the two of them, they had long, competitive one-on-one battles. Harry was a skilful footballer but his older brother had one weapon that could defeat him: strength.

'Come on, that's not fair!' Harry shouted as he picked himself up off the grass. 'You can't just push me off the ball like that.'

Charlie shrugged. 'That was a shoulder-to-shoulder challenge. It's not my fault that I'm bigger than you.'

It was no use complaining; Harry just had to find other ways to beat his brother. Luckily, he was very determined. A few times he stormed off angrily but most of the time, Harry tried and tried until he succeeded.

'You're definitely getting better, bro!' Charlie told him as they walked back home together for lunch.

Harry smiled proudly; that was his aim. He didn't want to just be an average player; he wanted to become a great player like his Tottenham heroes. He didn't care how much time and effort that would take. Harry played football before school, at break-time, at lunchtime, and then after school too.

'See you later, Mum!' he called out as he gulped down a glass of water and threw his bag down.

Kim didn't need to ask where her son was going. She knew exactly where he would be and what he'd be doing. 'Just be careful and make sure you're back for dinner,' was all she said.

In the summer, Harry and his friends played in the park all day. But in the winter, it was too dark so they swapped grass for tarmac. Under the streetlights, their games could go on much longer, although there were more obstacles to deal with.

'Stop!' Harry called out. 'Car coming!'

All shots had to be low and soft. A few broken flowers were fine but broken windows meant game over.

'Kev, don't blast it!'

'Mrs Curtis is watching at the curtain!'

Harry loved their street games because they really

helped him to improve his technique. In the tight
space between the pavements, his control had to be
excellent and he had to look up quickly to find the
pass. His movement had to be good too if he wanted
to escape from the defenders and score.

'Yes!' he would scream as he made a sudden run
towards goal. If he got it right, his marker wouldn't
have time to turn and catch him.

Harry's hero, Teddy Sheringham, was back as
Tottenham's Number 10. He watched him carefully
in every match and tried to copy his movement.
Teddy wasn't the quickest striker in the Premier
League but he was always alert and clever around
the penalty area.

'Stay tight on Harry,' his opponents would say.
'Don't switch off or he'll score!'

Normally, their street games were friendly and fun,
but not always. If the result came down to next goal
wins, everyone took it very seriously.

'No way! That went straight over the jumper –
that's not a goal.'

'What are you talking about? That was post and in!'

'Stop cheating!'

'You're the one who's cheating!'

Of course, there was no referee, so Harry often had to be the peacemaker. He wanted to win just as much as the other boys, if not more, but he always stayed calm. Getting angry didn't help anyone. If Harry ended up on the losing team one day, he just worked even harder the next day.

Harry's days started and ended with football. It was all he thought about. In bed, he lay there imagining his Tottenham debut:

It was 0–0 with ten minutes to go and he came on to replace Les Ferdinand up front. Darren Anderton got the ball in midfield and played a brilliant through-ball. Harry ran towards goal, and he was one-on-one with the goalkeeper. Could he stay calm and find the net?

Unfortunately, he fell asleep before he found out the answer.

CHAPTER 6

ARSENAL

Harry was used to seeing Premier League scouts at Ridgeway Rovers matches. There was lots of young talent in north east London and no club wanted to miss out on the next David Beckham. If he kept scoring, Harry believed that it could be him.

'Well played, today,' said Ian Marshall, the Chairman of Ridgeway Rovers, as he ruffled the boy's short hair. 'How many is that for the season now?'

Harry pretended to count but he knew the answer. 'Eighteen in fifteen games.'

'You're our little Alan Shearer!'

Harry shook his head. 'I prefer Sheringham.'

Ian laughed. 'Of course, Teddy it is then! Do you mind if I have a quick chat with your dad please?'

While Harry practised his keepie-uppies nearby, the adults chatted.

'We had an Arsenal scout here today,' Ian said. 'He wants your boy to go for a trial there.'

Pat wasn't surprised; he already knew that his son was a very good player. But he wanted to do what was best for him.

'What do you think?' he asked Ian. 'He's still only eight – is he too young to join an academy? I want Harry to keep enjoying his football.'

The Ridgeway Rovers coach nodded. 'I understand. Look, I don't think there's any harm in him trying it out. If he doesn't like it, he can just come back here. We'll always have a place for him.'

Pat thanked Ian. 'Harry loves everything about football but I just don't want to get his hopes up. It can be a very cruel business for youngsters.'

As soon as they were in the car, Harry wanted to know everything. 'What were you and Ian talking about?'

'Wait until we get home. I need to talk to your mum first.'

'Okay, but was it a Tottenham scout?'

'Harry!'

'A West Ham scout?'

'HARRY!'

After a whispered chat with Kim in the kitchen, Pat shared the good news with his son. 'Arsenal want to offer you a trial. What do you think?'

Harry's first thoughts were a mix of pride and disappointment. It was amazing news that a Premier League club wanted him, but why did it have to be Arsenal, Tottenham's biggest rivals?

'But we hate Arsenal, Dad!'

Pat laughed. 'We don't really hate them, son. It's just a football rivalry. They're a great club and they're doing very well at the moment.'

His dad was right; Arsenal were the second-best team in England, just behind Manchester United. They had exciting superstars like Dennis Bergkamp, Patrick Vieira and Thierry Henry. Tottenham, meanwhile, were down in mid-table.

That was enough to make Harry change his mind. 'Okay, so when can I start?'

For the big day, Harry decided not to wear his Tottenham shirt. He was already going to be the new kid at Arsenal and he didn't want to make things even harder.

'How are you feeling?' his mum asked on the journey to London Colney, Arsenal's training ground location.

'Fine,' Harry replied but really, he was getting more and more nervous in the backseat of the car. It was going to be a massive challenge for him, and what if he failed? What if he wasn't good enough and made a fool of himself? This wasn't Ridgeway Rovers anymore.

'You'll be brilliant,' Kim told him, giving his hand a squeeze. 'But maybe don't tell your new coaches that you're a Spurs fan straight away!'

Harry smiled and felt a bit more relaxed. As long as he tried his best, what more could he do?

As they drove into the Arsenal Training Centre, Harry couldn't believe his eyes. Compared to Ridgeway's Peter May Sports Centre, it looked like a whole city. There were ten perfect, full-size pitches, as well as lots of indoor facilities.

'Not bad, is it?' his dad joked.

Once the session began, Harry's nerves turned
into adrenaline. 'I can do this!' he told himself.
Everything felt better with a football at his feet.

In the drills, he showed off his best touch and
passing. Some of the other boys had incredible
technique already, but Harry didn't let that get him
down. He was waiting for his moment to shine –
shooting. When that moment arrived, the Arsenal
goalkeepers didn't have a chance. Bottom left, top
right, straight down the middle; Harry scored
every time.

'Great work!' the coach clapped.

That trial session soon turned into a whole
season at Arsenal. At first, it felt strange to play for
Tottenham's enemies but Harry soon forgot about
that. He was having so much fun. He wasn't as
skilful as some of his teammates, but that wasn't
really his role – he was the one who scored the goals.
He didn't play every minute of every match but he
tried to make the most of every opportunity.

At the end of the season, the Arsenal academy had to choose which youngsters to keep and which youngsters to let go. Harry crossed his fingers tightly for weeks but unfortunately, it was bad news. The coaches decided that he was too small for his age.

'I'm so sorry,' his dad said, giving him a hug. 'Be proud and keep going. Once you've had your growth spurt, Arsenal are going to regret it!'

For the next few days, Harry was so angry and upset that he wanted to give up. But luckily, that feeling didn't last long. He realised that he loved football too much to stop. If Arsenal didn't want him, he knew another team that hopefully still did.

'Dad, can I go and play for Ridgeway Rovers again?'

The Peter May Sports Centre would always feel like home.

'Welcome back, kid!' Ian said with a wink. 'What we're looking for is a goalscorer, a fox in the box – do you know of anyone like that?'

Harry grinned. 'Yes – me!'

CHAPTER 7

CHINGFORD FOUNDATION SCHOOL

After playing for Ridgeway Rovers, Harry was soon following in David Beckham's footsteps for a second time when he started at Chingford Foundation School. Becks' signed shirt hung proudly in the entrance lobby at Chingford. Harry looked at it every morning as he arrived at school, hoping that it would bring him luck, but especially on the day of the trial for the Year 7 football team. Chingford had one of the best track records in Greater London and Harry was ready to be their next star.

'I'm the striker that they need and I'll show them at the trial,' he told his brother, Charlie, on the way to school. He wasn't quite as confident as he sounded but he was as determined as ever.

Harry loved scoring goals. It was an amazing feeling when a shot hit the back of the net. But he could do a lot more than just that. During his year at Arsenal, he had improved his all-round game. He was good in possession, and creative too. Setting up chances for his teammates was almost as much fun as scoring.

'Just don't be too selfish,' Charlie warned. 'Mr Leadon hates a show-off!'

Harry didn't forget his brother's advice. After changing into his white Tottenham shirt, he made his way out onto the pitch with the other boys.

'Good luck!' Harry told his mates. They were all competing for places now.

After a warm-up and some passing exercises, Mark Leadon, Chingford's football coach, split the boys up and gave half of them orange bibs.

'I'm looking for team players today,' he told them. 'If you just want to show off how many tricks you can do, go do that in the playground. I want to see how you can work together and help each other to win. Right, let's play!'

Most of Harry's schoolmates knew that he was a good footballer because they had seen him play in the lunchtime games. They knew that he had played for Arsenal, but he was still quite small and he didn't have the flashy skills and speed to dribble past everyone. There were other boys who looked more talented but Harry hadn't played at his best. Yet.

'If we pass the ball around, they'll get tired and the chances will come,' he told his teammates. He had made himself the leader.

Harry was ready to be patient but he didn't need to be. The opposition defenders couldn't cope with his clever runs into space. As the cross came in, he made a late run to beat his marker to the ball.

Gooooooooooooooooooaaaaaaaaaaaaaaaaaaaallllllllllllllll llllllllllllllll!!!!!!!!!!!!!!!!!!!!!!!

Harry didn't run off and celebrate on his own; he ran straight to thank the teammate who had set him up. Together, they ran back for the restart. They had more goals to score.

'I like this kid,' Mark thought to himself on the sidelines. 'For an eleven-year-old, he really understands football. He knows where to go and he knows where his teammates are going to go too.'

Harry didn't stop running until Mark blew the whistle to end the game. By then, it had turned into a thrashing. When he found room to shoot, Harry shot and scored. When he could see another player in space, he passed for them to score instead. He was involved in every part of his team's victory.

They walked off the pitch together, with their arms around each other's shoulders. Their man of the match was right at the centre of the gang.

'Well played,' Mark said to them but he was looking straight at Harry.

'Thanks, sir,' he replied politely, but inside, he was buzzing with pride.

Mark was very impressed. Every year, he had excellent young footballers in his school team but this boy seemed special. He had technique, vision, movement *and* work-rate. Mark could tell that it was going to be a good season.

'So, how did it go?' Charlie asked when his brother got home from school that evening.

Harry smiled and shrugged modestly. 'It went okay, I think.'

Harry became the first name on a very successful teamsheet. His goals led Chingford to school cup glory.

'If you keep working hard, your shirt could be hanging up there with Becks one day!' Mark Leadon told him.

CHAPTER 8

HEROES AND DREAMS

'Welcome!' David Beckham announced to a group of sixteen boys and girls. The England superstar was in East London to launch his brand-new football academy. With his white Adidas tracksuit and trendy haircut, he looked so cool. 'Today, we're going to practise some of my favourite skills.'

Harry wasn't really listening; he was too busy staring at his hero. He was one of the Chingford Foundation School footballers who had been selected to go to the academy launch. So now, Becks was right next to him, giving him football tips! Surely, it was too good to be true? But no, it was really happening.

Like Becks, Harry wore an Adidas tracksuit, but their hairstyles didn't match. Harry's head was shaved short, like Becks way back in 2000, but Becks had tried five different looks since then! Harry felt very nervous. Not only was Becks watching him but there were also cameras everywhere. Still, he was desperate to impress. Harry dribbled the ball carefully from end to end, and kept his keepie-uppies simple.

'That's it, great work everyone!' Becks called out.

At the end of the day, he shook each of them by the hand and chatted with them. When it was Harry's turn, he was too nervous and shy to speak. Luckily, Becks went first.

'Well done today. Are you one of the lads from Chingford?' he asked.

Harry nodded. 'A-and I play for Ridgeway Rovers too.'

Becks smiled. 'Great club, so what's next? What's your dream?'

Harry didn't need to think about that one. 'I want to play for England at Wembley!'

'Good choice, it's the best feeling in the world. If you keep working hard, you can do it. Good luck!'

As Harry travelled home with his mum, he could still hear his hero's inspirational words in his head – 'you can do it'.

*

'Play the pass now!' Harry shouted, as he sprinted towards goal. It was only one of their street games, but that didn't matter. Every football match was important. The pass never arrived, however.

'Car!' one of his mates shouted, picking up the ball.

As he moved over towards the pavement, Harry noticed two strange things about this particular car. Firstly, it wasn't the typical old banger that usually drove through the area. It was a huge black Range Rover and it looked brand-new. Secondly, the car didn't speed off once they were out of the way. Instead, it stopped and the driver's door opened.

'Hey guys, do you fancy a game?' the man said with a big smile on his face.

Harry's jaw dropped. Was he dreaming? Was

Jermain Defoe, Spurs' star striker, really standing there asking to play with them?

'Yes, Jermain's on our team!'

'Hey, that's not fair!'

After a few minutes of arguing, the decision was made: Harry and Jermain would play on opposite teams.

'Let's see what you've got!' Jermain told him with a wink.

Harry loved a challenge but this one was impossible. He knew that he couldn't compete with a top Premier League striker yet but he did his best. He chased every pass and got on the ball as often as possible. He wanted to show off all his skills.

When he wasn't racing around the pitch, Harry tried to watch his superstar opponent in action. Jermain scored lots of goals but Harry was more interested in the rest of his play. With a powerful burst of speed, he could escape from any tackle. Jermain was always thinking one step ahead, playing quick passes to get his teammates into really dangerous areas. If there was a loose ball, or a goalmouth scramble, he was always the first to react.

First Becks and now Jermain; Harry was learning from the very best.

After half an hour, Jermain had to leave. 'Thanks for the game, lads!'

The boys all stood and watched as the black Range Rover drove away. Then they looked at each other, their faces full of wonder. It was a night that none of them would ever forget.

'They're not going to believe us at school, are they?' Harry said.

His mates shook their heads. 'Not in a million years.'

CHAPTER 9

TOTTENHAM AT LAST

'I can't believe you're leaving us again,' Ian Marshall said with a wink and a handshake. 'I hope it goes well for you, lad, but if not, just come back home!'

Harry would miss playing for Ridgeway Rovers but Watford had offered him a trial. They weren't as big as Arsenal or Tottenham, but they were a good Championship team. It was the sort of new challenge that he needed.

'Good luck!' Pat called from the car window as he dropped Harry off at the Watford training centre. His son hadn't said much during the journey and he hoped that he wasn't brooding on his experience at

Arsenal. Harry was at a different club now and there
was nothing to worry about.

But Harry wasn't worried; he was just focused
on doing his best. He might only have a few weeks
to impress his new coaches, so he had to get things
right. If Harry missed one shot, he had to score the
next one.

'How did it go?' Pat asked when he returned to
pick him up.

'It was good,' was all Harry said. This time, he was
taking it one step at a time. He didn't want to get
carried away. It was just nice to be training with a
professional team again.

But it turned out that Watford weren't the only
ones chasing him. Another club was also interested,
the only club in Harry's heart – Tottenham.

Tottenham's youth scout Mark O'Toole had been
watching Harry's Ridgeway Rovers performances
for nearly a year. Harry was easily the best player in
his team. He was a natural finisher and he had good
technique. So, what was Mark waiting for?

'He knows exactly where the goal is but most

strikers are either big or quick,' he discussed with the
other scouts. 'Harry's neither!'

Mark liked to be 100 per cent certain before
he told the Tottenham youth coaches to offer a
youngster a trial. But when he heard that Harry was
at Watford, he decided to take a risk, and advised the
coaches:

'I want you to take a look at a kid who plays for
Ridgeway Rovers. He scores lots of goals but he's
not a classic striker. I guess he's more like Teddy
Sheringham than Alan Shearer.'

'Interesting! What's his name?'

'Harry Kane.'

'Well, tell him to come down for a trial.'

When his dad told him the news, Harry thought
his family were playing a prank on him. How could
they be so mean? Surely, they knew how much he
wanted to play for his local club.

'No, I'm serious!' Pat told him. He tried to look
serious but he couldn't stop smiling. 'I got a call from
a Tottenham youth scout. They want you to go down
to the training centre next week.'

After checking a few times, Harry celebrated with a lap of the living room.

'I'm going to play for Tottenham! I'm going to play for Tottenham!'

He had only been training with Watford for about a month, but there was no way that he could say no to Spurs. His dream team was calling him.

Harry waited and worried but finally the big day arrived.

'How are you feeling?' Pat asked as they drove to Spurs Lodge in Epping Forest.

Harry nodded. His heart was beating so fast that he thought it might jump out of his mouth if he tried to speak.

'Just remember to enjoy it, son,' his dad told him. 'It's a big opportunity but you've got to have fun, okay?'

Harry nodded again. Nothing was as fun as scoring goals.

As they parked their car, Harry could see the other boys warming up on the pitch. In their matching club tracksuits, they seemed to be having a great time together. This was the Under-13s but they all looked at least fifteen. Harry was still waiting for his growth spurt. What if they didn't want a little kid to join their group? What if he made a fool of himself? No, he couldn't think like that. He had to keep believing in himself.

Mark O'Toole was there at the entrance to greet them. 'Welcome to Tottenham! Are you ready for this, kid?'

This time, Harry had to speak. 'Yes, thanks.'

After a deep breath, he walked out onto the pitch in his lucky Tottenham shirt. He had nothing to lose.

Two hours later, Harry was on his way back home, sweaty and buzzing.

'They scored first but I knew we would win it. We had all the best players. George is really good in midfield and Danny can dribble past anyone. I reckon he can kick it even harder than Charlie! The other team didn't stand a chance, really. We had to work hard but–'

'Whoa, slow down, kiddo!' his dad laughed. 'So, you had a good time out there?'

'It was so much fun! I scored the winning goal!'

'I know – it was a great strike too.'

Harry frowned. 'How do you know that?'

His dad laughed. 'I watched from the car! I didn't want to put extra pressure on you by standing there on the sidelines but I wasn't going to miss your first session. Well done, you played really well tonight.'

After six weeks on trial, Harry became a proper Spurs youth team player. It was the proudest moment of his life but he had lots of hard work ahead of him. He had been the best player at Ridgeway Rovers, but he was now just average at Tottenham. It was like starting school all over again.

Luckily, Harry was a quick and willing learner. If it meant he got to play for Spurs, he would do anything the coaches asked him to do.

'Excellent effort, Harry!' John Moncur, the head of youth development, shouted.

Harry was enjoying himself but as summer approached, he began to worry. Soon, it would be time for the end-of-season letters again. Would Spurs decide to keep him for another year? After his experience at Arsenal, he couldn't bear another rejection. The day the post arrived, Harry's hands were shaking.

'Open it!' his brother Charlie demanded impatiently.

When he tore open the envelope, Harry read the dreaded word and his heart sank: '*Unfortunately...*'. It was the release letter. He tried to hold back the tears but he couldn't. 'I don't understand – I had a good season!'

The phone rang and Pat went to answer it. Within seconds, the sadness was gone from his voice. Instead, he sounded relieved. 'Don't worry, these things happen...Yes, I'll tell him right now.'

'Panic over!' Pat called out as he returned to the living room. Harry looked up and saw a big smile on his dad's face. What was going on? 'They sent you the wrong letter by mistake. Spurs want you to stay!'

CHAPTER 10

ONE MORE YEAR

Alex Inglethorpe was Tottenham's Under-18s coach but once a week, he helped out with the Under-14s training. He liked to keep an eye on the younger age groups because the most talented boys would soon move up into his team. Ryan Mason and Andros Townsend were already making the step-up. Who would be next?

During the session, Alex offered lots of advice, especially to the team's best players. There were a couple of speedy full-backs, a tall centre-back and a classy playmaker. And then there was Harry.

Harry didn't really stand out as an amazing young footballer, but Alex loved the boy's attitude. He

KANE

played with so much desire and all he wanted to do
was score goals for his team. Harry understood that
he wasn't as strong or quick as the other strikers, but
he didn't let that stop him. He loved a challenge, and
competing with Tottenham's best young players was
certainly a challenge. With the pressure on, he never
panicked. He just made the most of his technique
and worked hard on his weaknesses.

'That's it, Harry! Shield the ball from the defender
and wait until the pass is on. Lovely!'

Harry was the perfect student. After most sessions,
he would stay behind for extra shooting practice. For
a youth coach, that desire was a very good sign.

'Let's wait and see what happens when he grows
a bit,' Alex kept telling everyone at the Tottenham
academy. But they couldn't wait forever. Next year,
Harry would be moving up to the Under-16s. Before
then, they had to make a big decision about his future.

'Thanks for coming,' the Under-14s coach said,
shaking hands with Harry's parents. 'I wanted to
talk to you about your son's progress. As you know,
everyone loves Harry here at Spurs. He works so

hard and he's a pleasure to work with.'

Pat and Kim could tell that there was a 'But' coming.

'But we're worried. He's still small for his age and he's not a speedy little striker like Jermain Defoe. Don't get me wrong, Harry's got a very good understanding of the game but he needs more than just that if he wants to play up front for Spurs.'

'Okay, so how long does he have to get better?' Pat asked. Once they knew the timeframe, they could make a plan.

The Under-14s coach frowned. 'Every age group is a big new challenge and unless we see real improvement, we don't think that Harry will make it in the Under-16s next year.'

So, one more year. When they got home, Pat sat Harry down in the living room and told him the news. He could see the tears building in his son's eyes. First Arsenal and now Tottenham...

'Don't worry, this isn't over,' Pat said, putting an arm around Harry's shoulder. 'We just have to work even harder to prove them wrong. We believe in you. Do you want to give up?'

Harry shook his head firmly. 'No.'

His dad smiled. 'Good, that's my boy! We'll make a plan tomorrow.'

For the next twelve months, Harry trained with Tottenham as normal, but he also did extra sessions away from the club.

'I want to help but me and you kicking a ball around in the garden won't cut it anymore,' his dad joked. 'It's time to get serious!'

At first, 'serious' just meant lots of boring running and not much actual football. Harry did short sprints until he could barely lift his legs. 'What's the point of this?' he thought to himself as he stood there panting in the rain. This wasn't the beautiful game that he loved.

'Let's have a chat,' his coach said. He could tell that Harry was hating every second of it. 'Look kid, you're never going to be a 100-metre champion but a short burst of pace can make a huge difference for a striker.'

Harry thought back to Jermain Defoe during that

street game a few years earlier. He was really good at making space for the shot and his reaction speed was amazing. That was what Harry needed. If the ball dropped in the penalty area, he had to get there first. If a goalkeeper made a save, he had to win the race to the rebound.

'Brilliant, Harry!' his coach cried out a few minutes later. 'That's your best time yet!'

Soon, they moved on to ball work. Harry practised his hold-up play, his heading and, of course, his shooting. He could feel the improvement and so could Tottenham. After a few months, Harry was looking fitter and much more confident on the pitch. Most importantly, he was a better striker and he was scoring more goals.

'Congratulations, kid!' Alex told him after another brilliant performance. 'I knew you'd prove them wrong. You're getting taller every time I see you.'

Yes, Harry was finally growing! Everything was falling into place at just the right time. Thanks to lots of extra effort, Spurs wanted him to stay. Now, Harry just needed to grow into his tall new body.

CHAPTER 11

MEXICO AND SWITZERLAND

By the time he turned fifteen, Harry had become one
of Tottenham's hottest prospects. He still played a lot
of games for the Under-16s but he was also getting
experience at higher levels. No matter who he played
against, Harry kept scoring goals.

'That kid is one of the best natural finishers I've
ever seen,' Spurs coach Tim Sherwood told Alex
Inglethorpe. 'Why have I never heard of him until
now?'

The Under-18s coach laughed. 'He's a late
developer!'

'Okay, well look after him carefully – he could be
our next goal machine.'

At the start of the 2008–09 season, Jonathan Obika had been Alex's number one striker in the Spurs academy side but the team played lots of matches and it was good to have competition for places.

'Welcome to the squad!' Alex said as he gave Harry the good news. 'At first, you'll be on the bench but if you keep making the most of your opportunities, you'll force your way into the starting line-up. You deserve this.'

Harry was delighted. Not only was he moving up but he was joining a very good side. There was Steven Caulker at the back, Ryan Mason in the middle and Andros Townsend on the wing. With teammates like that, he was going to get plenty of chances to score. Harry couldn't wait.

'If I grab a few goals, I could be playing for the first team soon!' he told Charlie excitedly.

It was his older brother's job to keep his feet on the ground. 'And if you miss a few sitters, you could be playing for the Under-16s again!' Charlie teased.

Luckily, that didn't happen. Harry kept on scoring and soon he was off on an exciting international adventure.

'I'm going to Mexico!' he told his family in December. 'I made the Spurs team for the Copa Chivas.'

'Never heard of it!' Charlie replied with a smile. He was very proud of his younger brother, but it wasn't very cool to show it.

Kim was more concerned about Christmas. 'When do you leave?' she asked.

Harry shrugged; he wasn't bothered about the details. He was playing football for Tottenham; that was all he needed to know. 'In January, I think.'

It was going to be the trip of a lifetime. He couldn't wait to have lots of fun with Ryan, Steven and Andros and win the tournament. What an experience it would be!

'Just you behave yourself,' his mum told him at the airport. 'Don't let the older boys get you into trouble!'

After a long flight, the squad arrived in Guadalajara

and found the familiar Tottenham cockerel on the side of a big coach.

'We're famous!' Ryan joked as they all got on board.

In the Copa Chivas, Tottenham faced teams from Spain, Costa Rica, Brazil, Paraguay, Norway and, of course, Mexico.

'Come on boys, we're representing England here!' Harry said, looking down at their white Spurs shirts.

It was hard work in the heat but Tottenham did well. In eight matches, Harry managed to score three goals.

'Only Ryan got more than me!' he told his parents proudly when he returned to Chingford. It had been the best trip ever, but he was glad to get back to his own bedroom and home cooking.

A few months later, Harry was off again. Tottenham were playing in the *Torneo Bellinzona* in Switzerland against big clubs like Sporting Lisbon and Barcelona.

'Barca who?' Steven joked. They weren't scared of anyone.

Harry started two of their five matches and, although he didn't score, he played a big role in helping his team to win the tournament.

'I like setting up goals too, you know!' he reminded Ryan after their final win. It was a great feeling but nothing beat scoring goals.

Harry had really enjoyed his travels and he had learnt a lot from playing against teams from other countries. But back in England, it was time to think about his Spurs future. With his sixteenth birthday coming up, would Tottenham offer him a scholarship contract? He felt like he was improving all the time but he didn't want to get his hopes up. As time went by, his fears grew.

'Harry, have you got any plans for Tuesday?' John McDermott, the head of the academy, asked him casually.

He quickly worked out the date in his head. 'That's my birthday! Why?'

John smiled. 'Do you think you'll have time to come in and sign your contract?

Harry had never felt so relieved. He couldn't wait

to tell his family and friends. After all his hard work, he was finally getting his reward. Signing with Spurs would be the best birthday present ever.

CHAPTER 12

GETTING CLOSER

Ahead of the 2009–10 season, the Tottenham Under-18s lined up for their squad photo. Harry had grown so much that the cameraman placed him on the back row next to the goalkeepers. He wasn't yet important enough to sit in the front row, but that was where he aimed to be next year.

Once everyone was in position, the cameraman counted down. '3, 2, 1… Click!'

Most of his teammates looked very serious in the photos but Harry couldn't help smiling. Why shouldn't he be happy? He was playing football for his favourite club in the world!

Harry's season started in Belgium at Eurofoot.

Ryan, Andros and Steven had all gone out on loan, so he was suddenly a senior member of the youth squad.

'A lot of excellent players have played in this tournament,' coach Alex Inglethorpe told them. 'This is going to be a great experience for all of you. We will be playing a lot of games while we're out here, so get ready to test your fitness!'

After his successful trips to Mexico and Switzerland, Harry couldn't wait for his next international adventure. He was a year older now and a much better striker. The tournament schedule was really tiring but Harry scored three goals in his first four games.

'You're on fire!' his strike partner Kudus Oyenuga cheered as they celebrated their win over Dutch team Willem II.

In the end, Tottenham didn't reach the semi-finals but Harry had his shooting boots on, ready for the Premier Academy League to begin. Or so he thought, anyway. But after four matches, he still hadn't scored.

'Just be patient,' Kudus kept telling him.

It was easy for Kudus to say; he had already found the net three times. 'But scoring goals is what I do best!' Harry argued.

'I think you're just trying too hard,' Tom Carroll, their tiny midfield playmaker, suggested. 'Just relax and I bet the goals will come.'

Harry was grateful for his teammates' support and advice. He scored in his next match against Fulham and once he started, he didn't stop. After two free-kick strikes against Watford, first-team coach Harry Redknapp picked him as a sub for the League Cup match against Everton.

'No way! This is too good to be true,' Harry said when he saw the squad list. His name was there next to top professionals like Jermaine Jenas and Vedran Ćorluka.

Alex laughed. 'No, it's for real! Just don't get your hopes up; you probably won't get off the bench.'

Harry didn't come on, but he got to train with his heroes and share a dressing room with them. The experience inspired him to keep working hard. He could feel himself getting closer and closer to his Tottenham dream.

By Christmas, Harry was the Under-18s top scorer with nine goals, and the new academy captain.

'Alex always had a good feeling about you,' John McDermott said as he congratulated Harry. 'You're certainly proving him right these days! If you keep it up, the future is yours.'

Harry celebrated by scoring his first hat-trick of the season against Coventry City. And the great news just kept coming. In January 2010, he was called up to the England Under-17s for the Algarve Tournament in Portugal.

'Welcome!' the coach John Peacock said at his first squad meeting. 'I guess you must know a lot of these guys from the Premier Academy League?'

'Yes,' Harry replied, trying to hide his nerves. He had played against Benik Afobe, Ross Barkley and Nathaniel Chalobah before but they probably didn't even remember him. He was the new kid and he suddenly felt very shy. Luckily, his new teammates were very friendly.

'Nice to meet you, we needed a new striker,'
Nathaniel grinned. 'Benik already thinks he's Thierry
Henry!'

Harry soon felt like one of the gang. Off the pitch,
they had lots of fun together but on the pitch, they
were a focused team. The Under-17 European
Championships were only a few months away, and
so the Algarve Tournament was a chance for players
to secure their places.

As he walked onto the pitch wearing the Three
Lions on his shirt for the first time, Harry had to
pinch himself to check that he wasn't dreaming. A
few years earlier, Spurs had been close to letting him
go – but now look at him! It was hard to believe.
Harry didn't score against France or Ukraine but
he would never forget those matches. He was an
England youth international now.

Harry knew that if he played well until May, he
had a chance of going to the Euros in Liechtenstein.
That's what he wanted more than anything. He kept
scoring goals for the Tottenham Under-18s and the
Reserves, and crossed his fingers. He finished with

eighteen goals in only twenty-two Premier Academy League games. Surely that would be enough to make the England squad?

In the end, Harry never found out because he was too ill to go to the tournament. Instead of representing his country at the Euros, he had to sit at home and watch Nathaniel, Ross and Benik winning without him. When England beat Spain in the final, Harry was both delighted and devastated.

'Congratulations, guys!' he texted his teammates but inside, he was very jealous. He should have been there with them, lifting the trophy.

'You'll get more chances,' his mum told him as he lay on the sofa feeling sorry for himself.

It didn't seem that way at the time, but Harry always bounced back from disappointments. There was a new season to prepare for, and a first professional Tottenham contract to sign. That was more than enough to lift him out of his bad mood. It was the best feeling in the world as he signed his name on the papers.

'Thanks for always believing in me,' Harry told

Alex as they chatted afterwards. 'I couldn't have done this without you.'

His Under-18s coach shook his head. 'You did it all yourself but you haven't achieved anything yet, kid. The next step is the hardest but you've got what it takes.'

Harry smiled. It was true; he wouldn't give up until he made it into the Spurs first team.

CHAPTER 13

EXPERIENCE NEEDED

At seventeen, Harry was on his way to becoming
a Spurs superstar but he still had a lot to learn.
Luckily, there were plenty of teachers around him
at Tottenham. In the Reserves, he often played
alongside first team stars who were recovering from
injuries, like David Bentley and Robbie Keane. Harry
loved those matches. He was always watching and
listening for new tips.

'If you need to, take a touch but if you hit it early,
you might catch the keeper out.'

'Don't just assume that he's going to catch it. Get
there in case he drops it!'

By 2010, Harry was also training regularly with

Harry Redknapp's squad. It was hard to believe
that he was sharing a pitch with world-class players
like Gareth Bale, Luka Modrić and Rafael van der
Vaart. But best of all, Harry was working with his
hero, Jermain Defoe. Eventually, he plucked up the
courage to talk about that street game.

'Oh yeah, I remember that!' Jermain laughed.
'That was you? Wow, I feel *really* old now!'

Jermain became Harry's mentor and invited him to
his extra shooting sessions.

'You're a natural goalscorer, H, but it takes more
than instinct to become a top striker. You need to
practise, practise, practise! What are you aiming for
when you shoot?'

It seemed like a really stupid question. 'The goal,'
he replied.

'Okay, but what part of the goal? Top corner,
bottom corner?'

'Err, I don't know, I guess I–'

Jermain interrupted Harry. 'No, no, no! You've got
to know exactly what you're aiming at, H. Before
you hit this one, I want you to picture the goal in

your head and then aim for the top right corner.'

Harry took his time and placed the ball carefully into the top right corner.

'Good, but you won't get that long to think in a real match.'

Jermain called a young defender over: 'As soon as I play the pass to Harry, close him down.'

Under pressure, Harry hit the target again but his shot went straight down the middle of the goal. 'No, the keeper would have saved that,' Jermain said. So Harry tried again and again until he hit that top right corner.

'Nice! Now let's work on making that space to shoot. Let's hope you're quicker than you look!' Jermain teased.

He was very impressed by Harry's attitude. Not only did he love scoring goals but he also loved improving his game. That was a winning combination. Jermain kept telling the Spurs coaches, 'If you give him a chance, I promise you he'll score!'

But for now, Redknapp already had Jermain, Roman Pavlyuchenko and Peter Crouch in his squad.

Harry would have to wait for his chance. He was doing well for the Reserves but was that the best place for him to develop? Spurs' youth coaches didn't think so.

'He's a great kid and a talented player but what's his best position?' Les Ferdinand asked Tim Sherwood.

That was a difficult question. Harry was a natural finisher but he was also good on the ball. He could read the game well as a second striker, linking the midfield and attack.

Sherwood's silence proved Ferdinand's point. 'That's the big issue. He's a goalscorer but he's not strong enough to battle against big centre-backs.'

'Not yet, no.'

'Plus, he's not quick enough to get in behind the defence.'

This time, Sherwood disagreed. 'He's quicker than he looks and he's lethal in the box.'

After a long discussion, the Spurs coaches agreed on an action plan – Harry would go out on loan in January 2011 to a lower league club.

'We've spoken to Leyton Orient and they want to take you for the rest of the season,' Sherwood told him in a meeting.

At first, Harry was surprised and upset. He didn't want to leave Tottenham, even if it was only for a few months.

'Look, kid, a spell in League One will be good for you,' Sherwood explained. 'You need first-team experience and you're not going to get that here at the moment, I'm afraid. We also need to toughen you up a bit, put some muscle on that skinny frame. Don't worry – we're not going to forget about you!'

Harry spoke to his parents and he spoke to his teammates. They all agreed that it was a good idea.

'Everyone goes out on loan at some point,' Ryan told him. 'It's better than being stuck in the Reserves, trust me!'

'I was at Orient last season,' Andros told him. 'It's a good club and they'll look after you. At least, Spurs aren't asking you to go miles from home. Leyton is just up the road!'

They were right, of course. If a loan move to

Leyton Orient would help him to improve and get into the Tottenham first team, Harry would go. It really helped that he wouldn't be going alone.

'Let's do this!' Tom cheered as they travelled to their first training session together.

CHAPTER 14

LEYTON ORIENT

Rochdale's pitch looked bad even before the match kicked off. Where had all the grass gone? As the Leyton Orient squad warmed up, they kept away from the boggy penalty areas and corners. They didn't want to make things worse. When Harry tried a short sprint, his boots sank into the squelch and it was difficult to lift them out. How was he supposed to make runs into the box?

Orient's striker Scott McGleish watched and laughed. 'Welcome to League One, kid!'

The Spotland Stadium was certainly no White Hart Lane. After seventy minutes of football and heavy rain, it looked more like a mud bath than a pitch. On the bench, Harry sat with his hood up, shaking his legs to keep warm. The score was 1–1, perfect for a super sub…

'Harry, you're coming on!' the assistant manager Kevin Nugent turned and shouted.

This was it – his Leyton Orient debut. Harry jumped to his feet and took off his tracksuit. As he waited on the touchline, he didn't even notice the rain falling. He was so focused on making a good first impression for his new club.

'It's fun out there today!' Scott joked, high-fiving Harry as he left the field.

Harry grinned and ran on. He was desperate to make a difference, either by scoring or creating the winning goal. He chased after every ball but before he knew it, the final whistle went.

'Well done, lad,' his manager Russell Slade said, slapping his wet, muddy back.

Harry had enjoyed his first short battle against the big League One centre-backs. They wanted to teach the Premier League youngster about 'real football', and he wanted to show them that this Premier

League youngster could cope with 'real football'.
Scott was right; it *was* fun!

'So, how did you find it?' Kevin asked back in
the dressing room. Alex Inglethorpe had left him in
charge of Harry and Tom during their loan spell at
the club.

'It's different, that's for sure!' Harry replied after a
nice hot shower. 'I need to get stronger but I'm ready
for the challenge.'

Orient's assistant manager was impressed. The kid
had a great attitude and that was very important
in professional football. He could see the hunger in
his eyes.

Harry was picked to start the next home game
against Sheffield Wednesday. It was a big responsibility
for a seventeen-year-old. He fought hard up front but
it wasn't easy against really experienced defenders. At
half-time, it was still 0–0.

'You're causing them lots of problems,' Kevin
reassured him. 'Keep doing what you're doing and
be patient.'

Harry felt more confident as he ran out for the

second half. He had fifteen, or maybe twenty, minutes to grab a goal before the manager took him off. 'I can do this,' he told himself.

When Orient took the lead, the whole team breathed a sigh of relief. They started passing the ball around nicely and creating more chances. Harry only needed one. When it arrived, he steadied himself and placed his shot carefully.

Goooooooooooooooaaaaaaaaaaaaaaaaaalllllllllllllllllll llllll!!!!!!!!!!!!!!!!!!!!!

He had scored on his full debut! Harry ran towards the Orient fans to celebrate. It felt like the start of big things.

'You're one of us now!' Scott cheered as they high-fived on the touchline.

*

'So, how is Harry getting on?' Alex asked Kevin when they met up a few months later.

The Orient assistant manager chuckled. 'That boy's a real fighter, isn't he? His legs are no bigger than matchsticks but he's fearless. He's good in front of goal, too.'

'What about that red card against Huddersfield?'

Kevin shook his head. 'The second yellow was very harsh,' he explained. 'I'm not sure he even touched the guy! You know that's not Harry's way. He's one of the good guys.'

Tottenham's youth coach nodded. He knew all about Harry's character. Some youngsters really struggled to adapt to new environments, but clearly not him. Alex never had any doubt that Harry would make the most of his first-team experience.

With Orient chasing a playoff spot, Harry was back on the bench for the last few matches of the season. It wasn't where he wanted to be but he was pretty pleased with his record of five goals in eighteen games. It was a decent start to his professional career.

'Welcome back, stranger!' Ryan joked when Harry returned to Tottenham in May.

Despite going out on loan, he had never really left his beloved club. After training with Orient, Harry often went back to do extra sessions with the Spurs Under-21s. They couldn't get rid of him that easily.

Over the summer of 2011, Redknapp sold Peter

Crouch and Robbie Keane, and replaced them with Emmanuel Adebayor. Harry was feeling positive about his sums.

'Two strikers left and only one came in,' he thought to himself. 'That means one spare spot for me!'

It looked that way at the start of the 2011–12 season. In August, Harry made his Tottenham debut at White Hart Lane, against Hearts in the UEFA Europa League. They were already 5–0 up from the first leg, so Redknapp threw him straight into the starting line-up, with Andros and Tom. Harry had never been so excited.

'I'm keeping Jermain out of the team!' he joked with his brother.

'What shirt number did they give you?' Charlie asked.

'37.'

'And what number is Jermain?'

'18.'

'Well, you're not the star striker yet then, bro!'

But Harry wasn't giving up until he *was* Tottenham's star striker. In the twenty-eighth minute, he chased after Tom's brilliant through-ball. It was a move that they had practised so many times in the Spurs youth teams. Harry got there first, just ahead of the Hearts keeper, who tripped him. Penalty!

Harry picked himself up and walked over to get the ball. This was *his* penalty, a great opportunity to score on his Spurs debut. He placed it down on the spot and took a few steps back. He tried to ignore the goalkeeper bouncing on his line. He pictured the goal in his head, just like Jermain had taught him.

After a deep breath, he ran towards the ball but suddenly, doubts crept into his head. Was it a bad idea to shoot bottom left like he usually did? He paused just before he kicked it and that gave the keeper time to make the save. Harry ran in for the rebound but it was no use; he had missed the penalty.

Harry was devastated but he didn't stand there with his head in his hands. The nightmares could wait until after the match. For now, he kept hunting for his next chance to become a Tottenham hero...

CHAPTER 15

MILLWALL

'Go out there and score!' Jermain shouted as Harry ran on to replace him.

Tottenham were already 3–0 up against Shamrock Rovers. There was still time for him to grab a fourth.

Danny Rose's cross flew over Harry's head but Andros was there at the back post. As he knocked it down, Harry reacted first and shot past the defender on the line.

Gooooooooooooooooooaaaaaaaaaaaaaaaaallllllllllllllll llllllll!!!!!!!!!!!!!!!!!!!!

Harry turned away to celebrate with Andros. What a feeling! He roared up at the sky. He was a Tottenham goalscorer now, and he could put that awful penalty miss behind him.

Unfortunately, however, that was the end of Tottenham's Europa League campaign. It was a real blow for their young players because the tournament was their big chance to shine. What would happen now? There wasn't space for them in Spurs' Premier League squad, so they would either have to go back to the Reserves or out on loan again.

'Right now, I just want to play week in week out,' Harry told his dad. 'I don't care where!'

Pat smiled. 'Be careful what you wish for. You wouldn't like the cold winters in Russia!'

In the end, Harry and Ryan were sent on loan to Millwall in January 2012. The Lions were fighting to stay in the Championship and they needed goals.

'We only scored one goal in the whole of December,' Harry's new manager Kenny Jackett moaned. 'We played five matches, that's over 450 minutes of football!'

Harry's job was clear and he couldn't wait to help his new team. In his Millwall debut against Bristol City, he had a few chances to score but he couldn't get past former England goalkeeper David James. When City won the match with a last-minute goal, Harry couldn't believe it. He trudged off the pitch with tears in his eyes.

'Hard luck, kid,' Jackett said, putting an arm around his shoulder. 'You played well. The goals will come.'

His new strike partner, Andy Keogh, gave him similar advice. 'Just forget about the misses. If you keep thinking about them, you'll never score!'

The Millwall players and coaches liked Harry and they wanted him to do well. Despite his talent, he wasn't an arrogant wonderkid who thought he was way too good for them. He was a friendly guy, who worked hard for the team and always wanted to improve.

But six weeks later, Harry was still waiting for his first league goal for Millwall. It was the longest drought of his whole life. What was going wrong? Why couldn't he just put the ball in the net? Eventually, he did it away at Burnley.

He made the perfect run and James Henry played

the perfect pass. Harry was through on goal. Surely, he couldn't miss this one! The goalkeeper rushed out to stop him but he stayed calm and used his side foot to guide the ball into the bottom corner.

Goooooooooooooooooaaaaaaaaaaaaaaaaalllllllllllllllllll lllllllllllll!!!!!!!!!!!!!!!!!!!!

Harry pumped his fists and jumped into the air. It was finally over! James threw himself into Harry's arms.

'Thanks mate!' Millwall's new goalscorer shouted above the noise of the fans. 'There's no stopping me now!'

With his confidence back, Harry became a goal machine once more. The Championship defenders just couldn't handle his movement. He was deadly in the penalty area, hitting the target with every shot and header. But he was also brilliant when he played behind the striker. In a deeper role, he had the technique and vision to set up goals.

'Cheers!' Andy shouted after scoring from his perfect pass.

Harry also loved to hit a long-range rocket. Against

Peterborough, he spun away from his marker and chased after the ball. It was bouncing high and he was on his weaker left foot, but Harry was feeling bold. Why not? Jermain and Robbie had taught him a very important lesson at Tottenham – if you shoot early, the keeper won't be ready. Harry struck his shot powerfully and accurately into the far corner.

Goooooooooooooooooooooooaaaaaaaaaaaaaaaaaalllllll llllllllllllllllllllll!!!!!!!!!!!!!!

Harry ran towards the fans and slid across the grass on his knees.

'You're on fire!' Andy cheered as they celebrated together.

With his nine goals, Harry won Millwall's Young Player of the Season award. It was a proud moment for him and a nice way to say goodbye to the club.

'We're going to miss you!' Jackett told him after his last training session. 'It's been a pleasure working with you. Good luck back at Spurs – you're going to be great.'

Harry was sad to leave Millwall but he was also excited about returning to Tottenham. He had learnt a lot from his loan experience. He was now a stronger player, both physically and mentally. It was much harder to push him off the ball, and much harder to stop him scoring.

'2012–13 is going to be my season!' Harry told his family confidently.

But first, he was off to play for England at the UEFA European Under-19 Championships in Estonia. Nathaniel, Benik and Ross were in the squad too, along with some exciting new players: Eric Dier was a tough defender and Nathan Redmond was a tricky winger.

'There's no reason why we can't win this!' their manager Noel Blake told them.

Although he wore the Number 10 shirt, Harry played in midfield behind Benik and Nathan. He enjoyed his playmaker role but it made it harder for him to do his favourite thing – scoring goals. After a draw against Croatia and a win over Serbia, England needed to beat France to reach the semi-finals.

As the corner came in, most of the England attackers charged towards the goal. But not Harry.

He waited around the penalty spot because he had noticed that the French goalkeeper wasn't very good at catching crosses. When he fumbled the ball, it fell straight to Harry, who was totally unmarked. He calmly volleyed it into the net.

Goooooooooooooooooooooaaaaaaaaaaaaaaaallllllllllll llllllllllllllll!!!!!!!!!!!!!!!!!!!!!!!!!

2–1 to England! Harry pumped his fists and pointed up at the sky. He was delighted to score such an important goal for his country.

'You're a genius!' Eric cheered as the whole team celebrated.

Unfortunately, Harry wasn't there to be England's hero in the semi-final against Greece. He had to watch from the bench as his teammates lost in extra-time. It was such a horrible way to crash out of the tournament.

'At least we've got the Under-20 World Cup next summer!' Harry said, trying to make everyone feel a little bit better.

He focused once again on his top target – breaking into the Tottenham first team.

CHAPTER 16

TOUGH TIMES

On the opening day of the 2013–14 season, Harry
travelled up to Newcastle with the Tottenham squad.
New manager André Villas-Boas wanted to give his
young players a chance. Jake Livermore started the
match, and Harry and Andros waited impatiently on
the subs bench. Would this be the day when they
made their Premier League debuts?

'Is it bad to hope that someone gets injured?'
Andros joked.

With ten minutes to go, Newcastle scored a
penalty to make it 2–1. Harry's heart was racing;
surely, this was going to be his moment. Tottenham
needed to score again and he was the only striker on
the bench.

'Harry, you're coming on!'

He quickly took off his yellow bib, and then his grey tracksuit. He pulled up his socks and re-laced his boots. He tucked his navy-blue Spurs shirt into his white shorts.'37 KANE' was ready for action.

'Good luck!' Andros said as Harry walked down to the touchline.

'Get a goal!' Villas-Boas said as Harry waited to come on.

'Let's do this!' Jermain cheered as Harry ran on to join him up front.

Harry had less than ten minutes to score and become an instant Spurs hero. Anything was possible but Newcastle were in control of the game. Harry's Premier League debut was over before he'd really touched the ball.

'Don't worry, that was just a first taste of the action,' Jermain promised him.

Harry hoped that his mentor was right. He shook hands with his opponents and the match officials. Then he walked over to clap the Tottenham fans in the away stand. He had done his best to save the day for his club.

He couldn't wait for his next chance to play but he wasn't even a substitute for their next match against West Brom. With Emmanuel Adebayor back in the team, he was back in the Reserves. Harry was disappointed but he didn't give up.

'I'm still only nineteen,' he told himself. 'I've got plenty of time to shine.'

A few days later, he joined Norwich City on loan for the rest of the season. The Canaries were in the Premier League, so this was a great opportunity to show Spurs that he was good enough to play at the top level.

'Bring it on!' he told his new manager Chris Hughton.

Against West Ham, Harry came on with twenty minutes to go. That gave him plenty of time to score. He dribbled forward, cut inside and curled the ball just wide of the post.

'So close!' Harry groaned, putting his hands on his head.

Minutes later, he beat the West Ham right-back and pulled the ball back to Robert Snodgrass... but his shot was blocked on the line! Somehow, the match finished 0–0 but Harry was happy with his debut.

Afterwards, Hughton told the media, 'I think Kane will be a super player'.

Harry was delighted with the praise. His first start for Norwich soon arrived against Doncaster in the League Cup. He couldn't wait.

'I'm definitely going to score!' he told his teammates.

Sadly, Harry didn't score and he only lasted fifty minutes. He tried to carry on but he couldn't; his foot was way too painful. He winced and limped off the pitch.

'What happened?' his brother asked as he rested on the sofa back at home.

'I've fractured a metatarsal,' Harry explained.

'Isn't that what Becks did before the 2002 World Cup?' Charlie joked, trying to cheer his brother up. 'You've got to stop copying him!'

Harry smiled, but he was dreading the surgery and then the months without football. It would drive him crazy.

'You're a strong character,' Alex Inglethorpe told him when he returned to Tottenham, 'and you're going to come back even stronger!'

Harry's new girlfriend helped to take his mind off his injury. He and Katie had gone to the same primary and secondary schools but it was only later that they started dating. They got on really well and made each other laugh, even during the tough times.

Harry spent October and November in the gym, slowly getting his foot ready to play football again. It was long, boring work but he had to do it if he wanted to be playing again before the new year. That was his big aim. In December, Harry started training with the first team again, and starring for the Reserves.

'I'm feeling good!' Harry told his manager Chris Hughton with a big smile on his face. It was great to be playing football again. He had missed it so much.

On 29 December 2012, he was a sub for the

Manchester City match. By half-time, Norwich were losing 2–1.

'They're down to ten men, so let's get forward and attack,' Hughton told his players in the dressing room. 'We can win this! Harry, you're coming on to replace Steve.'

Harry's eyes lit up. He had been hoping for ten, maybe fifteen, minutes at the end but instead he was going to play the whole second half.

This was his biggest challenge yet. Harry was up against City's captain Vincent Kompany, one of the best centre-backs in the world. These were the big battles that he dreamed about. Harry held the ball up well and made clever runs into space. He didn't score but he was back in business.

'Boss, that was just the start!' he promised Hughton.

Before long, however, Harry was told that he had to return to Tottenham. Villas-Boas wanted a third striker as back-up for Jermain and Emmanuel. Harry was happy to help his club but he wanted to play regular football. What was the point of him being there if he wasn't even getting on the bench? A few weeks later, Villas-Boas sent him back out on loan to Leicester City.

'This is all so confusing!' Harry moaned to Katie. It had turned into a very topsy-turvy season. 'Do Spurs want me or not?'

It was a question that no-one could answer. Harry tried his best to adapt to another new club but soon after scoring on his home debut against Blackburn, he was dropped from the Leicester starting line-up. It was a massive disappointment. It felt like his career was going backwards.

'If I'm only a sub in the Championship, how am I ever going to make it at Spurs?' he complained to his dad on the phone. Leicester felt like a very long way away from Chingford.

Pat had seen his son looking this sad before. 'Remember when you were fourteen and Tottenham told you that you weren't good enough?' he reminded him. 'You didn't give up back then and you're not going to give up now!'

Harry nodded. He *was* good enough! All he

needed was a run of games and a chance to get back into goalscoring form. He just had to believe that the breakthrough would come.

CHAPTER 17

BREAKTHROUGH

'I'm not going anywhere this season,' Harry told
Tottenham firmly. After four loan spells, he was
determined to stay at the club. 'I'm going to prove
that I should be playing here week in, week out!'

Harry wasn't a raw, skinny teenager anymore.
He was now twenty years old and he looked like a
fit, powerful striker at last. That was thanks to his
Football League experience and lots of hard work in
the gym to build up his strength. He now had even
more power in his shot.

'Looking good, H!' Jermain said in pre-season
training. His encouragement was working. Harry was
getting better and better.

The 2013 U-20 World Cup in Turkey had been a very disappointing tournament for England, but not for Harry. He set up their first goal against Iraq with a brilliant header, and a few days later scored a great equaliser against Chile from outside the penalty area. He hit the ball perfectly into the bottom corner, just like he did again and again on the training ground.

'What a strike!' England teammate Ross Barkley said to Harry as they high-fived.

When he returned to England in July, Harry felt ready to become a Premier League star but again, Spurs had signed a new striker. Roberto Soldado cost £26 million after scoring lots of goals for Valencia in La Liga. Watching his rival in action, Harry didn't give up. He believed in himself more than ever.

For now, cup matches were Harry's chance to shine. In the fourth round of the League Cup, Spurs were heading for a disastrous defeat as opponents Hull took the lead in extra-time. Could Harry save the day?

When Jermain passed the ball to him, he had
his back to goal, and needed to turn as quickly
as possible. Harry used his strength and speed to
spin cleverly past his marker. With a second touch,
he dribbled towards the penalty area. He was in
shooting range now. There were defenders right in
front of him, blocking the goal, but he knew exactly
where the bottom corner was. Harry could picture
it in his head.

*Goooooooooooooooooooooaaaaaaaaaaaaaaaalllllllllll
lllllllllllllll!!!!!!!!!!!!!!!!!!*

Yes! Harry pumped his fists and ran towards the
fans. The job wasn't done yet but his strike had
put Spurs back in the game. When the tie went to
penalties, he was one of the first to volunteer.

'I've got this,' he told Spurs manager André Villas-
Boas. It was time to make up for that miss in the
Europa League.

Harry was Spurs' fifth penalty taker. The pressure
was on – he had to score, otherwise they were out
of the competition. This time, he felt confident. He
had a plan and he was going to stick to it, no matter

what. As the goalkeeper dived to the right, Harry slammed his shot straight down the middle. The net bulged – what a relief!

'Well done, you showed a lot of guts there,' Tim Sherwood told him afterwards, giving him a hug. 'Your time is coming!'

In December 2013, Sherwood took over as Tottenham manager for the rest of the season, after the sacking of Villas-Boas. Harry didn't want to get his hopes up but he knew that his former Under-21 coach believed in his talent. Hopefully, Sherwood would give him more opportunities now. By February, he was coming off the bench more regularly but only because Jermain had signed for Toronto FC in Canada.

'I can't believe you're leaving!' Harry told him as they said goodbye. It was one of his saddest days at White Hart Lane. 'It won't be the same around here without you.'

Jermain smiled. 'It's time for me to move on and it's time for you to step up. I want you to wear this next season.'

It was Jermain's Number 18 shirt. Harry couldn't believe it.

'Wow, are you sure?' he asked. It would be such an honour to follow in his hero's footsteps. 'I promise to do you proud!'

Harry did just that when he finally got his first Premier League start for Tottenham against Sunderland in April. After years of waiting, Harry's time had come. He had never been so nervous in his life.

'Relax, just do what you do best,' Sherwood told him before kick-off. He was showing lots of faith in his young striker. 'Score!'

In the second half, Christian Eriksen curled a beautiful cross into the six-yard box. As the ball bounced, Harry made a late run and snuck in ahead of the centre-back to steer the ball into the bottom corner.

Goooooooooooooooooooooaaaaaaaaaaaaaaalllllllllllllllll llllllllllll!!!!!!!!!!!!!!!!!!!!

Harry was buzzing. With his arms out wide like an aeroplane, he ran towards the Spurs fans near the corner flag. He had scored his first Premier League goal for Tottenham. It was time to celebrate in style.

Aaron Lennon chased after him and jumped up on his back. 'Yes, mate, what a goal!' he cheered.

Harry was soon in the middle of a big player hug. He was part of the team now and that was the greatest feeling ever.

There were six more league matches in the season and Harry started all of them. He was full of confidence and full of goals. Against West Bromwich, Aaron dribbled down the right wing and crossed into the six-yard box. Harry jumped highest and headed the ball past the defender on the line.

Goooooooooooooooooooooaaaaaaaaaaaaaaaaalllllllllllll llllllllllllllllll!!!!!!!!!!!!!!!!!!!

A week later, they did it again. Aaron crossed the ball and Harry flicked it in. 2–1 to Tottenham!

'You've scored in three games in a row,' Emmanuel Adebayor shouted over the White Hart Lane noise. 'You're a goal machine!'

Harry had also already become a favourite with

the fans. They loved nothing more than cheering for their local hero.

> *He's one of our own,*
> *He's one of our own,*
> *Harry Kane – he's one of our own!*

Even an own goal against West Ham didn't stop Harry's rise. In only six weeks, he had gone from sub to England's hottest new striker.

'What an end to the season!' Tim Sherwood said as they walked off the pitch together. 'You'll be playing for a different manager next season, but don't worry. If you keep banging in the goals, you're going to be a Tottenham hero, no matter what!'

CHAPTER 18

EXCITING TIMES AT TOTTENHAM

'Do you think he'll bring in a big new striker?' Harry asked Andros during preseason.

His friend and teammate just shrugged. They would have to wait and see what the new Tottenham manager, Mauricio Pochettino, would do.

As the 2014–15 season kicked off, Spurs had signed a new goalkeeper, some new defenders and a new midfielder. But no new striker! That left only Emmanuel, Roberto and Harry. Harry was feeling really good about his chances. He worked extra hard to impress Pochettino.

'Great work, you've certainly got the desire that I'm looking for in my players,' his manager told him.

'This could be a huge season for you!'

Emmanuel started up front against West Ham in the Premier League but it was Harry, not Roberto, who came on for the last ten minutes. That was a good sign. If he kept scoring goals in other competitions, surely Pochettino would have no choice but to let him play. Harry got five goals in the Europa League and three in the League Cup.

'Kane needs to start in the Premier League!' the fans shouted in the stands.

Harry was making a name for himself with the England Under-21s too. He loved representing his country, especially in the big games. Against France, he positioned himself between the two centre-backs and waited like a predator. When Tom Ince played the through-ball, Harry was already on the move, chasing after it. He was too smart for the French defenders and he chipped his shot over the diving goalkeeper.

Goooooooooooooooooooaaaaaaaaaaaaaaaaaaaalllllllllll llllllllllllll!!!!!!!!!!!!!!!

Two minutes later, Tom crossed from the right and

Harry was there in the six-yard box to tap the ball into the net.

'That's a proper striker's goal!' his teammate told him as they celebrated together.

Tom was right. Harry was a real goalscorer now, always in the right place at the right time. 'That's thirteen goals in twelve games!' he replied proudly.

By November 2014, there was lots of pressure on Pochettino to give Harry more game-time in the Premier League. Away at Aston Villa, he came on for Emmanuel with half an hour to go.

'Come on, we can still win this match!' his old friend Ryan Mason told him. Soon, Andros was on the pitch too. They were all living their Spurs dreams together.

In injury time, Tottenham won a free kick just outside the penalty area. It was Harry's last chance to save the day for Spurs. Érik Lamela wanted to take it but Harry wasn't letting his big opportunity go. He took a long, deep breath to calm his beating heart. He looked down at the ball and then up at the goal. 'This is going in!' he told himself.

He pumped his legs hard as he ran towards the ball. He needed as much power as possible. But rather than kicking it with the top of his boot, he kicked it with the side. As the ball swerved through the air, it deflected off the head of a Villa defender and past their scrambling keeper.

Gooooooooooooooooaaaaaaaaaaaaaaaaaaallllllllllllllllll llllllllll!!!!!!!!!!!!!!!!!!!

It was the biggest goal that Harry had ever scored. He ran screaming towards the corner flag with all of his teammates behind him. In all the excitement, Harry threw himself down onto the grass for his favourite childhood celebration – the Klinsmann dive. Soon, he was at the bottom of a pile of happy players.

'What a beauty!' Danny Rose cheered in his face.

After scoring the match-winner, Harry was the talk of Tottenham. The fans had a new local hero and they wanted him to play every minute of every game. Against Hull City, Christian Eriksen's free kick hit the post but who was there to score the rebound? Harry!

Even when he didn't score for a few matches, Pochettino stuck with Harry. As a young player, he was still learning about playing at the top level.

'I believe in you,' his manager told him. 'You've got lots of potential and you've got the hunger to improve.'

With Pochettino's support, Harry bounced back against Swansea City. As Christian whipped in the corner kick, Harry made a late run into the box. He leapt high above his marker and powered his header down into the bottom corner.

Goooooooooooooooooooooaaaaaaaaaaaaaalllllllllllllll lllllllllll!!!!!!!!!!!!!!!!!

Once he started scoring, Harry couldn't stop. He was such a natural finisher. On Boxing Day, Harry even scored against one of his old teams. Only eighteen months earlier, he had been sitting on the Leicester City bench. Now, he was causing them all kinds of problems as Tottenham's star striker. With hard work and great support, he was proving everyone wrong yet again.

Pochettino was delighted with his young striker's

form but he didn't want him to burn out. 'Get some rest because we've got big games coming up.'

Harry was so excited about the 2015 fixture list ahead – Chelsea on New Year's Day and then a few weeks later, the biggest game of them all: The North London Derby – Tottenham vs Arsenal.

'Don't worry, boss,' he said with a big smile. 'I'll be ready to score some more!'

CHAPTER 19

GOALS, GOALS AND MORE GOALS

As the Tottenham team walked out of the tunnel at White Hart Lane, Harry was second in line, right behind their goalkeeper and captain, Hugo Lloris. He had come so far in the last eighteen months – it was still hard to believe. There were thousands of fans in the stadium, cheering loudly for their team, and cheering loudly for him.

He's one of our own,
He's one of our own,
Harry Kane – he's one of our own!

Harry looked down at the young mascot who was

holding his hand. Ten years before, that had been one of his biggest dreams – to walk out on to the pitch with his Spurs heroes. Now, he was the Spurs hero, so what was his new dream? Goals, goals and more goals, starting against their London rivals Chelsea.

'Come on, we can't let them beat us again!' Harry shouted to Ryan and Andros. They were all fired up and ready to win.

Chelsea took the lead, but Harry didn't let his head drop. It just made him even more determined to score. He got the ball on the left wing and dribbled infield. He beat one player and then shrugged off another. He only had one thing on his mind – goals. When he was just outside the penalty area, he looked up.

He was still a long way out and there were lots of Chelsea players in his way, but Harry could shoot from anywhere. The Premier League would soon know just how lethal he was. For now, however, the defenders gave him just enough space. His low, powerful strike skidded across the wet grass, past the keeper and right into the bottom corner.

Goooooooooooooooaaaaaaaaaaaaaaaaalllllllllllllllllllllllllllll!!!!!!!!!!!!!!!!!!!!!!!!

Game on! Harry ran towards the Tottenham fans and jumped into the air. He was used to scoring goals now, but this was one of his best and most important.

'You could outshoot a cowboy!' Kyle Walker joked as he climbed up on Harry's back.

At half-time, Spurs were winning 3–1 but Harry wanted more. 'We're not safe yet,' he warned his teammates. 'We've got to keep going!'

As the pass came towards him, Harry was just inside the Chelsea box with his back to goal. It didn't look dangerous at first but one lovely touch and spin later, it was very dangerous indeed. Harry stayed calm and placed his shot past the goalkeeper. It was like he'd been scoring top goals for years.

'Kane, that's gorgeous!' the TV commentator shouted. 'How good is *he*?'

The answer was: unstoppable. Even one of the best defences in the world couldn't handle him.

The match finished 5–3. It was a famous victory for Tottenham and Harry was their hero. After shaking hands with the Chelsea players, he walked around the pitch, clapping the supporters. Harry loved making them happy.

'If we play like that against Arsenal, we'll win that too!' he told Andros.

Harry got ready for the big North London Derby by scoring goals, goals and more goals. The timing was perfect; he was in the best form of his life just as Arsenal were coming to White Hart Lane. Revenge would be so sweet for Harry. Arsenal would soon realise their big mistake in letting him go.

After five minutes, Harry cut in from the left and curled a brilliant shot towards goal. He got ready to celebrate because the ball was heading for the bottom corner yet again. But the Arsenal keeper made a great save to tip it just round the post. So close! Harry put his hands to his head for a second but then kept going. If at first you don't score, shoot, shoot again.

At half-time, Tottenham were losing 1–0. 'We're

still in this game,' Pochettino told his players in the dressing room. 'If we keep creating chances, we'll score!'

When Érik took the corner, Harry stood lurking near the back post. He was waiting for the rebound. The keeper saved Mousa Dembélé's header but the ball bounced down in the box. Before the Arsenal defenders could react, Harry pounced to sweep it into the net.

Goooooooooooooooooooaaaaaaaaaaaaaaaallllllllllllllll llllllllll!!!!!!!!!!!!!!!!!!!

Harry roared and pumped his fists. Scoring for Spurs against Arsenal meant the world to him. He had dreamed about it ever since his first trip to White Hart Lane.

'Right, let's go and win this now!' Harry told his teammates.

With five minutes to go, it looked like it was going to be a draw. As Nabil Benteleb's cross drifted into the box, Harry's eyes never left the ball. He took a couple of steps backwards and then leapt high above Laurent Koscielny. It was a very difficult chance. To score, his header would have to be really powerful and really accurate.

As soon as the ball left his head, Harry knew that he had got the angle right. It was looping towards the corner but would the keeper have time to stop it? No, Harry's perfect technique gave David Ospina no chance.

Goooooooooooooooooaaaaaaaaaaaaaaaaallllllllllllllllll llllll!!!!!!!!!!!!!!!!!!!

As the ball landed in the net, Harry turned away to celebrate. What a moment! With the adrenaline flooding through his veins, he slid across the grass, screaming. As he looked up, he could see the Spurs fans going crazy in the crowd. All that joy was because of him!

The final minutes felt like hours but eventually, the referee blew the final whistle. Tottenham 2, Arsenal 1! The party went on and on, both down on the pitch and up in the stands.

'I might as well retire now!' Harry joked with Ryan. 'Nothing will ever beat scoring the winner in the North London Derby.'

'Not even playing for England?' his teammate asked him. 'Mate, Roy Hodgson would be a fool not to call you up to the squad!'

Harry was desperate to play for his country. Like his hero Becks, he wanted to be the national captain one day. After doing well for the Under-21s, he was now ready to step up into the senior team. He had won both the January and February Premier League Player of the Month awards. Then, in March, Harry got the call he had been waiting for.

'I'm in!' he told his partner Katie excitedly. He wanted to tell the whole world.

'In what?' she asked. 'What are you talking about?'

'The England squad!'

The amazing news spread throughout his family. Everyone wanted a ticket to watch his international debut.

'I might not even play!' Harry warned them, but they didn't care.

He was glad to see that lots of his Tottenham teammates were in the England team too. Training with superstars like Wayne Rooney and Gary Cahill would be a lot less scary with Kyle, Andros and Danny by his side. A week later, Ryan also joined the Spurs gang.

'Thank goodness Fabian Delph got injured!' he laughed. 'I was gutted to be the only one left behind.'

They were all named as substitutes for the Euro 2016 qualifier against Lithuania at Wembley. But would any of them get to come on and play? They all sat there on the England bench, crossing their fingers and shaking with nerves.

With seventy minutes gone, England were winning 3–0. It was time for Roy Hodgson to give his young players a chance. Harry's England youth teammate Ross Barkley was the first substitute and Harry himself was the second. He was replacing Wayne Rooney.

'Good luck!' Ryan and Andros said, patting him on the back.

Harry tried to forget that he was making his England debut at Wembley. That was something he could enjoy later when the match was over. For now, he just wanted to score.

As Raheem Sterling dribbled down the left wing, Harry took up his favourite striking position near the back post. Raheem's cross came straight towards him; he couldn't miss. Harry had all the time in the world to place his header past the keeper.

Goooooooooooooooooaaaaaaaaaaaaaaaalllllllllllllllllll llllllllllll!!!!!!!!!!!!!!

In his excitement, Harry bumped straight into the assistant referee. 'Sorry!' he called over his shoulder as he ran towards the corner flag.

'Was that your first touch?' Danny Welbeck asked as they celebrated.

'No, it was my third or fourth,' Harry replied with a cheeky grin. 'But I've only been on the field for about a minute!'

There had been so many highlights for Harry during the 2014–15 season already, but this was the best of all. He had scored for England on his debut. All of his dedication had paid off and he felt so proud of his achievements. Harry's childhood dream had come true.

CHAPTER 20

HARRY AND DELE

'So, do you think you can score as many this season?'
Charlie asked his brother.

Lots of people thought Harry's twenty-one Premier
League goals were a one-off, a fluke. They argued that
the PFA Young Player of the Year wouldn't be as good
in 2015–16 because defenders would know all about
him now. They would mark him out of the game.

But Harry knew that wasn't true. 'Of course I can.
In fact, I'm aiming for even more this time!'

Charlie smiled. 'Good, because when you scored
those goals against Arsenal, the guys in the pub
bought me drinks all night. Sometimes, it's fun being
your brother!'

Harry was still getting used to his fame. It was crazy! Every time he took his Labradors Brady and Wilson out for a walk, there were cameras waiting for him. They even took photos of Katie when she went out shopping.

'Our normal life is over!' she complained as she flicked through the newspapers.

After a very disappointing Euro 2015 with the England Under-21s, Harry was really looking forward to the new season. It would be his first as Tottenham's top striker. With Emmanuel gone, Harry now wore the famous Number 10 shirt. He was following in the footsteps of Spurs legends Jimmy Greaves, Gary Lineker and Harry's own hero, Teddy Sheringham.

Pochettino had strengthened the Spurs squad over the summer. They had signed Son Heung-min, a goal-scoring winger, and Dele Alli, a young attacking midfielder.

Harry and Dele clicked straight away. After a few training sessions, Dele knew where Harry would run, and Harry knew where to make space for Dele.

It was like they had been playing together for years. Soon, they were making up cool goal celebrations.

'It's like you guys are back in the school playground!' captain Hugo Lloris teased, but it was great to see them getting along so well.

Despite all of his excitement, Harry didn't score a single goal in August 2015. The newspapers kept calling him a 'one-season wonder' but that only made him more determined to prove them wrong.

'You're playing well and working hard for the team,' Pochettino reassured him. 'As soon as you get one goal, you'll get your confidence back.'

Against Manchester City, Christian's brilliant free kick bounced back off the post and landed right at Harry's feet. He was in lots of space and the goalkeeper was lying on the ground. Surely he couldn't miss an open goal? Some strikers might have passed the ball carefully into the net to make sure but instead, Harry curled it into the top corner.

Gooooooooooooooooooaaaaaaaaaaaaaaaaalllllllllllllllllll llllllllll!!!!!!!!!!!!!!!!!!!

Harry was delighted to score but most of all, he was relieved. His goal drought was over. Now, his season could really get started.

'Phew, I thought you were going to blaze that one over the bar!' Dele joked.

After that, Harry and Dele became the Premier League's deadliest double act. Between them, they had power, skill, pace and incredible shooting. By the end of February 2016, Tottenham were only two points behind Leicester City at the top of the table.

'If we keep playing like this, we'll be champions!' Pochettino told his players.

Every single one of them believed it. Spurs had the best defence in the league and were also one of the best attacking sides. Dele, Érik and Christian created lots of chances, and Harry scored lots of goals. It was one big, happy team effort. The pranks and teasing never stopped.

'How long do you have to wear that thing for?' Dele asked during training one day. 'Halloween was months ago, you know!'

'Very funny,' Harry replied, giving his teammate a friendly punch. He was wearing a plastic face mask to protect his broken nose. 'Who knows, maybe it will bring me luck and I'll wear it forever!'

'Let's hope not!' Christian laughed.

Next up was the game that Harry had been waiting months for – the North London Derby. Could they win it again? Arsenal were only three points behind Spurs, so the match was even more important than usual.

'Come on lads, we've got to win this!' Harry shouted in the dressing room before kick-off, and all of his teammates cheered.

The atmosphere at White Hart Lane was incredible. The fans never stopped singing, even when Tottenham went 1–0 down. They believed that their team would bounce back, especially with Harry up front.

Early in the second half, Harry thought he had scored the equaliser. The goalkeeper saved his vicious shot, but surely he was behind the goal-line?

'That's in!' Harry screamed to the referee. But the

technology showed that a tiny part of the ball hadn't crossed the line.

It was very frustrating but there was no point in complaining. Harry would just have to keep shooting until he got the whole ball into the net.

In the end, it was Toby Alderweireld who made it 1–1. Tottenham were playing well, but they needed a second goal to take the lead.

The ball was heading out for an Arsenal goal-kick but Dele managed to reach it and flick it back to his best friend, Harry. It looked like an impossible angle but with the supporters cheering him on, anything seemed possible. In a flash, Harry curled the ball up over the keeper and into the far corner.

Goooooooooooooooooooooaaaaaaaaaaaaaaaaaaaaaallll llllllllllllllllll!!!!!!!!!!!!!!!

It was one of the best goals Harry had ever scored. He felt on top of the world. He took off his mask as he ran and slid across the grass. Dele was right behind him and gave him a big hug.

'Maybe you *should* keep wearing that!' he joked.

Tottenham couldn't quite hold on for another big

victory. A draw wasn't the result that Spurs wanted, but Harry would never forget his incredible goal.

'We're still in this title race,' Pochettino urged his disappointed players. 'We just have to win every match until the end of the season.'

Harry and Dele did their best to make their Premier League dream come true. Dele set up both of Harry's goals against Aston Villa and they scored two each against Stoke City. But with three games of the season to go, Tottenham were seven points behind Leicester.

'If we don't beat Chelsea, our season's over,' Harry warned his teammates.

At half-time, it was all going according to plan. Harry scored the first goal and Son made it 2–0. They were cruising to victory but in the second half, they fell apart. All season, the Spurs players had stayed cool and focused but suddenly, they got angry and made silly mistakes. It finished 2–2.

'We threw it away!' Harry groaned as he walked off the pitch. He was absolutely devastated. They had worked so hard all season. And for what?

'We've learnt a lot this year,' Pochettino told his players once everyone had calmed down. 'I know you feel awful right now but you should be so proud of yourselves. Next season, we'll come back stronger and win the league!'

There was one bit of good news that made Harry feel a little better. With twenty-five goals, he had won the Premier League Golden Boot, beating Sergio Agüero and Jamie Vardy.

'And they said I was a one-season wonder!' Harry told his brother Charlie as they played golf together. A smile spread slowly across his face. He loved proving people wrong.

CHAPTER 21

ENGLAND

When Harry first joined the England squad back
in 2015, he was really nervous. It was a massive
honour to represent his country but there was a lot
of pressure too. If he didn't play well, there were lots
of other great players that could take his place. Plus,
it was scary being the new kid.

'You'll get used to this,' Wayne Rooney reassured
him. 'I remember when I first got the call-up. I was
only seventeen and it was terrifying! Just try to
ignore the talk and enjoy yourself.'

Wayne helped Harry to feel more relaxed around
the other senior players. They had fun playing golf
and table tennis together. They were nice guys and
Harry soon felt like one of the lads.

'France, here we come!' he cheered happily.

England qualified for Euro 2016 with ten wins out of ten. Harry added to his debut goal with a cheeky chip against San Marino and a low strike against Switzerland.

'At this rate, you're going to take my place in the team!' Wayne told him.

Harry shook his head. 'No, we'll play together up front!'

When Roy Hodgson announced his England squad for Euro 2016, Harry's name was there. He was delighted. There were four other strikers – Wayne, Jamie Vardy, Daniel Sturridge and Marcus Rashford – but none of them were scoring as many goals as him.

'You'll definitely play,' his brother Charlie told him.

Harry couldn't wait for his first major international tournament. His body felt pretty tired after a long Premier League season with Tottenham, but nothing was going to stop him.

'I really think we've got a good chance of winning it,' he told Dele, who was in the squad for France too.

His friend was feeling just as confident. 'If we play like we do for Spurs, we can definitely go all the way!'

Harry and Dele were both in the starting line-up for England's first group match against Russia. With Wayne now playing in midfield, Harry was England's number-one striker. He carried the country's great expectations in his shooting boots.

'I *have* to score!' he told himself as the match kicked off in Marseille.

England dominated the game but after seventy minutes, it was still 0–0. Harry got more and more frustrated. He was struggling to find the burst of pace that got him past Premier League defences. What was going wrong? His legs felt heavy and clumsy.

'Just be patient,' Wayne told him. 'If you keep getting into the right areas, the goal will come.'

When they won a free kick on the edge of the Russia box, Harry stood over the ball with Wayne and his Tottenham teammate Eric Dier. Everyone expected Harry to take it but as he ran up, he dummied the ball. Eric stepped up instead and curled the ball into the top corner. 1–0!

'Thanks for letting me take it,' he said to Harry as they celebrated the goal.

'No problem!' he replied. England had the lead and that was all that mattered.

But just as they were heading for a winning start to the tournament, Russia scored a late header. As he watched the ball flying towards the top corner, Harry's heart sank. He was very disappointed with the result and with his own performance in particular. It wasn't good enough. If he didn't improve, he would lose his place to Jamie or Daniel or Marcus.

'I believe in you, we all believe in you,' Hodgson told him after the game. 'So, believe in *yourself*!'

Harry tried not to read the player ratings in the English newspapers. Instead, he focused on bouncing back. If he could score a goal against Wales in the next game that would make everything better again.

But at half-time, it was looking like another bad day for Harry and England. He worked hard for the team but his goal-scoring touch was gone. The ball just wouldn't go in. When Gareth Bale scored a free kick to put Wales 1–0 up, Harry feared the worst.

'We need a quick goal in the second half,'
Hodgson told the team in the dressing room. 'Jamie
and Daniel, you'll be coming on to replace Harry and
Raheem.'

Harry stared down at the floor. Was that the end
of his tournament? He was really upset but he had to
accept the manager's decision.

Harry watched the second half from the bench
and cheered on his teammates. He was a good team
player. When Jamie scored the equaliser, he joined in
the celebrations. When Daniel scored the winner in
injury time, he sprinted to the corner flag to jump
on him.

'Get in!' he screamed.

It was only after the final whistle that Harry started
worrying again. Had he lost his place in the team, or
would he get another chance against Slovakia?

'I'm sorry but I've got to start Daniel and Jamie in
the next match,' Hodgson told him. 'Rest up and get
ready for the next round. We need you back, firing!'

Without Harry, England couldn't find a goal, but
0–0 was enough to take them through to the Round

of 16. He would get one more opportunity to score against Iceland, and he was pumped up for the biggest game of his international career.

It started brilliantly. Raheem was fouled in the box and Wayne scored the penalty. 1–0! It was a huge relief to get an early goal but two minutes later, it was 1–1.

'Come on, focus!' Joe Hart shouted at his teammates.

Harry and Dele both hit powerful long-range strikes that fizzed just over the crossbar. England looked in control of the game, but then Iceland scored again.

'No!' Harry shouted. His dream tournament was turning into an absolute nightmare.

England needed a hero, and quickly. Daniel crossed the ball to Harry in his favourite position near the back post. It was too low for a header so he went for the volley. Harry watched the ball carefully onto his foot and struck it beautifully. Unfortunately, it just wasn't his day, or his tournament. The goalkeeper jumped up high to make a good save. So close! Harry put his hands to his face – he was so desperate to score.

As the minutes ticked by, England started panicking. Harry's free kick flew miles wide. What a disaster! The boos from the fans grew louder.

'Stay calm, we've got plenty of time!' Hodgson called out from the touchline.

That time, however, ran out. At the final whistle, the Iceland players celebrated and the England players sank to their knees. They were out of the Euros after a terrible, embarrassing defeat.

As he trudged off the pitch, Harry was in shock. It was the worst feeling ever. He felt like he had really let his country down. Would they ever forgive him?

To take his mind off the disappointment, Harry watched American Football and focused on his future goals. With Tottenham, he would be playing in the Champions League for the first time, and trying to win the Premier League title. With England, he would be playing in the qualifiers for World Cup 2018. There were lots of exciting challenges ahead.

'I need to make things right!' Harry told himself.

CHAPTER 22

TOTTENHAM FOR
THE TITLE?

'Argggghhhhhhhhhhhhhhhhhh!' Harry screamed as he lay down on the turf. He tried to stay calm but it felt like really bad news. As he waved for the physio, the pain got worse and worse. White Hart Lane went quiet. The Spurs fans waited nervously to see whether their star striker could carry on.

'You're not singing anymore!' the opposing Sunderland fans cheered bitterly.

If only Harry hadn't slid in for the tackle. Tottenham were already winning 1–0 thanks to his goal. That was his job: scoring goals, not making tackles. But Harry always worked hard for the team. As he went to block the Sunderland centre-back, his right ankle twisted awkwardly in the grass. If the injury wasn't too serious, Harry promised himself that he would never defend again.

Unfortunately, it *was* serious. Harry tried to get up and play on but that wasn't possible. He hobbled over to the touchline and sat down again. The Spurs fans cheered and clapped their hero but Harry's match was over. He was carried down the tunnel on a stretcher.

'There's good news and there's bad news,' the doctor told him after the X-rays. 'The good news is that there's no fracture. The bad news is that there's ligament damage.'

Harry wasn't a medical expert but he knew that 'ligament damage' meant no football for a while. 'How long will I be out of action?' he asked, fearing a big number.

'It's too early to say but you should prepare yourself for eight weeks out. Hopefully, it won't be that long.'

Eight weeks! If everything went well, Harry would be back before December but it was still a big blow. His 2016–17 season had only just started. He had only played in one Champions League match.

Tottenham needed him.

'Who's going to get all our goals now?' he asked.

'Without you hogging all the chances, I'll score loads more!' Dele replied.

It was good to have Katie and his teammates around to cheer Harry up. It was going to be a boring, difficult couple of months for him. He would just have to recover as quickly as possible. To keep himself going, Harry picked out a key date in the calendar: 6 November. The North London Derby – that was what he was aiming for.

'I always score against Arsenal!' Harry reminded everyone.

Thanks to lots of hard work in the gym, he made it just in time. Harry was delighted to be back on the pitch, even if he wasn't at his best. Early in the second half, Tottenham won a penalty and Harry quickly grabbed the ball. It was the perfect chance to get a comeback goal.

He took a long, deep breath and waited for the referee's whistle. As the Arsenal keeper dived to his left, Harry placed it down the middle.

*Goooooooooooooooooaaaaaaaaaaaaaaaalllllllllllllllll
lllllll!!!!!!!!!!!!!!!!!!!!!!!*

He was back! Harry pumped his fists at the crowd
as his teammates jumped on him.

'What a cool finish!' Son cheered.

Harry didn't last the full match, but he was pleased
with his return. 'If I want to win the Golden Boot
again, I've got some catching up to do!' he told
Pochettino.

Tottenham got knocked out in the Champions
League Group Stage, but Harry still had time to grab
his first goals in the competition.

'Never mind, we've just got to focus on the
Premier League title now,' he told Dele. 'We'll
conquer Europe next year!'

After all his goals, Harry became a transfer target
for Real Madrid and Manchester United. Tottenham
wanted to keep their local hero for as long as
possible, so they offered Harry a big new contract
until 2020. Saying no didn't even cross his mind.

'I can't leave!' Harry said happily. 'This is my home
and we've got trophies to win.'

To celebrate, he went on another scoring spree. Two against Watford, three against West Brom, three against Stoke, two against Everton. By March, he was up to nineteen goals and at the top of the goal-scoring charts again.

'Congratulations, you're back where you belong,' Katie told him.

Harry was pleased but the Premier League title was his number one aim. Spurs were in second place behind Chelsea. Harry would give his all to catch them.

For Harry, winning the 2017 FA Cup was aim number two. In the quarter-finals, Tottenham faced his old club Millwall. So much had changed in the five years since his loan spell there. He would always be grateful to the Lions for their support but that didn't mean he would take it easy on them. Trophies always came first.

As soon as the ball came to him, Harry shot at goal. The Millwall keeper saved it but Harry didn't even notice. He was lying on the grass in agony.

'Is it your right ankle again?' the physio asked after rushing over to him.

Harry just nodded. Was it the same injury all over again? He couldn't bear to think about another eight weeks on the sidelines. He managed to limp off the pitch and down the tunnel. He didn't need to use the stretcher this time and that was a good sign.

'There is ligament damage,' the doctors confirmed, 'but it's not as serious as before. We'll do our best to get you back for the semi-final.'

With a target to aim for, Harry was determined to recover in time. He was back in action two weeks before their big cup match against Chelsea. There was even time for him to score a goal.

'See, I'm feeling sharp!' he promised Pochettino. There was no way that he could miss playing in the FA Cup semi-final. He was a big game player and his team needed him.

The atmosphere at Wembley was electric. As usual, Harry was the second Spurs player out of the tunnel. As he looked up, he could see big blocks of white in the crowd.

'*Tottenham! Tottenham! Tottenham!*'

If the stadium was this loud for the semi-final, what

would the final be like? But Harry couldn't get ahead of himself. He had to focus on beating Chelsea first.

The Blues took the lead but with Harry on the pitch, Spurs were always in the game. He stayed onside at the front post to flick on Christian's low cross. Thanks to his clever touch, the ball flew right into the bottom corner.

Goooooooooooooooooooaaaaaaaaaaaaaaaaaaaallllllllllll llllllllllllllllll!!!!!!!!!!!

'It's like you've got eyes in the back of your head!' Christian cheered as they hugged.

'Why would I need that?' Harry asked. 'The goal doesn't move – it's always in the same place!'

Despite his best efforts, Chelsea scored two late goals to win 4–2. It was very disappointing but Tottenham's season wasn't over yet.

'We've got five Premier League matches left,' Harry told Dele. 'If we can get all fifteen points, the pressure is on Chelsea.'

The first three points came at White Hart Lane in the North London Derby against Arsenal. Dele got the first goal and Harry scored the second from the penalty spot. The dream was still alive! But at West Ham a week later, Spurs fell apart again. Harry, Dele and Christian tried and tried but they couldn't get the goal they needed. In the second half, Tottenham panicked and conceded a silly goal. The 1-0 defeat left them seven points behind Chelsea.

'No, the title race isn't over yet,' Pochettino told his players. 'Come on, let's finish on a high!'

There was no chance of Harry relaxing. Even if he didn't win the Premier League, he could still win the Golden Boot. He was only three goals behind Everton's Romelu Lukaku with three games to go. Harry closed the gap to two with a neat flick against Manchester United.

'Three goals against Leicester and Hull? I can do that!' he told Dele.

'But what if Lukaku scores again?'

Dele was right; Harry needed to aim even higher. Against Leicester, his first goal was a tap-in, his second was a header and the third was a rocket from the edge of the penalty area. Harry had another amazing hat-trick but he wasn't finished yet. In injury time, he got the ball in the same position and scored again!

Harry was pleased with his four goals but he couldn't help asking himself, 'Why couldn't I do that against West Ham?' He was never satisfied.

Harry would have to think about that later, though. With one game to go, he was on 26 goals and Lukaku was on 24. At the final whistle in the Arsenal vs Everton game, Lukaku was up to 25 goals for Everton thanks to a penalty, but meanwhile Harry was way ahead on 29! With two fantastic finishes and a tap-in, he had grabbed yet another hat-trick against Hull.

'Wow, you were only two goals off the Premier League record,' his proud dad told him. 'And you missed eight games through injury!'

Harry was delighted with his second Golden Boot in a row but it didn't make up for another season without a trophy. Tottenham kept getting so close to glory but would they ever be crowned champions? Harry, the local hero, never stopped believing.

CHAPTER 23

ONE OF EUROPE'S FINEST

Harry jumped up in the England wall but the free kick flew past him and into the top corner. As he watched, his heart sank. Scotland were winning 2–1 at Hampden Park with a few minutes to go.

'Come on, we can't lose this!' Harry shouted to his teammates.

England were unbeaten in qualification for the 2018 World Cup and this, in June 2017, was a key match against their British rivals. It was also Harry's first match as the national captain. For all of these reasons, he refused to let it end in an embarrassing defeat.

With seconds to go, Kyle Walker passed to Raheem

Sterling on the left wing. Harry was surrounded by Scottish defenders but he was clever enough to escape. The centre-backs watched Raheem's high cross sail over their heads and thought they were safe. But they weren't. They had missed Harry's brilliant run to the back post.

There wasn't enough time or space to take a touch, so Harry went for a side-foot volley. With incredible technique and composure, he guided his shot past the keeper.

Gooooooooooooooooooooaaaaaaaaaaaalllllllllllllllll lllll!!!!!!!!!!!!!!

It was another big goal in a big game. Under pressure, Harry hardly ever failed.

'You're a born leader,' England manager Gareth Southgate told him after the match. 'That's why I gave you the captain's armband.'

At twenty-four, Harry wasn't a bright young talent anymore. After three excellent seasons, he was now an experienced player with lots of responsibility for club and country. Now he felt ready to take the next step and become one of Europe's finest.

'I might not have as much skill as Cristiano Ronaldo and Lionel Messi but I can score as many goals,' he told Dele.

Harry was full of ambition ahead of the 2017–18 season. It was time to shine in the Champions League as well as the Premier League. But first, he had to get August out of the way.

'Maybe I should just take the month off!' Harry joked at home with Katie.

No matter how hard he tried and how many shots he took, he just couldn't score. He was trying to ignore all the talk about his August goal curse. Their beautiful baby daughter was certainly helping to take his mind off things.

'Yes, you could stay home and change Ivy's nappies with me!' Katie replied with a smile. She knew that Harry could never stay away from football. He loved it so much.

On 1 September, he travelled with England to play against Malta. 'Don't worry, I've got this,' he told his teammates. 'August is over!'

As Dele twisted and turned in the penalty area,

Harry got into space and called for the pass. The goalkeeper rushed out but he calmly slotted the ball into the net.

Goooooooooooooooooooaaaaaaaaaaaaaaaallllllllllllllll llllllll!!!!!!!!!!!!!!!!!

On the touchline, Southgate pumped his fists. Tottenham fans all over the world did the same. Their goal machine was back.

'Finally!' Dele teased him. 'What would you do without me?'

Harry was too relieved to fight back. 'Thanks, you're the best!' he replied.

Once he scored one, Harry usually scored two. He did it against Malta and then he did it against Everton in the Premier League. As always, Harry's timing was perfect. Tottenham were about to start their Champions League campaign against German giants Borussia Dortmund.

'They picked the wrong time to face me!' he said confidently.

Harry won the ball on the halfway line, headed it forward and chased after it. He wasn't letting anyone get in his way. As he entered the Dortmund penalty area, the defender tried to push him wide. Harry didn't mind; he could score from any angle! Before the keeper could react, the ball flew past him.

The Tottenham fans went wild.

> *He's one of our own,*
> *He's one of our own,*
> *Harry Kane – he's one of our own!*

Harry went hunting for another goal and he got it.

'He just gets better and better!' the commentator marvelled.

It was Harry's first Champions League double, but he wanted a third. He was always hungry for more goals. With a few minutes to go, Pochettino took him off.

'The hat-trick will have to wait until next week!' he told his star striker, patting him on the back.

The APOEL Nicosia defence was prepared for Harry's arrival but there was nothing that they could do to stop him. He made it look so easy. He scored his first goal with his left foot and the second with his right. There was half an hour left to get his third but he only needed five minutes.

Kieran Trippier curled the ball in from the right and Harry ran from the edge of the box to glance it down into the bottom corner. All that heading practice had been worth it.

Gooooooooooooooooooooooaaaaaaaaaaaaaaaalllllllllll llllllllllllll!!!!!!!!!!!!!!!

Harry ran towards Kieran and gave him a big hug. He was always grateful for the assists but this one was particularly special. Harry had his first ever Champions League hat-trick.

'That was perfect!' he told Son afterwards, clutching the match ball tightly.

'Yeah, it was a good win,' his teammate replied.

'No, I mean it was a perfect hat-trick,' Harry explained. 'One with my right foot, one with my left, and one with my head. That's the first time I've ever done that!'

Son laughed. 'You score so many goals. How can you remember them all?'

Every single goal was important to Harry and he often watched videos of his matches to help him improve. He never stopped working on his game.

'Is Kane the best striker in Europe right now?' the newspapers asked. Harry had already scored thirty-six goals by September and he still had three months of the year to go!

To keep his feet on the ground, Harry thought back to his early football days. Arsenal had rejected him and Tottenham had nearly done the same. As an eleven-year-old boy, he had told his hero David Beckham that he wanted to play at Wembley for England. Thanks to lots of practice and determination, Harry had achieved that dream and so much more.

His shirt now hung next to Becks' shirt in the hallway at Chingford Foundation School. Harry had the future at his goalscoring feet. He would do everything possible to lead England to World Cup glory in Russia.

CHAPTER 24

FOOTBALL'S COMING HOME!

Harry couldn't wait for the biggest challenge of his football career so far. Not only was he on his way to Russia to play in his first World Cup, but the England manager, Gareth Southgate, had also picked him to captain his country.

With Three Lions on his shirt and the armband on his sleeve, could Harry lead his nation to glory again, after fifty-two years of hurt? It looked unlikely. At the 2014 World Cup, England had finished bottom of their group and at Euro 2016, they had lost to Iceland in the second round. Harry, however, was full of confidence – as always.

'I believe we can win the World Cup,' he told

the media. 'We're going to fight and give everything we've got.'

The England team spirit was growing stronger and stronger every day. Yes, they were young but they weren't going to let that stop them. They had the talent to succeed and they got on really well together, no matter which Premier League club they played for. Kyle was one of Harry's best friends – so what if he had moved from Tottenham to Manchester City?

'We're all playing for *England* now!' everyone agreed.

It was time to give the fans something to cheer about. That task began against Tunisia, one of the top African nations. After the peace and quiet of their base camp, the England players finally experienced the amazing World Cup atmosphere. All that noise, all that colour – what a buzz!

'This is it,' Harry told his teammates, 'this is what we've been dreaming about since we were kids!'

With the adrenaline pumping through their bodies, England started brilliantly. John Stones lept up high to head Ashley Young's corner towards the top corner. Surely, it was going in...no, *saved*! But yet again, Harry was in the right place at the right time for the rebound.

Goooooooooooooooooooooooaaaaaaaaaaaaaaaaaa aaaaaaaalllllllllllllllllllllllllllllllll!!!!!!!!!!!!!!!!!!!!

Harry had his first World Cup goal already! He ran towards the corner flag and slid gleefully across the grass. Soon, he was at the bottom of an England team bundle.

When he finally escaped, Harry stood in front of the cheering crowd and held up the Three Lions on his red shirt. 'Come on!' he roared.

Even when Tunisia made it 1–1 from the penalty spot, Harry kept believing.

'There's still plenty of time to score again!'

Even when defenders wrestled him to the ground in the box but the referee shook his head, Harry kept believing.

'We'll find a way!'

Even with seconds to go, Harry kept believing.

'We can do this!'

Harry Maguire flicked Kieran Trippier's corner

towards goal. Harry Kane was waiting at the back post, totally unmarked. What a chance to become England's World Cup hero! He calmly steered his header past the goalkeeper.

Gooooooooooooooooooooooooooaaaaaaaaaaaaaaaaaa aaaaaaaallllllllllllllllllllllllllllllllllllll!!!!!!!!!!!!!!!!!!!!!

Another game, another two goals for Harry, England's big game player. And in a World Cup, too! It was the best feeling ever.

'H, what would we do without you?' Ashley screamed.

On the bench, Southgate punched the air. What an important goal, what an important win!

England's next victory, against Panama, was a lot more comfortable.

Kieran crossed and John headed home. 1–0!

Harry smashed in an unstoppable penalty. 2–0!

Jesse curled a long-range shot into the top corner. 3–0!

John finished off a brilliant team move. 4–0!

Harry was wrestled to the ground in the box again and this time, the referee pointed to the spot. 5–0!

The England fans couldn't believe what they were seeing, but Harry could.

'This is awesome!' he laughed in the dressing room at half-time. 'More of the same!'

Harry was on a hat-trick, after all. A fifth goal would take him above Belgium's Romelu Lukaku as the top scorer at the 2018 World Cup.

With 30 minutes to go, Harry looked over at the bench and saw Jamie Vardy warming up. He was about to come off – was there time for one last shot? No, but Ruben Loftus-Cheek's shot flicked up flukily off Harry's heel.

Goooooooooooooooooooooooooaaaaaaaaaaaaaaaaaa aaaaaaaallllllllllllllllllllllllllllllllllllllllll!!!!!!!!!!!!!!!!!!!!!

'H, that's the worst hat-trick ever!' Jesse Lingard joked.

Harry shrugged and smiled. 'Whatever, there's no such thing as a bad hat-trick!'

Every goal counted, especially for a Number 9. Harry would treasure his World Cup matchball forever. With England through to the Round of 16, suddenly the fans were full of hope and excitement:

It's coming home, it's coming home,
It's coming, FOOTBALL'S COMING HOME!

The players, however, had to keep their feet on the ground. A 1–0 defeat to Belgium in the final game of the group stage set up a second-round match against Colombia.

'This is a massive test for us,' Southgate told his players, 'but we're ready!'

Harry battled bravely against the big centre-backs. When he made a run to head Kieran's corner, Carlos Sánchez pushed him to the floor.

'Foul!' Harry cried out.

Penalty! The Colombian players argued for ages with the referee and they even tried to scuff up the spot, but nothing could stop an ice-cold striker like Harry. He just waited calmly and, when the referee blew the whistle, slotted it coolly home.

Goooooooooooooooooooooooooaaaaaaaaaaaaaaaaaa aaaaaaaallllllllllllllllllllllllllllllllllllll!!!!!!!!!!!!!!!!!!!!!

What a tournament he was having – that was goal number six already!

England were on their way to the World Cup
quarter-finals, but in the last minute, Colombia
equalised. As Harry watched the ball cross the goal-
line, he put his hands on his head. Oh no, what now?

'Dig deep!' he shouted to his struggling
teammates.

Could England win a World Cup penalty shoot-out
for the first time ever? They had been practising for
weeks. Harry could barely walk but he knew that
his nation needed him. As captain, he had to lead
by example.

'I'll go first,' he said firmly.

With all eyes on him and a yellow wall of
Colombia fans in front of him, Harry stepped up
slowly and…SCORED, of course!

He pumped his fist and re-joined his teammates
on the half-way line. Even when Jordan Henderson's
penalty was saved, Harry knew that it wasn't over.
He trusted their other Jordan – Jordan Pickford – to
make at least one super save in the shoot-out.

Carlos Bacca ran up and…there was the super save!

Now, Eric Dier just needed to keep cool and…

*Goooooooooooooooooooooooaaaaaaaaaaaaaaaaaaa
aaaaaalllllllllllllllllllllllllllllllllllll!!!!!!!!!!!!!!!!!!!!!*

What a moment – England were through to
the World Cup quarter-finals after WINNING ON
PENALTIES! Harry raced over to hug his keeper.

'Jordan, you hero!' he screamed. It was time for an
even bigger England team bundle.

Was football *really* coming home? The impossible
now seemed possible. Harry watched all the amazing
videos of the celebrations back home.

'Look what we've started, lads,' he told his
teammates before their quarter-final against Sweden.
'Come on, we can't stop now!'

England weren't ready to go home yet. Harry
Maguire scored a thumping header.

'If one Harry doesn't get you, the other one
will!' the TV commentator screamed – and then
Dele grabbed a second to send England into the
World Cup semi-finals for the first time in twenty-
eight years. The whole nation was going football
crazy!

'Is it coming home?' a journalist asked afterwards.

Harry grinned. 'We'll have to wait and see, but hopefully!'

Against Croatia, England made another brilliant start when Kieran curled a fantastic free-kick into the top corner – 1–0!

'It's coming home, it's coming home,
It's coming, FOOTBALL'S COMING HOME!'

Could England score a second goal to settle the semi-final? Jesse threaded a great pass through to Harry in the penalty area.

He just had the goalkeeper to beat...*SAVED!*

He got to the rebound first...*OFF THE POST!*

Harry couldn't believe his bad luck, and neither could the fans. England's superstar striker was usually so lethal!

Croatia fought their way back into the match – 1–1! Suddenly, the England players looked nervous and tired. Harry did his best to urge his team on but could they hang on for penalties? No- in the 110th minute, Mario Mandžukić won it for Croatia.

At the final whistle, Harry sank to his knees,

surrounded by his band of football brothers. They had all given absolutely everything.

It was devastating to get so close to the final but they were still a huge success story. They hadn't brought the World Cup home but they had brought football home: England had fallen in love with its national team again. Thousands of fans stayed behind in the stadium to clap and cheer for their heroes.

'It hurts a lot,' Harry tweeted later that night. 'We can be proud and we'll be back. Thanks for all your support. #ThreeLions.'

England lost their third place play-off against Belgium but Harry did finish his first World Cup with an individual award – the Golden Boot for top scorer! It was a great achievement, even if it wasn't the team trophy that he really wanted.

There was plenty of time for that. This was just the beginning for Southgate's England side. Harry couldn't wait to lead his country to glory at Euro 2020 and World Cup 2022.

KANE

(10) THE FACTS

NAME: HARRY EDWARD KANE

DATE OF BIRTH: 28 July 1993

AGE: 25

PLACE OF BIRTH: Walthamstow, London

NATIONALITY: England

BEST FRIEND: Dele Alli

CURRENT CLUB: Tottenham

POSITION: ST

THE STATS

Height (cm):	188
Club appearances:	239
Club goals:	126
Club trophies:	0
International appearances:	30
International goals:	19
International trophies:	0
Ballon d'Ors:	0

★ ★ ★ **HERO RATING: 88** ★ ★ ★

GREATEST MOMENTS

Type and search the web links to see the magic for yourself!

 7 APRIL 2014, TOTTENHAM 5-1 SUNDERLAND

https://www.youtube.com/watch?v=3XnvmoUOAXk
Harry's first Premier League goal was a long time coming. After four loan spells, he finally got his chance at Tottenham under Tim Sherwood. Against Sunderland, Christian Eriksen curled a brilliant ball into the six-yard box and Harry beat his marker to score. It was a real striker's finish and a sign of the great things to come.

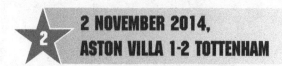

2 NOVEMBER 2014,
ASTON VILLA 1-2 TOTTENHAM

https://www.youtube.com/watch?v=VYIDn3ohqo8

This was the goal that changed Harry's career at White Hart Lane. He has definitely scored better goals but this last-minute free kick won the match for Tottenham. Before this, Harry was a substitute. After this, he became the star striker we know and love.

7 FEBRUARY 2015,
TOTTENHAM 2-1 ARSENAL

https://www.youtube.com/watch?v=y62kN8PGHFo

This was the day that Harry became a true Tottenham hero. In the big North London Derby, he scored two goals to secure a famous victory. Harry's first goal was a tap-in but the second was a world-class header. He used his power and technique to direct the ball right into the corner of the Arsenal goal.

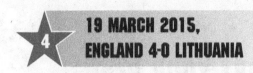

19 MARCH 2015, ENGLAND 4-0 LITHUANIA

https://www.youtube.com/watch?v=OPBjwNKhoKc
It was Harry's international debut at Wembley and he
had only been on the pitch for 80 seconds. Raheem
Sterling crossed from the left and, as usual, Harry was
in the right place at the right time. He scored with a
simple header at the back post and then bumped into
the match official!

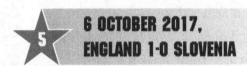

6 OCTOBER 2017, ENGLAND 1-0 SLOVENIA

https://www.youtube.com/watch?v=yMloUtQRHos
On a tense night at Wembley, the new England
captain led his country to the 2018 World Cup in
Russia. In the last minute, Kyle Walker crossed from
the right and Harry stretched out his lethal right leg to
poke the ball past the keeper.

PLAY LIKE YOUR HEROES

THE HARRY KANE FINISH

SEE IT HERE You Tube

https://www.youtube.com watch?v=EAWRV0GThIs&t=314s

STEP 1: Make a clever forward run between the defenders.

STEP 2: When you get the ball, control it perfectly. That first touch is really important!

STEP 3: Use your skill and strength to escape your marker and open up a bit of space to shoot.

STEP 4: Don't wait! Strike the ball as early as possible to surprise the keeper.

STEP 5: Keep it low! When the ball zips across the grass, it's harder for the keeper to save.

STEP 6: Aim for the corner! Picture the goal in your head and pick your spot. Go for the right or the left but never go down the middle.

STEP 7: As the ball hits the back of the net, run towards the fans in the corner with your arms out wide and a big grin on your face.

TEST YOUR KNOWLEDGE

QUESTIONS

1. Who was Harry's first Tottenham hero?

2. What position did Harry first play at Ridgeway Rovers?

3. Which other England legend also played for Ridgeway Rovers?

4. Which three clubs did Harry have trials with when he was a youngster?

5. Name three of Harry's teammates in the Tottenham youth team.

6. How many loan spells did Harry have before settling at Spurs?

7. Who was the Spurs manager when Harry made his first Premier League start?

8. Who gave Harry his Number 18 shirt when he left Tottenham?

9. Harry scored on his England debut – True or False?

10. How many goals did Harry score for England at Euro 2016?

11. How many Premier League Golden Boots has Harry won so far?

Answers below. . . No cheating!

1. Teddy Sheringham 2. Goalkeeper 3. David Beckham 4. Arsenal, Watford and Tottenham 5. Any of Tom Carroll, Jonathan Obika, Kudus Oyenuga, Ryan Mason, Andros Townsend and Steven Caulker 6. Four – Leyton Orient, Millwall, Norwich City and Leicester City 7. Tim Sherwood 8. Jermain Defoe 9. True – Harry scored after only 80 seconds against Lithuania! 10. 0 11. 3

The 2018 World Cup saw your favourite football heroes go head-to-head for the ultimate prize – the World Cup.

Complete your collection with six limited-edition international Ultimate Football Heroes.

AVAILABLE NOW

FOLLOW IN THE FOOTSTEPS OF LEGENDS. . .

Bridge the gap between past and present by stepping into the shoes of six classic World Cup heroes and reading their exciting stories – from the playground to the pitch, and to superstardom!